$15 A

12-3

HarperCollins

GREECE

LANGUAGE SURVIVAL GUIDE

THE VISUAL PHRASE BOOK AND DICTIONARY

HarperResource
An Imprint of HarperCollins*Publishers*

HarperCollins books may be purchased for educational, business, or sales promotional use. For information please write: Special Markets Department, HarperCollins Publishers Inc., 10 East 53rd Street, New York, NY 10022.

First published 2003 by HarperCollins Publishers in the United Kingdom.

Consultant: Juliet A Quincey

Photography: Juliet A Quincey
Map: Heather Moore
Additional photography: Athens Metro (pp 27, top; 30, centre left; 31, right); Artville (pp 91, 2; 92, 1; 93, 1; 94, 1; 95, 2; 96, 2; 97, 1; 98, 1; 99, 1; 100, 2); The Anthony Blake Photo Library (pp 92, 1; 93, 1; 94, 2; 95, 1; 97, 2; 100, 1; 101, 3).
Layout: The Printer's Devil, Glasgow

Other titles in the HarperCollins Language Survival Guide series:
France (0-06-053692-6)
Spain (0-06-053740-X)
Italy (0-06-053693-4)
Portugal (0-06-057977-3)

ISBN 0-06-057975-7

04 05 06 07 08 10 9 8 7 6 5 4 3 2 1

Printed in Italy by Amadeus SpA

CONTENTS

USEFUL WEBSITES

Currency Converters

www.x-rates.com

Foreign Office Advice

www.fco.gov.uk/travel/countryadvice.asp

Passport Office

www.ukpa.gov.uk

Health Advice

www.thetraveldoctor.com

www.doh.gov.uk/traveladvice

Driving Abroad

www.drivingabroad.co.uk/driving_tips_countries/greece/driving_in_greece.htm

Pets

www.defra.gov.uk/animalh/quarantine/qindex.shtml

Weather

www.bbc.co.uk/weather

Facts

www.cia.gov/cia/publications/factbook/geos/gr.html

Internet Cafes

www.cybercafes.com

Transport

www.greekferries.gr

www.ferries.gr

www.dolphins.gr *(hydrofoil service to Greek islands)*

www.osenet.gr/eng.htm *(Hellenic Railways Organisation)*

www.travelinfo.gr/train.htm *(schedules)*

Tourism

www.greektourism.gr *(Greek Naitonal Tourism Organisation)*

www.visiteurope.com/greece

www.travelinfo.gr

www.greektravel.com

www.travelgreece.com

Accommodation

www.greekhotels.gr

www.greecetravel.com/campsites *(camping)*

www.europeanhostels.com/fall/listings/greece *(hostels)*

Food & Wine

www.gourmed.gr

Other

www.xo.gr/en/index.jsp *(Greek Yellow Pages in English)*

INTRODUCTION

As technology sweeps across the world, travellers aren't just faced with the prospect of speaking a foreign language – they also have foreign machines to contend with. Machines for parking, for dispensing cash, for buying tickets and food. Often there is nobody about to ask how they work. *Collins Language Survival Guides* address this problem by showing photographically signs and situations you might come across.

The things that throw you are often the ones that look familiar – such as buses, trains or phones – but which operate slightly differently.

There are usually codes to how things operate and though you might not think you are aware of them, you are probably using them everyday: the colour-coding for roads (blue for motorways, green for major roads, yellow for temporary signs) or when buying milk (generally blue for whole milk, green for semi-skimmed and red for skimmed). It's when these familiar codes don't work in the same way, that you feel slightly at a loss and probably more unsure than you need be. By making a note of how these types of things work and knowing a few keywords, you will feel much more confident.

The unique combination of practical information, photos and phrases found in this book provides the key to hassle-free travel and the colour-coding below shows how information is presented and how to access it as quickly as possible.

General, practical information which will provide useful tips on getting the best out of your trip.

keywords

δεξιά
*dheksee**a***
on/to the right
αριστερά
areestera
on/to the left

◀ **keywords**
these are words that are useful to know both when you see them written down or when you hear them spoken

key talk ▶
short, simple phrases that you can change and adapt to suit your own situation

excuse me!
*seeghn**o**mee*
συγνώμη!

can you help me?
*bor**ee**te na me voeeth**ee**sete*
μπορείτε να με βοηθήσετε;

do you know where...?
*k**se**rete poo...*
ξέρετε πού...;

talking

The **Food Section** allows you to choose more easily from what is on offer both for snacks and at restaurants.

The practical 5000-word English–Greek, Greek–English **Dictionary** means that you will never be stuck for words.

SPEAKING GREEK

In the pronunciation system in this book, Greek sounds are represented by spellings of the nearest possible sounds in English. When you read the pronunciation, sound the letters as if you were reading English (but make sure you also pronounce vowels at the end of a word). The vowels in ***heavy type*** show where the stress falls (in the Greek script it is marked with an accent).

The following notes should help:

	REMARKS	EXAMPLE	PRONOUNCED
gh	*like **r** at back of throat*	γάλα	*gh**a**la*
dh	*like **th** in this*	δάχτυλο	*dh**a**khteelo*
th	*like **th** in thin*	θέατρο	*th**e**atro*
ks	*like **x** in fox*	ξένος	*ks**e**nos*
r	*slightly trilled **r***	ρόδα	*r**o**dha*
kh	*like **ch** in loch*	χάνω	*kh**a**no*
	*like a rough **h** before e or ee*	χέρι	*kh**e**ree*

Here are a few tricky letter combinations:

αι	*met*	***e***	γυναίκα	*gheen**e**ka*
αυ	*café*	***af***	αυτό	*aft**o***
	or have	***av***	αύριο	***a**vreeo*
ει	*meet*	***ee***	είκοσι	***ee**kosee*
ευ	*effect*	***ef***	Δευτέρα	*dheft**e**ra*
	or every	***ev***	Ευρώπη	*evr**o**pee*
γγ	*hang*	***ng***	Αγγλία	*angl**ee**a*
γκ	*get*	***g***	γκάζι	*g**a**zee*
	hang	***ng***	άγκυρα	***a**ngeera*
ντ	*hand*	***nd***	αντίο	*and**ee**o*
	dog	***d***	ντομάτα	*dom**a**ta*
μπ	*bag*	***b***	μπλούζα	*bl**oo**za*
οι	*meet*	***ee***	πλοίο	*pl**ee**o*
ου	*moon*	***oo***	ούζο	***oo**zo*

The letters **η**, **ι**, **υ**, **οι**, and **ει** have the same sound **ee**. Also, **αι** and **ε** have the same sound **e** (as in m**e**t).

Vowel combinations to look out for are **ευ** and **αυ**. **ευ** is pronounced *ef* or *ev*, and **αυ** *af* or *av*. So **ευρώ** (euro) is pronounced *evr**o*** and **αυτό** (it, this) is pronounced *aft**o***.

You should also note that the Greek question mark is a semi-colon, i.e. ***;***.

EVERYDAY TALK

There are two forms of address in Greek, formal and informal. Greek people will use the formal until they are on a first-name basis, so for the purposes of this book we will use the formal. The important thing for foreign visitors, though, is that they 'have a go' at Greek. Don't worry too much about formal and informal, or about making mistakes in general – the Greeks will be very happy to hear you try to speak their language!

yes
ne
ναι

no
***o**khee*
όχι

ok/that's fine
*end**a**ksee*
εντάξει

please
*parakal**o***
παρακαλώ

thank you
*efkhareest**o***
ευχαριστώ

thanks very much
*efkhareest**o** pol**ee***
ευχαριστώ πολύ

don't mention it
*parakal**o***
παρακαλώ

never mind
*dhen peer**a**zee*
δεν πειράζει

hello/hi *and* **goodbye/bye**
*y**a** sas (formal) / y**a** soo (informal)*
γειά σας / γειά σου

hello
*kh**e**rete (formal)*
χαίρετε

goodbye
*and**ee**o (formal)*
αντίο

good morning
*kaleem**e**ra*
καλημέρα

good afternoon/evening
*kaleesp**e**ra*
καλησπέρα

good night
*kaleen**ee**khta*
καληνύχτα

excuse me! / sorry!
*seeghn**o**mee*
συγνώμη!

I am sorry
*leep**a**me*
λυπάμαι

excuse me
*me seeghkhor**ee**te*
με συγχωρείτε

I don't understand
*dhen katalav**e**no*
δεν καταλαβαίνω

I don't know
*dhen ks**e**ro*
δεν ξέρω

Addressing people

When addressing someone for the first time, or attracting attention, use Κύριε *k**ee**ree-e* (Mr), Κυρία *keer**ee**a* (Mrs/Ms) or Δεσποινίς *dhespeen**ee**s* (Miss). These titles may be used without a name, like French *Monsieur* and *Madame*. It is also quite common to use Κύριος *k**ee**reeos* etc with the person's first name.

welcome
*kal**o**s **ee**rthate / kal**o**s or**ee**sate*
καλώς ήρθατε / καλώς ορίσατε

(reply to this)
*kal**o**s sas vr**ee**kame*
καλώς σάς βρήκαμε

how are you?
*pos **ee**ste*
πώς είστε;

fine, thanks
*pol**ee** kal**a** efkhareest**o***
πολύ καλά ευχαριστώ

and you?
*es**ee**s*
εσείς;

Asking for something in a shop or bar, you would ask for what you want, adding ***parakalo****.*

Keywords

1	ένα	*ena*
2	δύο	*dheeo*
3	τρία	*treea*
4	τέσσερα	*tesera*
5	πέντε	*pende*
6	έξι	*eksee*
7	επτά	*efta*
8	οκτώ	*okhto*
9	εννέα	*ene-a*
10	δέκα	*dheka*

a...
ena... ('ο' words)
ένα...

an iced coffee
ena frape
ένα φραπέ

2 iced coffees
dheeo frape
δύο φραπέ

meea... ('η' words)
μία...

a beer
meea beera
μία μπίρα

2 beers
dheeo beeres
δύο μπίρες

ena... ('το' words)
ένα...

a bottle
ena bookalee
ένα μπουκάλι

2 bottles
dheeo bookaleea
δύο μπουκάλια

a coffee and two beers
enan kafe ke dheeo beeres
έναν καφέ και δύο μπίρες

a tea please
ena tsaee parakalo
ένα τσάι παρακαλώ

the menu please
ton katalogho parakalo
τον κατάλογο παρακαλώ

the bill please
to logharyasmo parakalo
το λογαριασμό παρακαλώ

another/more... *('ο' & 'το' words)*
alo ena...
άλλο ένα...

('η' words)
alee meea...
άλλη μία...

another iced coffee
alo ena frape
άλλο ένα φραπέ

another beer
alee meea beera
άλλη μία μπίρα

2 more beers
ales dheeo beeres
άλλες δύο μπίρες

2 more iced coffees
aloos dheeo frape
άλλους δύο φραπέ

To catch someone's attention

The easiest way to catch someone's attention is with **συγνώμη!** *seeghnomee*. Note that the word no in Greek, **όχι** *okhee*, is often accompanied by an upward tilting of the face, or slight raising of the eyebrows and a click of the tongue. You may think that this is a nod for yes, rather than a no!

excuse me!
seeghnomee
συγνώμη!

can you help me?
boreete na me voeetheesete
μπορείτε να με βοηθήσετε;

do you know where...?
kserete poo...
ξέρετε πού...;

By combining key words and phrases you can build up your language and adapt the phrases to suit your own situation.

ekhete
do you have?

do you have a map?
ekhete ena khartee
έχετε ένα χάρτη;

do you have a room?
ekhete ena dhomateeo
έχετε ένα δωμάτιο;

poso kanee
how much?

how much is the cheese?
poso kanee to teeree
πόσο κάνει το τυρί;

how much is the ticket?
poso kanee to eeseeteereeo
πόσο κάνει το εισιτήριο;

tha eethela...
I'd like ...

I'd like a slice of gateau
tha eethela meea pasta
θα ήθελα μία πάστα

I'd like an ice cream
tha eethela ena paghoto
θα ήθελα ένα παγωτό

khreeazome...
I need ...

I need a taxi
khreeazome ena taksee
χρειάζομαι ένα ταξί

I need a receipt
khreeazome meea apodheeksee
χρειάζομαι μία απόδειξη

pote
when?

when does it open?
pote aneeghee
πότε ανοίγει;

when does it close?
pote kleenee
πότε κλείνει;

when does it leave?
pote fevyee
πότε φεύγει;

when does it arrive?
pote ftanee
πότε φτάνει;

poo eene...
where is...?

where is the bank?
poo eene ee trapeza
πού είναι η τράπεζα;

where is the hotel?
poo eene to ksenodhokheeo
πού είναι το ξενοδοχείο;

ekhee...
is there...?

is there a market?
ekhee la-eekee aghora
έχει λαϊκή αγορά;

where is there a market?
poo ekhee la-eekee aghora
πού έχει λαϊκή αγορά;

dhen ekhee...
there is no...

there is no bread
dhen ekhee psomee
δεν έχει ψωμί

there is no hot water
dhen ekhee zesto nero
δεν έχει ζεστό νερό

boro na...
can I...?

can I smoke?
boro na kapneeso
μπορώ να καπνίσω;

can I hire a car?
boro na neekyaso ena aftokeeneeto
μπορώ να νοικιάσω ένα αυτοκίνητο;

where can I buy bread?
poo boro na aghoraso psomee
πού μπορώ να αγοράσω ψωμί;

eene
is it?

is it near?
eene konda
είναι κοντά;

is it far?
eene makreea
είναι μακριά;

These are a selection of small but very useful words to know.

μεγάλο
meghalo
big

μικρό
meekro
little

λίγο / πολύ
leegho / polee
a little / a lot

αρκετά
arketa
enough

κοντά / μακριά
konda / makreea
near / far

κοντινότερο
kondeenotero
nearest

πολύ ακριβό
polee akreevo
too expensive

και
ke
and

με / χωρίς
me / khorees
with / without

... μου
... moo
my...

αυτό / εκείνο
afto / ekeeno
this one / that one

αμέσως
amesos
straight away

αργότερα
arghotera
later

a large car
ena meghalo aftokeeneeto
ένα μεγάλο αυτοκίνητο

a small beer
meea meekree beera
μία μικρή μπίρα

a little please
leegho parakalo
λίγο παρακαλώ

a lot please
polee parakalo
πολύ παρακαλώ

that's enough thanks
arketa efkhareesto
αρκετά ευχαριστώ

where is the nearest chemist?
poo eene to kondeenotero farmakeeo
πού είναι το κοντινότερο φαρμακείο;

it is too expensive
eene polee akreevo
είναι πολύ ακριβό

it is too small
eene polee meekro
είναι πολύ μικρό

a tea and an iced coffee
ένα τσάι και ένα φραπέ
ena tsaee ke ena frappé

with milk
me ghala
με γάλα

with ice
me paghakeea
με παγάκια

without sugar
khorees zakharee
χωρίς ζάχαρη

without ice
khorees paghakeea
χωρίς παγάκια

for me
για μένα
ya mena

for her
γι' αυτήν
yafteen

for him
γι' αυτόν
yafton

for us
για μας
ya mas

my passport
to dheeavateereeo moo
το διαβατήριό μου

my key
to kleedhee moo
το κλειδί μου

I'd like this one
tha eethela afto
θα ήθελα αυτό

I'd like that one
tha eethela ekeeno
θα ήθελα εκείνο

I need a taxi straight away
khreeazome taksee amesos
χρειάζομαι ταξί αμέσως

is it safe?
eene asfales
είναι ασφαλές;

I'll phone back later
tha ksanaparo arghotera
θα ξαναπάρω αργότερα

It is always good to be able to say a few words about yourself to break the ice, even if you won't be able to tell your life story.

what's your name?
*pos se **le**ne*
πώς σε λένε;

my name is...
*me **le**ne...*
με λένε...

I'm from England
***ee**me ap**o** teen angl**ee**a*
είμαι από την Αγγλία

I'm from America
ee**me ap**o** teen amereek**ee
είμαι από την Αμερική

where do you live?
*poo m**e**nees*
πού μένεις;

where do you live? *(plural)*
*poo m**e**nete*
πού μένετε;

I'm single
***ee**me el**e**fther-os(-ee)*
είμαι ελεύθερος(-η)

I'm married
***ee**me pandrem**e**n-os(-ee)*
είμαι παντρεμένος(-η)

I'm divorced
***ee**me khoreesm**e**n-os(-ee)*
είμαι χωρισμένος(-η)

I have...
***e**kho...*
έχω ...

a boyfriend
***e**na f**ee**lo*
ένα φίλο

a girlfriend
*m**ee**a f**ee**lee*
μία φιλη

I have ... children
e**kho ... pedhee**a
έχω ... παιδιά

I have no children
*dhen **e**kho pedhee**a***
δεν έχω παιδιά

I'm here on holiday
*vr**ee**skome edh**o** ya dheeakop**e**s*
βρίσκομαι εδώ για διακοπές

I'm here for work
*vr**ee**skome edh**o** ya dhoolee**a***
βρίσκομαι εδώ για δουλειά

where do you live?
*poo m**e**nees*
πού μένεις;

I live in Glasgow
*zo stee ghlask**o**vee*
ζω στη Γλασκώβη

you have a beautiful home
***e**khete or**e**o sp**ee**tee*
έχετε ωραίο σπίτι

the meal was delicious
*to fagheet**o** **ee**tan nosteem**o**tato*
το φαγητο ήταν νοστιμότατο

this is a gift for you
***ee**ne **e**na dh**o**ro ya sas*
είναι ένα δώρο για σας

pleased to meet you
*kh**a**reeka ya tee ghnoreem**ee**a*
χάρηκα για τη γνωριμία

this is my husband
*ap**o** dho o s**ee**zeegh**o**s moo*
από 'δω ο σύζυγός μου

this is my wife
*ap**o** dho ee s**ee**zeegh**o**s moo*
από 'δω η σύζυγός μου

thanks for your hospitality
*efkharees**to** ya teen feelokse**nee**a*
ευχαριστώ για την φιλοξενία

I've enjoyed myself very much
*p**e**rasa pol**ee** or**a**ya*
πέρασα πολύ ωραία

what is your address?
*pya **ee**ne ee dhee**e**ftheens**ee** sas*
ποιά είνα η διεύθυνσή σας;

Although problems are not something anyone wants, you might come across the odd difficulty, and it is best to be armed with a few phrases to cope with the situation.

excuse me!
*seeghn**o**mee*
συγνώμη!

can you help me?
*bor**ee**te na me voeeth**ee**sete*
μπορείτε να με βοηθήσετε;

I don't speak Greek
*dhen meel**a**o eleeneek**a***
δεν μιλάω Ελληνικά

do you speak English?
*meel**a**te angleek**a***
μιλάτε Αγγλικά;

I'm lost
e**kho khath**ee
έχω χαθεί

how do I get to...?
*pos bor**o** na p**a**o sto / stee...*
πώς μπορώ να πάω στο / στη...;

I've lost...
***e**khasa...*
έχασα...

my purse
*to portof**o**lee moo*
το πορτοφόλι μου

my passport
*to dheeavat**ee**ree**o** moo*
το διαβατήριό μου

my keys
*ta kleedhy**a** moo*
τα κλειδιά μου

I've left my bag in...
*ks**e**khasa teen ts**a**nda moo...*
ξέχασα την τσάντα μου...

on the bus
*sto leofor**ee**o*
στο λεωφορείο

on the boat
*sto pl**ee**o*
στο πλοίο

I've missed...
***e**khasa...*
έχασα...

my flight
*teen pt**ee**see*
την πτήση

my connection
*teen andap**o**kreesee moo*
την ανταπόκριση μου

I'm late
***e**kho argh**ee**see*
έχω αργήσει

I need to get to...
*pr**e**pee na ft**a**so sto...*
πρέπει να φτάσω στο...

I have no money
*dhen **e**kho khr**ee**mata*
δεν έχω χρήματα

my luggage hasn't arrived
*ee aposkev**e**s moo dhen **e**ftasan*
οι αποσκευές μου δεν έφτασαν

this is my address
*aft**ee** **ee**ne **ee**ne ee dhee**e**ftheensee moo*
αυτή είναι η διεύθυνση μου

I'm sorry
*leep**a**me*
λυπάμαι

I didn't know
*dhen **ee**ksera*
δεν ήξερα

this is broken
e**spase aft**o
έσπασε αυτό

where can I get this repaired?
*poo tha moo to epeeskev**a**soon*
πού θα μου το επισκευάσουν;

someone's stolen my...
*k**a**peeos moo **e**klepse...*
κάποιος μου έκλεψε...

handbag
*teen ts**a**nda*
την τσάντα

traveller's cheques
*tees takseedheeoteek**e**s epeetay**e**s*
τις ταξιδιωτικές επιταγές

leave me alone!
*af**ee**ste me **ee**seekho*
αφήστε με ήσυχο!

go away!
*f**ee**yete*
φύγετε!

Greeks like to receive good service and quality. They will complain when things are not as they ought to be.

there is no...
*dhen **e**khee...*
δεν έχει...

there is no hot water
*dhen **e**khee zest**o** ner**o***
δεν έχει ζεστό νερό

it is dirty
***ee**ne vr**o**meeko*
είναι βρώμικο

it is broken
*kh**a**lase*
χάλασε

the shower doesn't work
*to doos dhen dhool**e**vee*
το ντους δεν δουλεύει

there is no toilet paper
*dhen **e**khee khart**ee** tooal**e**tas*
δεν έχει χαρτί τουαλέτας

there is no bread
*dhen **e**khee psom**ee***
δεν έχει ψωμί

the bath is dirty
*to b**a**nyo **ee**ne vr**o**meeko*
το μπάνιο είναι βρώμικο

can you repair it?
*bor**ee**te na to epeedheeorth**o**sete*
μπορείτε να το επιδιορθώσετε;

the light
to fos
το φως

the toilet
*ee tooal**e**ta*
η τουαλέτα

the telephone
*to teel**e**fono*
το τηλέφωνο

the heating
*ee th**e**rmansee*
η θέρμανση

...doesn't work
*...dhen dhool**e**vee*
...δεν δουλεύει

...doesn't work
*...dhen dhool**e**vee*
...δεν δουλεύει

it is too noisy
***e**khee pol**ee** th**o**reevo*
έχει πολύ θόρυβο

I didn't order this
*dhen z**ee**teesa aft**o***
δεν ζήτησα αυτό

I want a refund
*th**e**lo ta left**a** moo p**ee**so*
θέλω τα λεφτά μου πίσω

we've been waiting for a long time
*pereem**e**noome pol**ee** **o**ra*
περιμένουμε πολή ώρα

it's very expensive
ee**ne pol**ee** akreev**o
είναι πολύ ακριβό

where is the manager?
*poo **ee**ne o dheeeftheent**ee**s*
πού είναι ο διευθυντής;

I want to complain
*th**e**lo na k**a**no par**a**pona*
θέλω να κάνω παράπονα

we're in a hurry
ee**maste veeasteek**ee
είμαστε βιαστικοί

there is a mistake
***e**gheene l**a**thos*
έγινε λάθος

EVERYDAY GREECE

The next four pages should give you an idea of the type of things you will come across in Greece.

▲ **ENTRANCE** ***ee**sodhos*

▲ **EXIT** ***e**ksodhos*

▲ **PULL** ***ee**lthate*

▲ **PUSH** *oth**ee**sate*

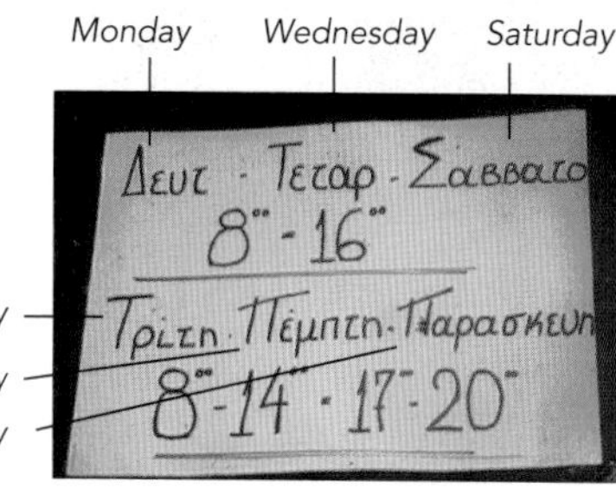

▲ Shops generally open in the morning (8–9 am until 1–2 pm) and again in the evening (approx 5–8 pm). They close in the afternoon and all day Sun. However, in busy tourist areas they usually open all day every day.

◀ The euro symbol. Greece is in the euro zone.

▲ Kiosk (*per**ee**ptero*). These kiosks sell all kinds of things including maps, postcards, stamps, cigarettes, snacks and drinks. They often have a payphone and will give directions.

▲ Tickets on sale for the lottery, which is drawn twice a week.

talking

do you have...?
***e**khete...*
έχετε...;

where can I buy...?
*poo bor**o** na aghor**a**so...*
πού μπορώ να αγοράσω...;

stamps
*ghramat**o**seema*
γραμματόσημα

bread
*psom**ee***
ψωμί

phonecards
*teelek**a**rtes*
τηλεκάρτες

tickets
*eeseet**ee**reea*
εισιτήρια

welcome Greek people may say this (*kal**o**s **ee**lthate*) to you. They like you to feel welcome in their country, and appreciate it if you try to speak the language, ◀ however tentatively.

ΔΩΜΑΤΙΑ

▲ **ROOMS** *dhom**a**teea*
All over Greece you can find rooms to rent, usually with car-parking space. If there are no signs, just ask.

▲ **OPEN** *aneekt**o***

κλειστο

▲ **CLOSED** *kleest**o***

◀ Greece is full of friendly little cafe-bars. Greeks are generally welcoming towards foreigners, although in Athens people are usually less friendly than elsewhere, and can seem rude.

The Greek alphabet can seem daunting. But if you learn it, the ▼ language will come alive.

δ Δ = d
η Η = e
λ Λ = l
μ Μ = m
ν Ν = n
ξ Ξ = x
π Π = p
ρ Ρ = r

Capital letters are written differently from lower case letters. These are ones that might fool you.

ΤΑΜΕΙΟ

▲ **PAY HERE/CASH DESK** *tam**ee**o*

◀ Greek post boxes are yellow and it is usually quite easy to find one. Red boxes are for express post around Athens. Times of collections are sometimes on the box. ΕΛΤΑ is the Greek postal company.

talking

excuse me!
*seeghn**o**mee*
συγνώμη!

can you show me?
*bor**ee**te na moo dh**ee**ksete*
μπορείτε να μου δείξετε;

how does this work?
*pos dhool**e**vee aft**o***
πώς δουλεύει αυτό;

what does this mean?
*tee seem**e**nee aft**o***
τι σημαίνει αυτό;

▲ **INFORMATION**
Feel free to ask for all kinds of information, about the local area and Greece in general.

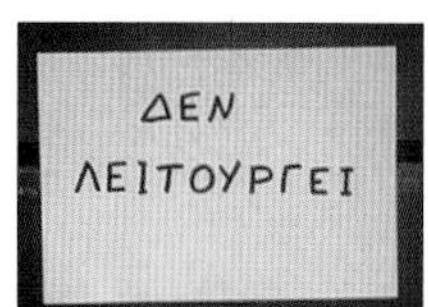

▲ **OUT OF ORDER**

◀ British & US papers are sold in cities and tourist areas in the summer.

▲ **CLOSED** *happy holidays!*

▲ **DANGER** *k**ee**ndheenos*

▼ **NO SMOKING**

A service charge is generally included in bills and tipping is a matter of choice. Some Greeks tip, some don't, so there is no obligation. It's entirely up to you. ▶

talking

can I smoke here?
*bor**o** na kapn**ee**so edh**o***
μπορώ να καπνίσω εδώ;

do you mind if I smoke?
*sas peer**a**zee na kapn**ee**so*
σας πειράζει να καπνίσω;

I don't smoke
*dhen kapn**ee**zo*
δεν καπνίζω

please don't smoke
*parakal**o** mee kapn**ee**zete*
παρακαλώ μην καπνίζετε

an ashtray please
*__e__na tass**a**kee parakal**o***
ένα τασάκι παρακαλώ

a non-smoking table please
*ena trap**e**zee ya mee kapneest**e**s parakal**o***
ένα τραπέζι για μή καπνιστές παρακαλώ

There are a few public toilets in Greece, but not many. There may be a small charge. Otherwise look for toilets in shopping centres, department stores and petrol stations. Bars, snack bars etc will let you use the toilet but of course it's polite to buy a drink first – cans of soda or small bottles of water are cheap! It is wise to carry tissues at all times. A word about Greek plumbing: because of the sewerage system, all (yes, ***all****) toilet paper* ***must*** *be deposited in the bin beside the toilet, not thrown into the toilet bowl. This applies wherever you are in Greece. It may seem strange, but please abide by this rule, otherwise the drains get blocked and some unfortunate person has the task of removing all the toilet paper from the pipes.*

▲ **GENTS** *andhr**o**n*

ΤΟΥΑΛΕΤΕΣ

▲ **TOILETS** *tooal**e**tes*

▼ **LADIES** *yeenek**o**n*

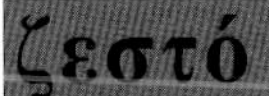

κρύο

▲ **HOT** *zest**o*** **COLD** *kr**ee**o*

Watch out as sometimes you find that someone has swapped the tap colours round and you get hot water from the cold tap!

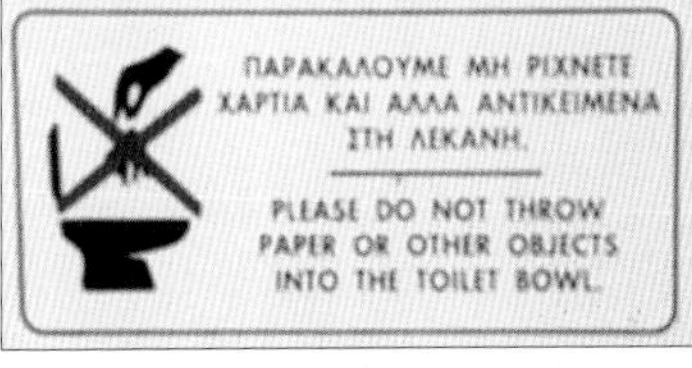

◀ Greek toilets have very narrow plumbing and you must put toilet paper in the wastebins provided, rather than in the toilet.

talking talking

excuse me! where is the toilet?
*seeghn**o**mee! poo **ee**ne ee tooal**e**ta*
συγνώμη! πού είναι η τουαλέτα;

may I use the toilet?
*bor**o** na p**a**o steen tooal**e**ta*
μπορώ να πάω στην τουαλέτα;

do you have toilets for the disabled?
***e**khete tooal**e**tes ya an**a**peeroos*
έχετε τουαλέτες για ανάπηρους;

the toilet doesn't work
*ee tooal**e**ta dhen leetoory**ee***
η τουαλέτα δεν λειτουργεί

do I need a key?
*khree**a**zome kleedh**ee***
χρειάζομαι κλειδί;

ASKING THE WAY

*Tourist offices usually have free maps, in addition to brochures and leaflets about local attractions, trips etc. They can also help you with accommodation, transport and general information. You can buy all kinds of different maps at bookshops, newsagents and at traditional Greek kiosks (**pereeptera**). **Pereeptera** can be seen on many street corners. They sell a multitude of things and often have a pay phone, too.*

▲ Office of tourism *Syntagma Square*

▲ TOURIST INFORMATION OFFICE

Local maps are often available free from Tourist Offices. You can also buy them cheaply at newsagent's or kiosks. ▶

excuse me!
*seeghn**o**mee*
συγνώμη!

where is...?
*poo **ee**ne...*
πού είναι...;

where is the hotel?
*poo **ee**ne to ksenodhokh**ee**o*
πού είναι το ξενοδοχείο;

I'm looking for...
*ps**a**khno ya to (with ο and το words) / tee (with η words)...*
ψάχνω για το / τη...

I'm looking for the station
*ps**a**khno ya to stathm**o***
ψάχνω για το το σταθμό

is it far?
ee**ne makree**a
είναι μακριά;

do you know where...?
*ks**e**rete poo **ee**ne...*
ξέρετε πού είναι...;

do you know where the tourist office is?
*ks**e**rete poo **ee**ne to ghraf**ee**o tooreesm**oo***
ξέρετε πού είναι το γραφείο τουρισμού

how do I get to...?
*pos bor**o** na p**a**o sto (with ο and το words) / stee (with η words)...*
πώς μπορώ να πάω στο / στη...;

where is the nearest...?
*poo **ee**ne to kondeen**o**tero...*
πού είναι το κοντινότερο...;

▲ Brown signs show the way to local places of interest. Plaka is the area beneath the Acropolis which is full of lively bars, shops and restaurants.

◀ *to the Holy Church of Saint Kharalambos*

◀ Sites of historical interest often have English translations.

▲ **ΟΔΟΣ** *odh**o**s* road, street
ΑΠΟ *ap**o*** from (8–2)

ΑΡΙΣΤΕΡΑ

▲ **LEFT** *areester**a***

RIGHT *dekhsee**a*** ▼

ΔΕΚΞΙΑ

δεξιά
*dekhsee**a***
to the right

αριστερά
*areester**a***
to the left

ευθεία
*efth**ee**a*
straight ahead

δρόμος
*dhr**o**mos*
road

πρώτο δρόμο δεξιά
*pr**o**to dhr**o**mo dheksee**a***
first on right

δεύτερο δρόμο αριστερά
*dh**e**ftero dhr**o**mo areester**a***
second on left

πλατεία
*plat**ee**a*
square

φανάρια
*fan**a**reea*
traffic lights

δίπλα στο
*dh**ee**pla sto*
next to

κοντά στο
*kond**a** sto*
near to

*apod**o** / apok**ee***
απο εδώ / από εκεί
this way / that way

πήγαινε / στρίψε
*p**ee**gene / str**ee**pse*
go / turn

απέναντι
*ap**e**nandee*
opposite

εκκλησία
*eklees**ee**a*
church

BANKS & MONEY

Banking hours are usually 8 am till 2 pm Mon to Thur and 8 am till 1 pm on Fri, but check opening-hours signs just to make sure. You can change cash and travellers' cheques at banks, travel agencies and at some hotels, but it's a good idea to check out the best exchange rate and ask about the commission before deciding where to change your money. It's also very easy to find a 24 hour ATM (cash dispenser). ATMs accept Switch, Maestro, Cirrus and most credit cards.

ΤΙΜΗ: 13, 60 ΕΥΡΩ

*price teem**ee***   *euro evr**o***

◀ The price of an item

▲ These are two of the major banks in Greece. The Greek word for bank is **τράπεζα** *tr**a**peza.*

24-hour indoor cash dispenser; swipe your card to get in ▼

You will find 24-hour cash-points at many banks and in tourist areas, with instructions in English, French, German and Italian. ▼

Cashpoint interface is as you would find at home. ▼

Travel agents as well as banks offer exchange services; these are ususally signed in English.

Greece's currency is the euro, ευρώ (*evr**o***), which breaks down into 100 euro cents. Euro notes are the same across Europe. The coins are officially cents, but Greek people call them λεπτά (*lept**a***) The reverse of the coins carry different designs in each European member country.

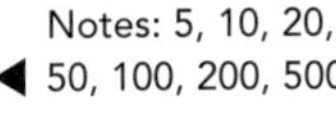

Notes: 5, 10, 20, 50, 100, 200, 500

Coins: 2 euro, 1 euro, 50 cent, 20 cent, 10 cent, 5 cent, 2 cent, 1 cent

keywords

ATM
ay tee em
cash dispenser

κωδικός PIN
*kodeek**o**s pin*
PIN number

συνάλλαγμα
*seen**a**laghma*
change

βάλε
*v**a**le*
insert

χαρτονομίσματα
*khartonom**ee**smata*
notes

μετρητά
*metreet**a***
cash

νόμισμα
*n**o**meesma*
coin

πιστωτική κάρτα
*peestoteek**ee** k**a**rta*
credit card

talking

where can I change money?
*poo bor**o** na al**a**kso khr**ee**mata*
πού μπορώ να αλλάξω χρήματα;

where is there a bank?
*poo **ee**ne m**ee**a tr**a**peza*
πού είναι μία τράπεζα;

where is there a bureau de change?
*poo **ee**ne **e**na enalakt**ee**reeo seenal**a**ghmatos*
πού είναι ένα εναλλακτήριο συναλλάγματος;

when does the bank open?
*p**o**te an**ee**ghee ee tr**a**peza*
πότε ανοίγει η τράπεζα;

when does the bank close?
*p**o**te kl**ee**nee ee tr**a**peza*
πότε κλείνει η τράπεζα;

where is there a cash dispenser?
*poo **e**khee **e**na ay tee em*
πού έχει ένα ay tee em;

I want to cash these traveller's cheques
*tha **ee**thela na al**a**kso aft**a** ta takseedhyoteek**a** tsek*
θα ήθελα να αλλάξω αυτά τα ταξιδιωτικά τσεκ

WHEN IS...?

Greece is two hours ahead of Great Britain all year round.
Π.μ. *means a.m.* (**προ μεσημβρίας** *pro meseemvreeas – before midday).*
Μ.μ. *means p.m.* (**μετά μεσημβρίας** *meta meseemvreeas after midday).*

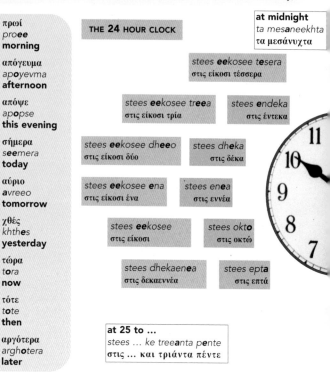

keywords

Greek	Pronunciation	English
πρωί	*proee*	**morning**
απόγευμα	*apoyevma*	**afternoon**
απόψε	*apopse*	**this evening**
σήμερα	*seemera*	**today**
αύριο	*avreeo*	**tomorrow**
χθές	*khthes*	**yesterday**
τώρα	*tora*	**now**
τότε	*tote*	**then**
αργότερα	*arghotera*	**later**

THE 24 HOUR CLOCK

at midnight
ta mesaneekhta
τα μεσάνυχτα

stees eekosee tesera
στις είκοσι τέσσερα

stees eekosee treea
στις είκοσι τρία

stees endeka
στις έντεκα

stees eekosee dheeo
στις είκοσι δύο

stees dheka
στις δέκα

stees eekosee ena
στις είκοσι ένα

stees enea
στις εννέα

stees eekosee
στις είκοσι

stees okto
στις οκτώ

stees dhekaenea
στις δεκαεννέα

stees epta
στις επτά

at 25 to ...
stees ... ke treeanta pente
στις ... και τριάντα πέντε

talking

when is the next...	**boat**	**bus**	**train**	**to...?**
pote fevyee to epomeno...	*pleeo*	*leoforeeo*	τραίνο	*ya...*
πότε φεύγει το επόμενο...;	πλοίο	λεωφορείο	*treno*	για...;

what time is...?	**breakfast**	**dinner**
tee ora serveerete...	*to proeeno*	*to vradheeno*
τι ώρα σερβίρεται...;	το πρωινό	το βραδυνό

when does it leave?
pote fevyee
πότε φεύγει;

when does it arrive?
pote ftanee
πότε φτάνει;

when does it open?
pote aneeyee
πότε ανοίγει;

when does it close?
pote kleenee
πότε κλείνει;

t midday
) *meseemeree*
• μεσημέρι

at a quarter past ...
stees ... ke tetarto
στις ... και τέταρτο

es dhodheka
: δώδεκα

stees meea
στις μία

stees dhekatreea
στις δεκατρία

stees dheeo
στις δύο

stees dhekatesera
στις δεκατέσσερα

stees treea
στις τρία

stees dhekapende
στις δεκαπέντε

stees teserees
στις τέσσερις

stees dhekaeksee
στις δεκαέξι

stees pende
στις πέντε

stees dhekaefta
στις δεκαεφτά

ees eksee
ις έξι

stees dhekaokto
στις δεκαοκτώ

at ... thirty
stees ... ke meesee
στις ... και μισή

keywords

Ιανουάριος
eeanooareeos
January

Φεβρουάριος
fevrooareeos
Febuary

Μάρτιος
marteeos
March

Απρίλιος
apreeleeos
April

Μάιος
maeeos
May

Ιούνιος
eeooneeos
June

Ιούλιος
eeooleeos
July

Αύγουστος
avghoostos
August

Σεπτέμβριος
septemvreeos
September

Οκτώβριος
oktovreeos
October

Νοέμβριος
noemvreeos
November

Δεκέμβριος
dhekemvreeos
December

talking

what time is it please?
tee ora eene parakalo
τι ώρα είναι, παρακαλώ;

it's 9 o'clock
eene enea ee ora
είναι εννέα η ώρα

in an hour's time
se meea ora
σε μία ώρα

in a while
se leegho
σε λίγο

two hours ago
preen apo dheeo ores
πριν από δύο ώρες

what's the date?
tee eemeromeeneea ekhoome seemera
τι ημερομηνία έχουμε σήμερα;

which month?
pyos meenas
ποιός μήνας;

it's the 5th of August 2003
eene ee pemtee avghoostoo dheeo kheeleeadhes treea
είναι η 5η Αυγούστου 2003

TIMETABLES

Key words to look out for are **καθημερινές** *(katheemereene**s**) meaning weekday (i.e. Mon–Sat) and* **Κυριακές και γιορτές** *(keereeyak**e**s ke yort**e**s) meaning Sundays and public holidays. Timetables vary according to whether they are* **θερινές** *(**thereenes** – summer) or* **χειμερινές** *(**kheemereenes** – winter).*

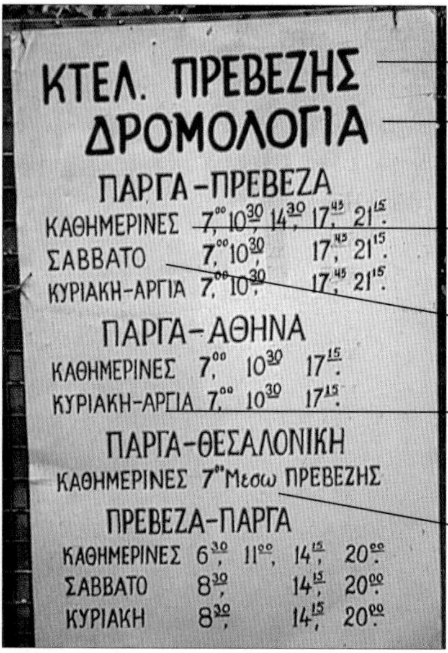

ΚΤΕΛ. ΠΡΕΒΕΖΗΣ
ΔΡΟΜΟΛΟΓΙΑ
ΠΑΡΓΑ-ΠΡΕΒΕΖΑ
ΚΑΘΗΜΕΡΙΝΕΣ 7,00 10,30 14,30 17,45 21,15
ΣΑΒΒΑΤΟ 7,00 10,30 17,45 21,15
ΚΥΡΙΑΚΗ-ΑΡΓΙΑ 7,00 10,30 17,45 21,15
ΠΑΡΓΑ-ΑΘΗΝΑ
ΚΑΘΗΜΕΡΙΝΕΣ 7,00 10,30 17,15
ΚΥΡΙΑΚΗ-ΑΡΓΙΑ 7,00 10,30 17,15
ΠΑΡΓΑ-ΘΕΣΑΛΟΝΙΚΗ
ΚΑΘΗΜΕΡΙΝΕΣ 7,00 Μεσω ΠΡΕΒΕΖΗΣ
ΠΡΕΒΕΖΑ-ΠΑΡΓΑ
ΚΑΘΗΜΕΡΙΝΕΣ 6,30 11,00 14,15 20,00
ΣΑΒΒΑΤΟ 8,30 14,15 20,00
ΚΥΡΙΑΚΗ 8,30 14,15 20,00

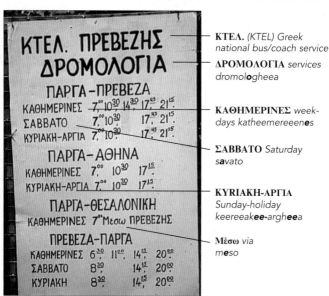

ΚΤΕΛ. *(KTEL) Greek national bus/coach service*

ΔΡΟΜΟΛΟΓΙΑ *services dromol**o**gheea*

ΚΑΘΗΜΕΡΙΝΕΣ *week-days katheemereeene**s***

ΣΑΒΒΑΤΟ *Saturday s**a**vato*

ΚΥΡΙΑΚΗ-ΑΡΓΙΑ *Sunday-holiday keereeak**ee**-argh**ee**a*

Μέσω *via m**e**so*

▲ Timetable for long-distance coaches to Preveza, Athens and Thessalonika

09.00 π.μ.

▲ **9 AM**

1 PM ▼

13.00 μ.μ.

ΟΡΧΗΣΤΡΑ ΠΑΡΓΑΣ
Τηλ: 0684 - 31.176 & 0944-28.27.42
ΣΗΜΕΡΑ

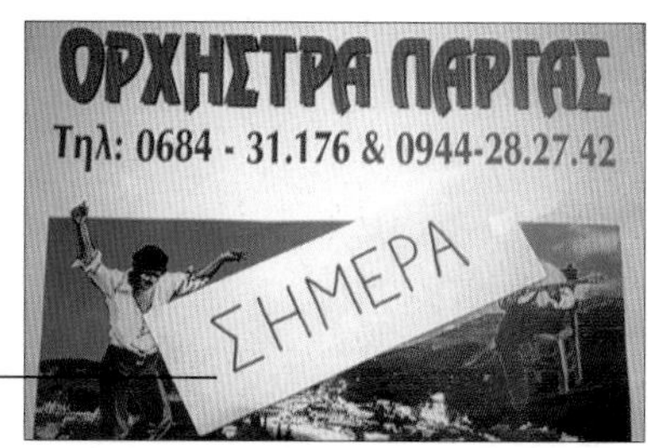

today

talk

have you a timetable?	when does it leave?	when does it arrive?
*ekhete to or**a**reeo*	*p**o**te f**e**vyee*	*p**o**te ft**a**nee*
έχετε το ωράριο;	**πότε φεύγει;**	**πότε φτάνει;**

▲Timetables, especially in tourist areas, will often have English translations alongside the Greek.

◀Bus station timetable board showing local and longer-distance routes.

αναχώρηση *anakh**o**reesee* **departure**

άφιξη ***a**feeksee* **arrival**

καθημερινά *katheemereen**a*** **daily**

λειτουργεί *leetoorgh**ee*** **operates**

εκτός λειτουργίας *ekt**o**s leetoorgh**ee**as* **no service**

έως / από ***e**os / ap**o*** **until / from**

διακοπές *deeakop**e**s* **holidays**

καλοκαίρι *kalok**e**ree* **summer**

χειμώνας *kheem**o**nas* **winter**

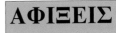

keywords keywords

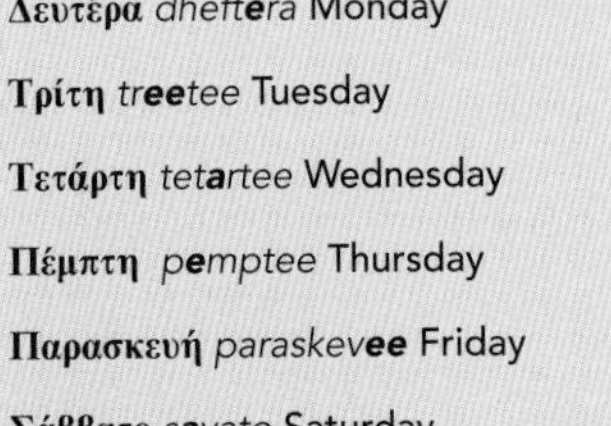
Δευτέρα *dheft**e**ra* Monday

Τρίτη *tr**ee**tee* Tuesday

Τετάρτη *tet**a**rtee* Wednesday

Πέμπτη *p**e**mptee* Thursday

Παρασκευή *paraskev**ee*** Friday

Σάββατο *s**a**vato* Saturday

Κυριακή *keereeak**ee*** Sunday

▲ In Greek days of the week begin with a capital letter, as do months of the year. Signs are often written in capital letters.

ΑΦΙΞΕΙΣ

▲ **ARRIVALS** *af**ee**ksees*

ΑΝΑΧΩΡΗΣΗ

▲ **DEPARTURES** *anakh**o**reesee*

▲ **TIME** ***o**ra*

TICKETS

In Athens, tickets for the Metro, bus, trolley-bus and trains must be validated. Keep your ticket till the end of your journey. On the Metro, buy your ticket (at the desk or from a machine) and validate it as you walk past the validating machines. On the buses you will see the validating machines as you get on. Other cities have a similar ticketing system to Athens, although Athens alone has a Metro. In the rural areas, buy a ticket and keep it throughout the journey.

▲ Athens local bus ticket

◀ You can buy a range of tickets for the Athens metro. This is a single-journey ticket.

▲ 24-hour unlimited travel on bus, trolley or metro.

note the Greek for euro

◀ Another type of Athens local bus ticket

Inter-city train ticket

▼ All information is printed in English as well as in Greek.

▲ You have to validate any ticket you buy for public transport in a validating machine. These are found at the entrance of buses, train platforms and metro stations, as shown here. Simply insert your ticket in the slot for punching.

▲ Cinema ticket booth

price of ticket

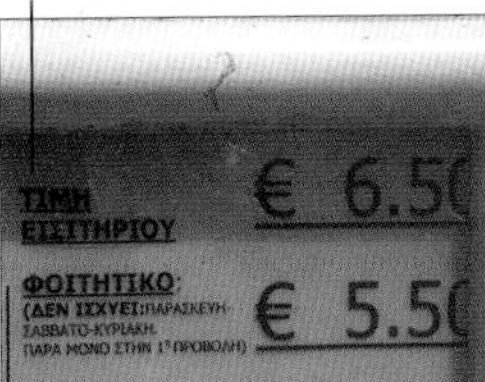

price for students

▲ Ticket prices

▼ Most signs will have translations. The word for ticket is *eeseet**ee**reeo* and the plural is *eeseet**ee**reea*

keywords

εισιτήριο
*eeseet**ee**reeo*
ticket

απλό
*apl**o***
single

με επιστροφή
*me epeestro-f**ee***
return

ημερήσιο εισιτήριο
*eemer**ee**seeo eeseet**ee**reeo*
all day ticket

εισιτήριο διαρκείας
*eeseet**ee**reeo deearkh**ee**as*
season ticket

ταξιδιωτικό πάσο
*takseedheeo-teek**o** p**a**so*
travel pass

ολόκληρο
*ol**o**kleero*
adult

παιδικό
*pedeek**o***
child

οικογενειακό
*eekoyeneeak**o***
family

φοιτητικό
*feeteeteek**o***
student

ηλικιωμένων
*eelee-keeom**e**non*
over 60

αναπηρικό
*anapeereek**o***
disabled

PUBLIC TRANSPORT

Buses and trains are reasonably priced and reliable. There are good bus services within cities and regular long-distance coaches catering for people in towns and in country villages. Tickets are bought from a ticket office or on the bus in rural areas. Because Greece is so mountainous, the railway system is more limited. There is a line from Athens to Thessalonika and from Thessalonika across to the Turkish border. There is also a line from Athens to Patras and around the Peloponnese, which is very scenic. You buy tickets at the stations.

◀ **BUS STATION**

A bus-stop in Athens showing where this Averof IKA stop is on the bus-route. ▼

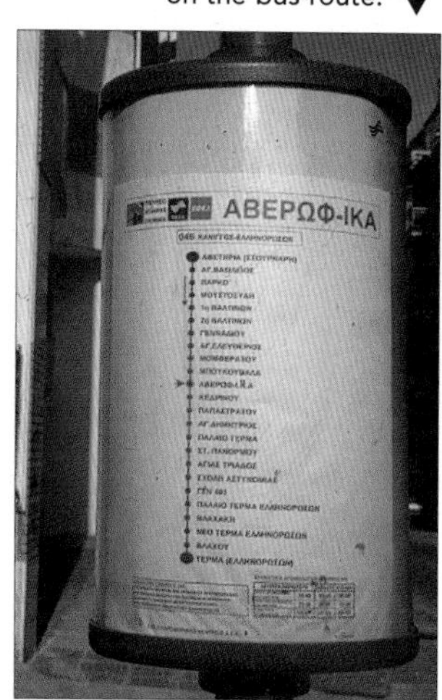

▲ Bus stop with route numbers

▶ Ticket office

▲ *bus-stop (s**ta**see)* ▼

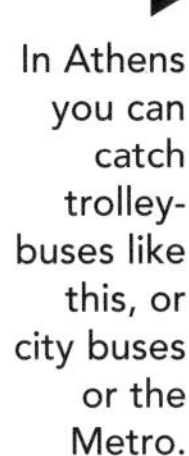

▶ In Athens you can catch trolley-buses like this, or city buses or the Metro.

You can buy bus and trolley-bus tickets here. ▼

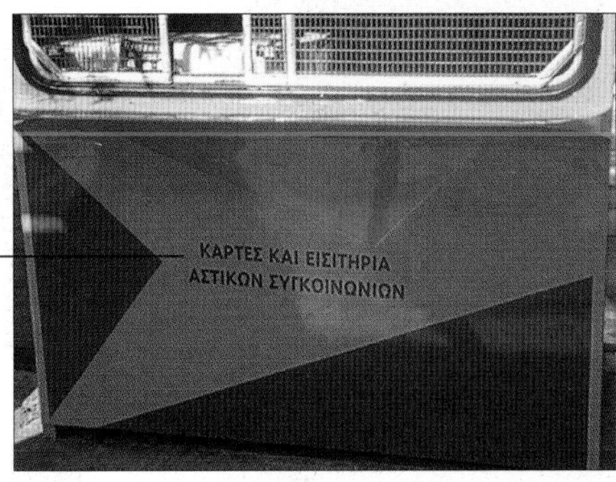

ΚΑΡΤΕΣ = *cards*
ΚΑΙ = *and*
ΕΙΣΙΤΗΡΙΑ = *tickets*

where is the bus station?
*poo **ee**ne o stathm**o**s leofor**ee**on*
πού είναι ο σταθμός λεωφορείων;

where is the bus stop?
*poo **ee**ne ee st**a**see too leofor**ee**oo*
πού είναι η στάση του λεωφορείου

where is the bus to the centre?
*poo **ee**ne to leofor**ee**o ya to k**e**ntro*
πού είναι το λεωφορείο για το κέντρο;

which bus goes to Pireus?
*pyo leofor**ee**o p**a**-ee ston peeray**a***
ποιο λεωφορείο πάει στον Πειραιά;

to the station
*sto stathm**o***
στο σταθμό

to the museum
*sto moos**ee**o*
στο μουσείο

to the Acropolis
*steen akr**o**polee*
στην Ακρόπολη

to Plaka
*steen pl**a**ka*
στην Πλάκα

where is this bus going?
*poo p**a**-ee aft**o** to leofor**ee**o*
πού πάει αυτό το λεωφορείο;

The new Metro in Athens is very impressive. It is built in pink and grey marble and contains many exhibits of archaeological discoveries made during construction. Security is high there: there is no smoking, no eating/drinking and most definitely no graffiti. It opens at 5.30 am and closes at midnight. A ticket is valid for one single journey of any length.You can also get a ticket valid for 24 hours (as many trips as you want) The 24 hour ticket is also valid for use on the buses, trolley-buses and trains in the same period of time.

◀ Metro symbol with station name and network map below.

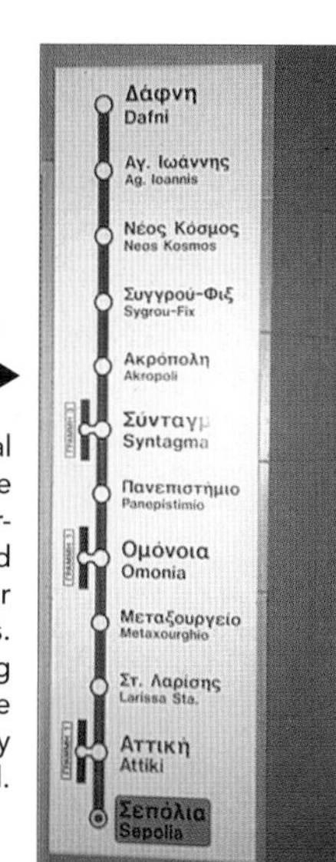

▶ Individual lines are colour-coded, and maps appear in stations. Connecting stations are clearly indicated.

Προς Δάφνη To Dafni

▲ Overhead direction indicator in station.

◀ Athens' Metro system is modern.

▼ Ticket office

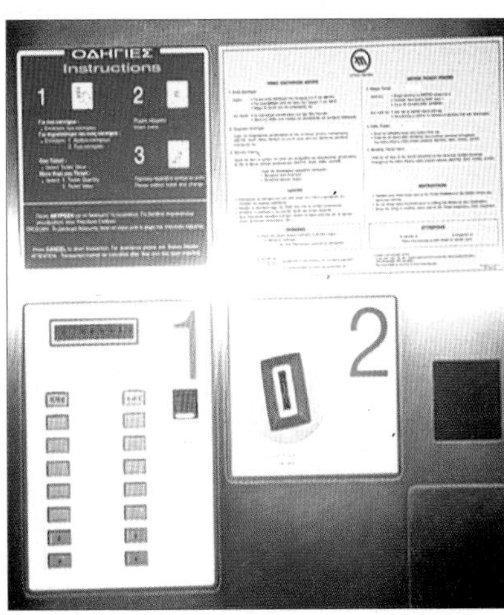

▲ Automatic ticket machines in the Athens Metro are easy to use and are multilingual.

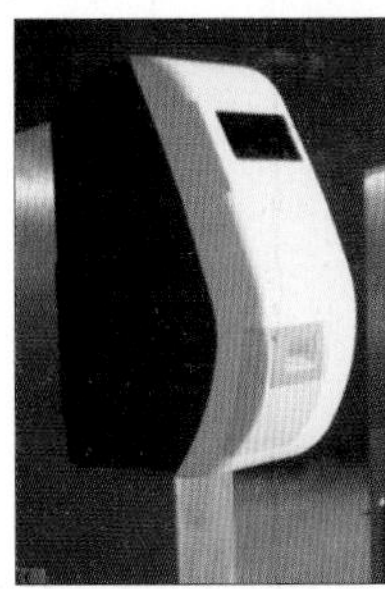

▲ In the Metro you must validate your ticket in one of these machines and then keep it during your journey.

where is the nearest metro station?
poo ***ee****ne o kondeen****o****teros stathm****o****s too metr****o***
πού είναι ο κοντινότερος σταθμός του μετρό;

a ticket / 4 tickets, please
e*na eeseet****ee****reeo /* ***t****essera eeseet****ee****reea parakal****o***
ένα εισιτήριο / τέσσερα εισιτήρια παρακαλώ

have you a map of the metro?
e*khete kh****a****rtee ya to metr****o***
έχετε χάρτη για το μετρό;

I want to go to...
*th****e****lo na p****a****o sto / stee...*
θέλω να πάω στο / στη...

do I have to change?
*pr****e****pee nal****a****kso ghram****ee***
πρέπει ν'αλλάξω γραμμή;

which line do I take?
*pya ghramm****ee*** *pr****e****pee na p****a****ro*
ποια γραμμή πρέπει να πάρω;

excuse me!
*me seeghkhor****ee****te*
με συγχωρείτε!

can I go by underground?
*bor****o*** *na p****a****o me to metr****o***
μπορώ να πάω με το μετρό;

where?
poo
πού;

I'm getting off
*kat****e****veno*
κατεβαίνω

Because Greece is so mountainous the train service is quite limited, but inexpensive. Trains tend to be rather slow and do not go to more remote areas or many places of archaeological interest. The initials of the Greek National Railway are **ΟΣΕ** *and you can visit their website for details of trains and timetables on www.ose.gr. Tickets can be bought at railway stations and travel agents. However, you must remember (as with all other forms of public transport) to validate your ticket at the validating machines in the station before you begin your journey.*

ΕΙΣΙΤΗΡΙΑ ΕΣΩΤΕΡΙΚΟΥ
ΠΛΗΝ ΑΜΑΞ/ΧΙΩΝ INTERCITY

▲ TICKETS WITHIN GREECE EXCEPT INTERCITY TICKETS

ATHENS STATION ▲

WAITING ROOM ▶

a single to...
__e__na apl__o__ eeseet__ee__reeo ya...
ένα απλό εισιτήριο για...

2 singles to...
dh__ee__o apl__a__ eeseet__ee__reea ya...
δύο απλά εισιτήρια για...

a return to...
__e__na eeseet__ee__reeo me epeestrof__ee__ ya...
ένα εισιτήριο με επιστροφή για...

2 returns to...
dh__ee__o eeseet__ee__reea me epeestrof__ee__ ya...
δύο εισιτήρια με επιστροφή για...

a child's ticket to...
__e__na pedheek__o__ eeseet__ee__reeo ya...
ένα παιδικό εισητήριο για...

he/she is ... years old
__ee__ne ... khron__o__n
είναι ... χρονών

I want to book 2 seats
th__e__lo na kl__ee__so dh__ee__o th__e__sees
θέλω να κλείσω δύο θέσεις

economy class
tooreesteek__ee__ th__e__see
τουριστική θέση

smoking
kapn__ee__zontes
καπνίζοντες

non smoking
mee kapn__ee__zontes
μη καπνίζοντες

is there a supplement to pay?
eep__a__rkhee epeepl__e__on epeev__a__reensee
υπάρχει επιπλέον επιβάρυνση;

Arrivals and departures board in the station. In major stations, information is displayed in both Greek and English, alternating continually. ▼

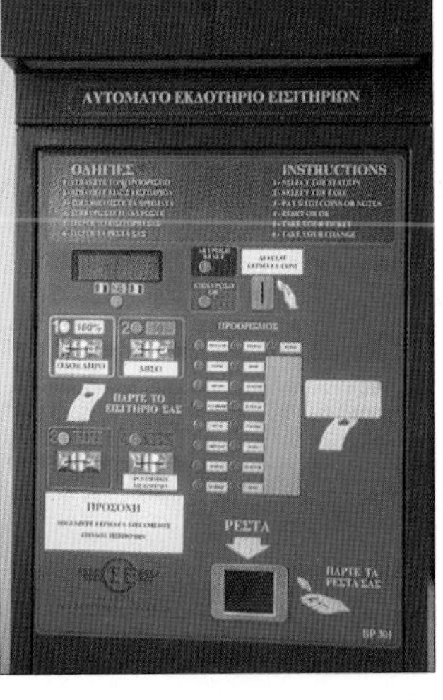

Automatic ticket machine in the railway station. Instructions are available in English as well as Greek. ◀

◀ Overhead departure board on platform

keywords

απλό
aplo
single

μετ επιστροφής
met epeestrofees
return

κράτηση
krateesee
reservation

επιτρέπεται το κάπνισμα
epeetrepete to kapneesma
smoking is allowed

απαγορεύεται το κάπνισμα
apagorevete to kapneesma
non-smoking

γραφείο εισιτηρίων
grafeeo eessee-teereeon
ticket office

γραφείο αποσκευών
grafeeo aposkevon
left luggage

βαγόνι
vagonee
carriage

πλατφόρμα
platforma
platform

talking

is this the train for...?
eene afto to treno ya...
είναι αυτό το τρένο για...;

is this seat free?
eene ee thesee elevtheree
είναι η θέση ελεύθερη;

which platform does it leave from?
apo peea platforma fevyee
από ποια πλατφόρμα φεύγει;

this is my seat
aftee eene ee thesee moo
αυτή είναι η θέση μου

TAXI

Taxis abound in Greece. Each town has its own colour for taxis. Taxis in Athens are yellow. It is easy to flag them down in cities, as the local people do. You can also ask at a kiosk for the phone number of a taxi firm, or ask your hotel to call a taxi for you. Tipping is not all that common in Greece but small tips are always gratefully received.

▲ Taxis are quite cheap, but you should still ask the price beforehand. The grey taxis are for long-distance journeys, i.e. town to town.

▲ You can ring for a taxi, wait at a stand or flag one down in the street.

A taxi stand and phone in a small town. ▼

All taxis have meters. ▼

where can I get a taxi?
poo bor**o** na vro taks**ee**
πού μπορώ να βρω ταξί;

to the airport
sto aerodhr**o**meeo
στο αεροδρόμιο

please take me to this address
se aft**ee**n teen dheee**v**theensee parakal**o**
σε αυτήν την διεύθυνση, παρακαλώ

how much will it cost?
p**o**so kost**ee**zee
πόσο κοστίζει;

it's too much
**ee**ne pol**ee** akreev**a**
είναι πολύ ακριβά

how much is to the centre?
p**o**so kost**ee**zee ya to k**e**ntro
πόσο κοστίζει για το κέντρο;

please order me a taxi
parakal**o** kal**e**ste **e**na taks**ee**
παρακαλώ καλέστε ένα ταξί

can I have a receipt?
bor**ee**te na moo dh**o**sete ap**o**dheeksee
μπορείτε να μου δώσετε απόδειξη;

keep the change
krat**ee**ste ta r**e**sta
κρατήστε τα ρέστα

CAR HIRE

You will find all the major car-hire companies in Greece, plus various local ones. You can also book a car from abroad, before your trip, and the car should be waiting for you at the airport – usually a cheap, easy option. Within Greece, restrictions vary. You HAVE to have held a driving licence for at least one year, but the minimum age differs between companies from 21 to 25. Some companies charge supplements for young drivers. A few local companies will let you rent a car at age 20.

I want to hire a car
thelo na neekyaso ena aftokeeneeto
θέλω να νοικιάσω ένα αυτοκίνητο

for one day
ya meea mera
για μία μέρα

for ... days
ya ... meres
για ... μέρες

I prefer a...
proteemo ena...
προτιμώ ένα ...

large
meghalo
μεγάλο

small
meekro
μικρό

car
aftokeeneeto
αυτοκίνητο

how much is it...?
poso kanee...
πόσο κάνει...;

per day
tee mera
τη μέρα

per week
tee vdhomadha
τη βδομάδα

how much is the deposit?
posee eene ee prokatavolee
πόση είναι η προκαταβολή;

is there a charge per kilometre?
yeenete khreosee ana kheeleeometro
γίνεται χρέωση ανά χιλιόμετρο;

how much?
poso kanee
πόσο κάνει;

what is included in the insurance?
tee pereelamvanete steen asfaleea
τι περιλαμβάνεται στην ασφάλεια;

I want to take out additional insurance
thelo na paro prosthetee asfaleea
θέλω να πάρω πρόσθετη ασφάλεια

what do I do if I break down?
tee tha kano an meeno apo vlavee
τι θα κάνω αν μείνω από βλάβη;

where are the documents?
poo eene ee adheea keekloforeeas ke ee asfaleea
πού είναι η άδεια κυκλοφορίας και η ασφαλεία;

DRIVING

The minimum age for driving in Greece is 18. Greek people generally drive carefully and the roads are good. Watch out when driving in Athens, though, as it can get quite chaotic. Take care at all times, especially on zebra crossings, as you will occasionally come across impatient drivers and people who overtake dangerously. Cars do not often stop for pedestrians – the zebra crossing is really just an accepted crossing point for pedestrians once the road is clear. There are many excellent new highways in Greece, linking major towns and cities. In Greece's mountainous areas, you will find twisting roads with hairpin bends but there won't usually be a lot of traffic about. Even the remotest roads nowadays have tarmac but you might still find the odd dirt track, linking tiny villages. If you take your own car to Greece, a Green Card may or may not be necessary – ask your Insurance Company to explain this in full. Keep your driving licence, car documents and passport with you at all times. Police often set up speed checks, especially where there is a small village along an otherwise deserted highway – so watch your speed! Seatbelts and motorbike helmets are compulsory and fines are issued. Occasionally you may see three people on one motorbike without a helmet in sight, but don't let this deceive you, fines are hefty for these offences!

Speed restrictions

built up area	50 km/h
(motorcycles)	40 km/h
main roads	90 km/h
(motorcycles)	70 km/h
motorway	120 km/h
(motorcycles)	90 km/h

▲ Speed restrictions vary for cars and motorcycles. It is compulsory to wear seatbelts.

▲ Each county has its own set of designated letters, 'ATE' is Athens. Only letters recognizable throughout Europe are used on numberplates.

caution

roadworks in progress

slow

◀ Greek main roads are all 'E' roads, with a number, similar to our 'A' roads.

caution

in progress

roadworks

speed 10 kph

Toll-free main roads are signed in blue, while you pay a toll on the motorways. ▼

*motorway (aftokeeneet**o**dhromos) signs are green in Greece*

▲ Beaches are well signposted

Από 00:00 π.μ.
Εως 07:00 π.μ.

◀ No motorbikes allowed at night. Note that it is compulsory to wear a crash helmet.

Από *apo* from

Έως ***e**os* till

Π.μ.. = am

Μ.μ. = pm

◀ Signpost indicating Vrahos tunnel

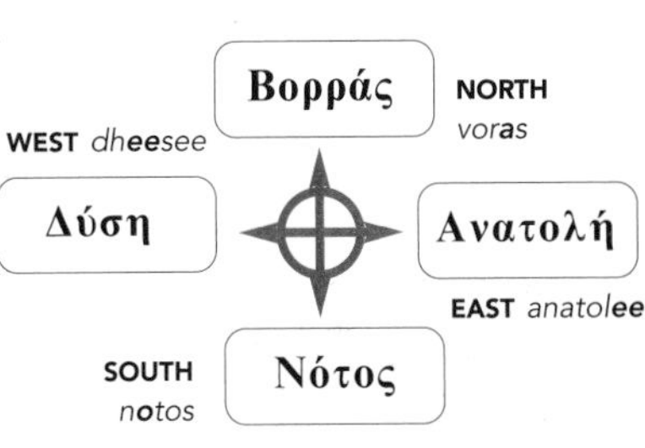

▲ Direction indicators

▲ No overtaking: Uneven surface

Caution: Road narrows : No overtaking ▼

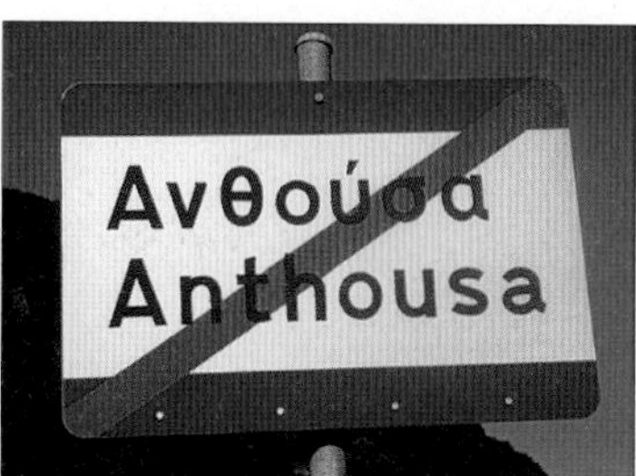

▲ A diagonal red line shows that you are leaving a town or village.

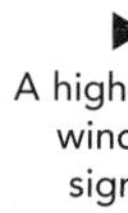

A high-wind sign

Restricted ▶ access times for heavy vehicles

from 10 am to 11 pm

talking

we're going to...
*py**e**noome sto...*
πηγαίνουμε στο...

what is the best route?
*py**a** **ee**ne ee kal**ee**teree dheeadhrom**ee***
ποια είναι η καλύτερη διαδρομή;

how do I get to the motorway?
*pos tha p**a**o steen ethneek**ee***
πως θα παω στην εθνική;

which junction is it for...?
*se py**a** dheeast**a**vrosee **ee**ne...*
σε ποια διαστάυρωση είναι...;

when is the best time to drive?
*py**a** **ee**ne ee kal**ee**teree **o**ra ya odh**ee**yeesee*
ποια είναι η καλύτερη ώρα για οδήγηση;

is the road good?
*ee**ne kal**o**s o dhr**o**mos*
είναι καλός ο δρόμος;

When driving on the motorway you pay a toll. Toll-stations are well signed and easy to deal with. Rates are quite low and you pay a fixed rate per section, e.g Patras to Corinth. You pay at the start of the motorway and should keep your ticket in case they check it on leaving. Keep your eye on the speed limit and watch out for occasional impatient overtaking.

◀ Signs give you lane directions as you approach the motorway toll-booths. Stay in cash-only lanes.

▼ Toll booth

Keep your toll receipt until you get off the motorway. ▼

T.E.O A.E.
ΕΟ ΑΘΗΝΩΝ-ΚΟΡΙΝΘΟΥ
ΣΔ ΕΛΕΥΣΙΝΙΩΝ
ΦΥΛΑΞΕΤΕ ΤΟ ΩΣ ΤΟ ΤΕΛΟΣ ΤΗΣ ΔΙΑΔΡΟΜΗΣ (Ν.1798/88)
KEEP THIS TICKET THROUGH OUT THE TRAVEL AND SHOW IT AT ANY CHECK OVER
ΑΠΟΔΕΙΞΗ ΠΛΗΡΩΜΗΣ ΔΙΟΔΙΩΝ
ΑΡ.ΚΥΚΛΟΦ / PLATE NO:
ΧΕΙΡ/OPER: 287 ΛΩΡΙΔΑ/LANE: 18
ΗΜΕΡ/DATE: 24/08/2002 ΩΡΑ/TIME: 17:26:12
ΚΑΤ/CAT: 2 CASH
ΤΙΜΗ/TAR: 1.40 EUR
ΑΡ.ΑΠΟΔ/TICK.NO: 1132
ΚΑΛΟ & ΑΣΦΑΛΕΣ ΤΑΞΙΔΙ / HAVE A NICE & SAFE TRIP
10240817261202

If you break down

For roadside help, dial 104. The Automobile and Touring Club of Greece provides 24-hour information to foreign tourists on 174.

can you help me?
*bor**ee**te na me voeeth**ee**sete*
μπορείτε να με βοηθήσετε;

my car has broken down
*to aftok**ee**neet**o** moo kh**a**lase*
το αυτοκίνητό μου χάλασε

I'm on my own *(female)*
***ee**me m**o**nee moo*
είμαι μόνη μου

there are children in the car
***e**kho pedy**a** sto aftok**ee**neeto*
έχω παιδιά στο αυτοκίνητο

the car is...
*to aftok**ee**neeto **ee**ne...*
το αυτοκίνητο είναι...

a blue Fiat
***e**na ble Fiat*
ένα μπλε Fiat

registration number...
*o areethm**o**s keekloforeeas...*
ο αριθμός κυκλοφορίας...

You can park by the roadside in small towns. In bigger places there will be various restrictions. A tow-away sign makes the situation fairly obvious, but other signs may be less easy to be sure about. If in doubt, ask before parking, as fines are high. The safest place to park in a big town is a 'parking' where you pay a fixed amount for a fixed length of time. In Athens you can leave your car long-term in a technologically operated 'robot' car-park, where it will be completely safe. Parking meters are very rarely seen.

▲ **NO PARKING** ▼

▼ **PARKING** *50m right*

prohibited *KTEL (bus) station*

entrance

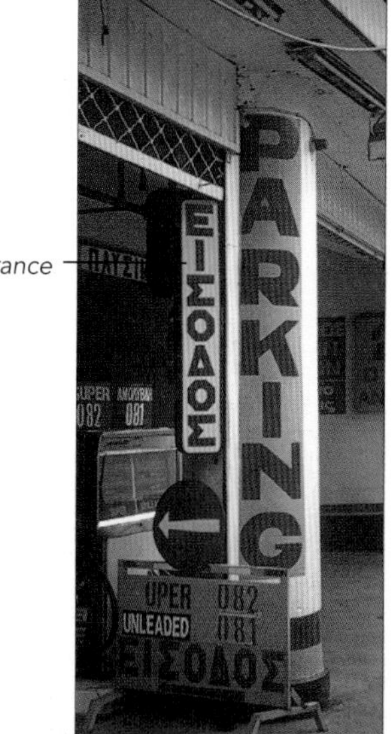

▲ *Parking*
ΔΕΧΟΜΕΘΑ = *receiving*
ΑΥΤΟΚΙΝΗΤΑ = *cars*
ΔΙΑΝΥΚΤΕΡΕΥΕΙ = *open all night*

Underground parking (private) ▲

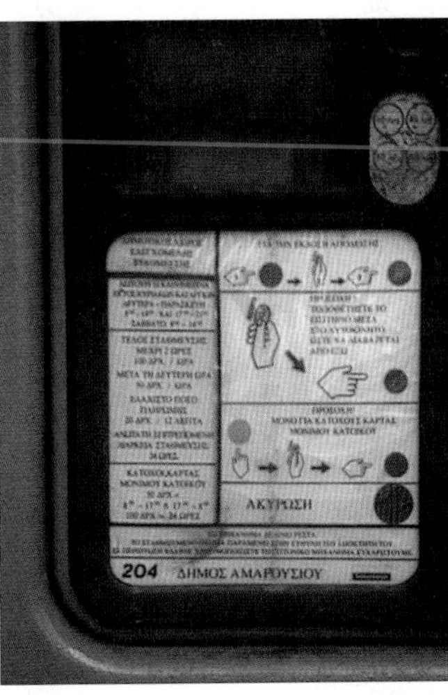

◀ There are not many pay-and-display parking meters in Greece, and you will probably find them only in Athens. Instructions for use are the same as the meters in the UK.

can I park here?
boro na parkaro edho
μπορώ να παρκάρω εδώ;

where is the best place to park?
poo eene kaleetera na parkaro
πού είναι καλύτερα να παρκάρω;

how long can I park here?
ya posee ora boro na parkaro edho
για πόση ώρα μπορώ να παρκάρω εδώ;

do I need a parking ticket?
khreeazome karta stathmefsees
χρειάζομαι κάρτα στάθμευσης;

is there a car park?
eeparkhee kapyo parking
υπάρχει κάποιο πάρκινγκ;

Petrol is relatively cheap and diesel even less. Opening hours of petrol stations vary, but they are plentiful and many open all day and into the evening. The attendant will fill your tank – there is no self-service. Filling stations also have air, oil, water and sometimes a carwash and vacuum cleaner, and some will mend punctures.

Πλυντήριο = *car wash*

Λιπαντήριο = *lubrication*

*air (a**e**ras)* *water (ner**o**)*

▶ Petrol pumps are generally labelled in English.

Auto car wash ◀

▶ *change of oil free of charge*

talking

is there a petrol station near here?
*eep**a**rkhee venzeen**a**dheeko edh**o** kond**a***
υπάρχει βενζινάδικο εδώ κοντά;

fill it up, please
*yem**ee**ste to parakal**o***
γεμίστε το, παρακαλώ

unleaded
*am**o**leevdhee*
αμόλυβδη

20 euros worth of unleaded petrol
***ee**kosee evr**o** am**o**leevdhee venz**ee**nee*
είκοσι ευρώ αμόλυβδη βενζίνη

You can find all the main dealerships in the major towns. There are also lots of smaller garages and auto-electricians. It's a good idea to ask the price of the repair first, as in any country. If you break down, there are a number of companies you can call, two of which are ELPA (tel 104) and Express Service (tel 154). Check their rates before you ask them to come out.

▲ Express Service and ELPA are breakdown services like the AA. Non-members can also phone for help but will pay a supplement.

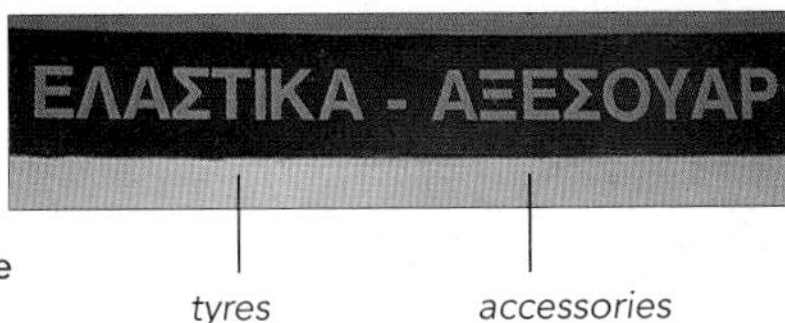

tyres *accessories*

I've broken down
khalase to aftokeeneeto moo
χάλασε το αυτοκίνητό μου

where is the nearest garage? *(for repairs)*
poo eene to pyo kondeeno garaz
πού είναι το πιο κοντινό γκαράζ;

is it serious?
eene sovaro
είναι σοβαρό;

the ... doesn't work properly
o/ee/to ... dhen dhoolevee kala
ο/η/το ... δεν δουλεύει καλά

the ... don't work properly
ee/ta ... dhen dhoolevoon kala
οι/τα ... δεν δουλεύουν καλά

I don't have a spare tyre
dhen ekho rezerva
δεν έχω ρεζέρβα

have you the parts?
ekhete ta andalakteeka
έχετε τα ανταλλακτικά;

could you please help me to change the tyre
boreete na me voeetheesete na alakso lasteekho
μπορείτε να με βοηθήσετε να αλλάξω λάστιχο;

when will it be ready?
pote tha eene eteemo
πότε θα είναι έτοιμο;

how much will it cost?
poso tha kosteesee
πόσο θα κοστίσει;

the car won't start
ee meekhanee dhen ksekeena
η μηχανή δεν ξεκινά

the battery is flat
ee batareea eene adheea
η μπαταρία είναι άδεια

the engine is overheating
afksanete ee thermokraseea tees mekhanees
αυξάνεται η θερμοκρασία της μηχανής

I have a flat tyre
me epyase lasteekho
με έπιασε λαστιχό

can you replace the windscreen?
boreete na ftyaksete to parbreez
μπορείτε να φτιάξετε το παρμπρίζ;

SHOPPING

When you go into a shop, especially a small one, it is polite to say **kaleemera** *or* **ya sas** *to the shopkeeper (even* **tee kanete** *if you're feeling really daring!) before asking/looking for what you want, as Greece is a much more 'personal' part of the world than more northernly countries. Our impersonal approach can sometimes seem rude! Shops generally open in the morning (8–9 am until 1–2 pm) and again in the evening (approx 5–8 pm). They close in the afternoon and all day on Sundays. However, in busy tourist areas they usually open all day every day (including Sunday) during the summer.*

keywords

φούρνος
*f**oo**rnos*
baker's

κρεοπωλείο
*krayopol**ee**o*
butcher's

ιχθυοπωλείο
*eetheeopol**ee**o*
fish shop

παντοπωλείο
*pandopol**ee**o*
grocer's

μανάβικο
*man**a**veeko*
greengrocer's

καπνοπωλείο
*kapnopol**ee**o*
tobacconist's

ζαχαροπλαστείο
*zakharoplast**ee**o*
cake shop

▲ **BAKERY** Bread is baked freshly every day at the baker's shop. For a big loaf, ask for **ένα κιλό** ***e**na keel**o*** (a kilo loaf). For a small loaf ask for **μισόκιλο** *mees**o**keelo* (a half kilo loaf). For a round sandwich bun ask for **ένα ψώμακι** ***e**na psom**a**kee. Many bakers sell sandwiches.* **ΑΡΤΟΣ** is the ancient Greek for bread (used in shop signs only).

BOOKSHOP ▶

optician
contact lenses

ΟΠΤΙΚΑ
ΦΑΚΟΙ ΕΠΑΦΗΣ
ΧΑΡΗ ΣΠΥΡΙΔΗ
(ΠΤΥΧ.ΟΠΤΙΚΟΣ)

In Greece, especially in big towns and cities, you will find well-stocked supermarkets and hypermarkets. There are both national and international chains. Some will open all day, others will open in the morning and evening only, depending on the size of the supermarket, time of year, etc. All kinds of food and drink are available in supermarkets and mini-markets. In most cases, though, fresh bread is best bought at the baker's.

◀ One of the large Greek supermarket chains

Co-operative supermarkets, like this one, tend to be cheaper. ▼

◀ Special offers at the supermarket

ΤΙΜΗ *teem**ee*** = *price*

co-op

where can I buy...?
*poo bor**o** na aghor**a**so...*
πού μπορώ να αγοράσω...;

matches
*sp**ee**rta*
σπίρτα

bread
*psom**ee***
ψωμί

water
*ner**o***
νερό

do you have...?
ekhete...
έχετε...;

milk
*gh**a**la*
γάλα

bread rolls
*psom**a**keea*
ψωμάκια

I'm looking for a present
*ps**a**khno ya **e**na dh**o**ro*
ψάχνω για ένα δώρο

I'd like a good wine
*tha **ee**thela **e**na kal**o** kras**ee***
θα ήθελα ένα καλό κρασί

how much does it cost?
*p**o**so kost**ee**zee*
πόσο κοστίζει;

can I pay with this card?
*bor**o** na pleer**o**so me aft**ee** teen k**a**rta*
μπορώ να πληρώσω με αυτή την κάρτα;

is there a market?
e**khee laeek**ee** aghor**a
έχει λαϊκή αγορά;

which day?
*py**a** m**e**ra*
ποια μέρα;

talking talking

*Quantities are expressed in kilos and grams. One kilo (**keelo**) is roughly equivalent to 2lb; half a kilo (**meeso keelo**) is equivalent to 1lb. If you want roughly a quarter ($\frac{1}{4}$lb) of something, ask for 100 grams (**ekato gramareea**). If you want to ask for ham, cheese, salami, etc in slices, ask for **fetes**. 10 slices is **dheka fetes**. Many towns have a weekly market which is great for fresh, local produce. It's best to go good and early. As well as food, markets sell clothes, shoes and all kinds of household items. It's a lot of fun, too!*

◀ Fruit and vegetables are generally sold by the kilo, although larger items, such as melons, are sold individually. Small supermarkets/mini-markets may well have no fish/meat or fruit/vegetables, so you have to get these from the fishmonger/butcher or greengrocer.

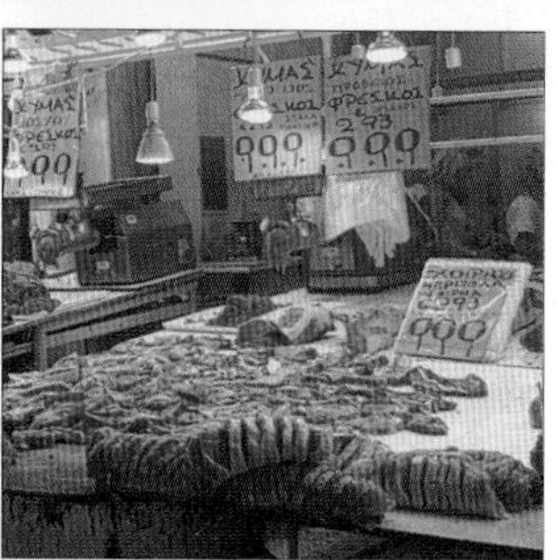

◀ Butcher's stall in the market.
ΜΟΣΧΑΡΙ *(moskh**a**ree) beef*
ΚΥΜΑΣ *(keem**a**s) mince*
ΧΟΙΡΙΝΟ *(kheereen**o**) pork*
ΜΠΡΙΖΟΛΑ *(bree**zo**la) chop*

milk

green: **Άπαχο** *(**a**pakho) = skimmed*

red: **Πλήρες** *(pl**ee**res) = full-cream*

Λιπαρά *(leepar**a**) = fat*

The colour-coding of milk **γάλα** *(gh**a**la)* cartons varies from one company to another. ▶

blue: **Ημίπαχο** *(eem**ee**pakho) = semi-skimmed*

pasta

1 calorie per 1 gram

boiled pasta

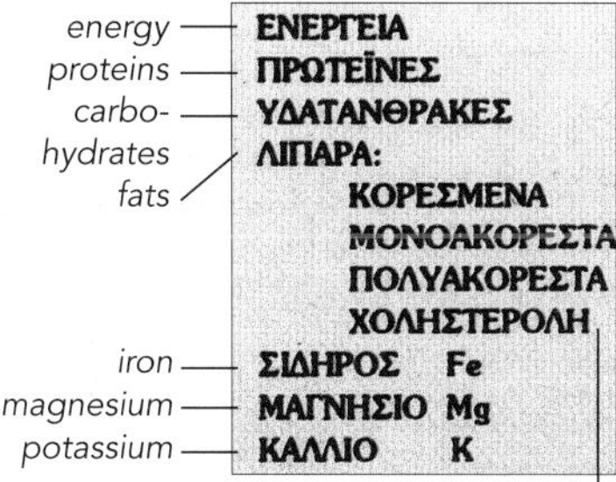

energy, proteins, carbohydrates, fats: saturated, monounsaturated, polyunsaturated, cholesterol; iron, magnesium, potassium

▼ **EAT BEFORE**

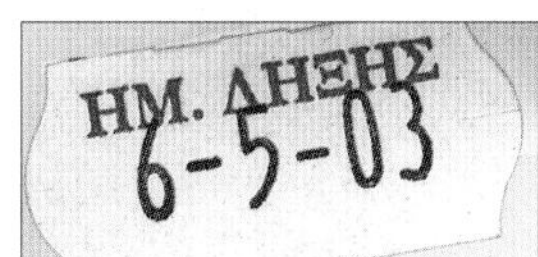

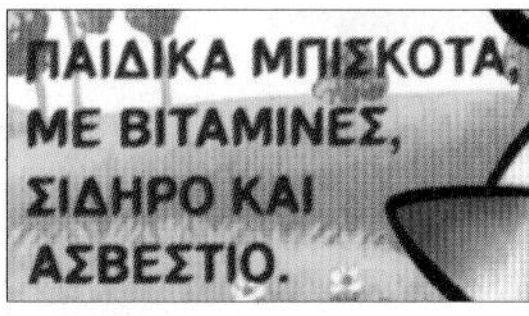

▲ *children's biscuits, with vitamins, iron and calcium*

a piece of cheese
ena komatee teeree
ένα κομμάτι τυρί

a little more
leegho akoma
λίγο ακόμα

a little less
leeghotero
λιγότερο

that's enough, thanks
ftanee efkhareesto
φτάνει ευχαριστώ

$\frac{1}{4}$ kilo feta cheese
ena tetarto keelo feta
ένα τέταρτο κιλό φέτα

3 tomatoes
trees domates
τρεις ντομάτες

10 slices of ham
deka fetes zambon
δέκα φέτας ζαμπόν

a litre of milk
ena leetro ghala
ένα λίτρο γάλα

bottled water
emfeealomeno nero
εμφιαλωμένο νερό

sparkling	**still**
aeryookho	*mee aeryookho*
αεριούχο	μη αεριούχο

a tin of tomatoes
ena kootee domates
ένα κουτί ντομάτες

half a kilo of green beans
meeso keelo fasolakya
μισό κιλό φασολάκια

a kilo of potatoes
ena keelo patates
ένα κιλό πατάτες

two cheese pies
dheeo teeropeetes
δύο τυρόπιτες

ΚΑΡΑΜΕΛΛΕΣ LIHN ΧΩΡΙΣ ΖΑΧΑΡΗ (ΜΕ ΣΟΡΒΙΤΗ)
ΜΕ ΑΡΩΜΑ ΦΡΟΥΤΟΥ

◀ *Sweets –* **χωρίς ζάχαρη** *(khorees zakharee) without sugar*

talking talking talking talking talking talking

Everyday Foods

biscuits τα μπισκότα *beesk**o**ta*

bread το ψωμί *psom**ee***

bread roll τα ψωμάκια *psom**a**keea*

butter το βούτυρο *v**oo**teero*

cereal τα δημητριακά *dheemeetreeak**a***

cheese το τυρί *teer**ee***

cheese pie η τυρόπιτα *teer**o**peeta*

chicken το κοτόπουλο *kot**o**poolo*

chips οι πατάτες τηγανητές *pat**a**tes teeghaneet**e**s*

chocolate η σοκολάτα *sokol**a**ta*

coffee *(instant)* το Νεσκαφέ *Nescafe®*

cream η κρέμα *kr**e**ma*

crisps τα πατατάκια *patat**a**keea*

eggs τα αβγά *avgh**a***

fish το ψάρι *ps**a**ree*

flour το αλεύρι *al**e**vree*

ham το ζαμπόν *zamb**o**n*

herbal tea το τσάι από βότανα *ts**a**ee ap**o** v**o**tana*

honey το μέλι *m**e**lee*

jam η μαρμελάδα *marmel**a**dha*

lamb το αρνάκι *arn**a**kee*

margarine η μαργαρίνη *marghar**ee**nee*

marmalade η μαρμελάδα πορτοκάλι *marmel**a**dha portok**a**lee*

meat balls οι κεφτέδες *keft**e**dhes*

milk το γάλα *gh**a**la*

mustard η μουστάρδα *moost**a**rdha*

olive oil το ελαιόλαδο *ele**o**ladho*

orange juice ο χυμός πορτοκάλι *kheem**o**s portok**a**lee*

pasta τα ζυμαρικά *zeemareek**a***

pepper το πιπέρι *peep**e**ree*

pork το χοιρινό *kheereen**o***

rice το ρύζι *r**ee**zee*

salt το αλάτι *al**a**tee*

spinach pie η σπανακόπιτα *spanak**o**peeta*

sugar η ζάχαρη *z**a**kharee*

tea το τσάι *ts**a**ee*

tomatoes *(tin)* οι ντομάτες κονσέρβα *dom**a**tes kons**e**rva*

tuna ο τόνος *t**o**nos*

vegetable oil το φυτικό λάδι *feeteek**o** l**a**dhee*

vinegar το ξύδι *ks**ee**dhee*

yoghurt το γιαούρτι *ya**oo**rtee*

Fruit

apples	τα μήλα *m**ee**la*
apricots	το βερύκοκκα *ver**ee**koka*
bananas	οι μπανάνες *ban**a**nes*
cherries	τα κεράσια *ker**a**seea*
figs	τα σύκα *s**ee**ka*
grapefruit	το γκρέιπφρουτ *gr**ei**pfroot*
grapes	τα σταφύλια *staf**ee**leea*
lemon	το λεμόνι *lem**o**nee*
melon	το πεπόνι *pep**o**nee*
nectarines	τα νεκταρίνια *nektar**ee**neea*
oranges	τα πορτοκάλια *portok**a**leea*
peaches	τα ροδάκινα *rodh**a**keena*
pears	τα αχλάδια *akhl**a**dheea*
pineapple	ο ανανάς *o anan**a**s*
plums	τα δαμάσκηνα *dham**a**skeena*
strawberries	οι φράουλες *fr**a**ooles*
watermelon	το καρπούζι *karp**oo**zee*

Vegetables

asparagus	τα σπαράγγια *spar**a**ngeea*
aubergine	η μελιτζάνα *meleetz**a**na*
basil	ο βασιλικός *vaseeleek**o**s*
bean *(haricot)*	το φασόλι *fas**o**lee*
(broad)	το κουκί *kook**ee***
cabbage	το λάχανο *l**a**khano*
carrots	τα καρότα *kar**o**ta*
cauliflower	το κουνουπίδι *koonoop**ee**dhee*
celery	το σέλινο *s**e**leeno*
chickpeas	τα ρεβίθια *rev**ee**theea*
courgettes	τα κολοκυθάκια *kolokeeth**a**keea*
cucumber	το αγγούρι *ang**oo**ree*
eggplant	η μελιτζάνα *meleetz**a**na*
garlic	το σκόρδο *sk**o**rdho*
green beans	τα φασολάκια *fasol**a**keea*
lettuce	το μαρούλι *mar**oo**lee*
mushrooms	τα μανιτάρια *maneet**a**reea*
olives	οι ελιές *ely**e**s*
onions	τα κρεμμύδια *krem**ee**dheea*
parsley	ο μαϊντανός *maeendan**o**s*
peas	ο αρακάς *arak**a**s*
peppers	οι πιπεριές *peeperee-**e**s*
potatoes	οι πατάτες *pat**a**tes*
spinach	το σπανάκι *span**a**kee*
tomatoes	οι ντομάτες *dom**a**tes*
zucchini	τα κολοκυθάκια *kolokeeth**a**keea*

In the cities there are many high-quality department stores. One of the most popular of these is the 'Hondos Centre' which has branches throughout Greece.

keywords

πολυκατάστημα
*poleekat**a**steema*
department store

υπόγειο
*eep**o**yo*
basement

ισόγειο
*ees**o**yo*
ground floor

πρώτος όροφος
*pr**o**tos **o**rofos*
1st floor

κατάστημα
*kat**a**steema*
department

ηλεκτρικά είδη
*eelektreek**a** **ee**dee*
electrical goods

κοσμήματα
*kosm**ee**mata*
jewellery

γυναικεία
*yeenek**ee**a*
ladies'

ανδρικά
*andreek**a***
men's

παιδικά
*pedeek**a***
children's

◀ **SHOE SHOP**
The word for shoes is **παπούτσια** (*pap**oo**tseea*) and for sandals **σανδάλια** (*sand**a**leea*).

▲ **4TH FLOOR** (*o**rofos*)

SALE ▼

Μόνο — (*m**o**no*) only

1.230 €

το άτομο — (*to **a**toma*) per person

FREE GIFT ▶ (*d**o**ro*)

Δώρο!

◀ The rural answer to the department store! In the country areas and smaller villages you will sometimes find vans like this selling clothes, food, linen, chairs and tables, even baby chicks. They have a megaphone to advertise their wares.

talking

where can I find...?
poo na vro...
πού να βρω...;

batteries for this
*batar**ee**es yee aft**o***
μπαταρίες γι' αυτό

toys
*peghn**ee**dhya*
παιγνίδια

shoes
*pap**oo**tsya*
παπούτσια

Women's clothes sizes

UK/Australia	8	10	12	14	16	18	20	22
Europe	36	38	40	42	44	46	48	50
US/Canada	6	8	10	12	14	16	18	20

Men's clothes sizes (suits)

UK/US/Canada	36	38	40	42	44	46
Europe	46	48	50	52	54	56
Australia	92	97	102	107	112	117

Shoes

UK/Australia	2	3	4	5	6	7	8	9	10	11
Europe	35	36	37	38	39	41	42	43	45	46
US/Canada women	4	5	6	7	8	9	10	11	12	-
US/Canada men	3	4	5	6	7	8	9	10	11	12

Children's Shoes

UK/US/Canada	0	1	2	3	4	5	6	7	8	9	10	11
Europe	15	17	18	19	20	22	23	24	26	27	28	29

can I try this on?
*bor**o** na to dhokeem**a**so*
μπορώ να το δοκιμάσω;

it's too big for me
*moo **ee**ne megh**a**lo*
μου είναι μεγάλο

it's too small for me
*moo **ee**ne pol**ee** sten**o***
μου είναι πολύ στενό

it's too expensive
ee**ne pol**ee** akreev**o
είναι πολύ ακριβό

I'll take this one
*tha to p**a**ro*
θα το πάρω

I take a size ...
*for**o** ... n**oo**mero*
φορώ ... νούμερο

where are the changing rooms?
*poo **ee**ne ta dhokeemast**ee**reea*
πού είναι τα δοκιμαστήρια;

have you a smaller one?
***e**khete meekr**o**tero n**oo**mero*
έχετε μικρότερο νούμερο;

have you a larger one?
***e**khete meghal**ee**tero n**oo**mero*
έχετε μεγαλύτερο νούμερο;

do you have this in my size?
***e**khete aft**o** sto n**oo**mer**o** moo*
έχετε αυτό στο νούμερό μου;

can you give me a discount?
*tha moo k**a**nete kal**ee**teree teem**ee***
θα μου κάνετε καλύτερη τιμή;

I like it
*moo ar**e**see*
μου αρέσει

I don't like it
*dhen moo ar**e**see*
δεν μου αρέσει

*Post Offices open in the morning, from 8–9 am until 1–2 pm, according to the location. They do not open in the afternoon or on Saturdays, with the exception of the main Post Office in Syntagma Square in Athens, which opens on Saturdays and Sundays in summer. Stamps can also be bought at kiosks (**pereeptero**) and at shops selling postcards.*

▲ Post Offices may be signposted

▲ Opening hours are sometimes printed in English. Post offices usually open only in the morning.

▶ Red post-boxes are for express mail in the Athens area. Yellow boxes are for general post, and often detail collection times.

talking

where is the post office?
*poo **ee**ne to takheedhrom**ee**o*
πού είναι το ταχυδρομείο;

do you sell stamps?
***e**khete ghrammat**o**seema*
έχετε γραμματόσημα;

where can I buy stamps?
*poo bor**o** na aghor**a**so ghramat**o**seema*
πού μπορώ να αγοράσω γραμματόσημα;

10 stamps
*dh**e**ka ghramat**o**seema*
δέκα γραμματόσημα

for postcards
*ya k**a**rtes*
για κάρτες

urgent mail
*ep**ee**ghon*
επείγον

to Britain
*ya angl**ee**a*
για Αγγλία

to America
*ya amereek**ee***
για Αμερική *amereek**ee***

I want to send this letter registered post
*th**e**lo na st**ee**lo aft**o** to ghr**a**ma seesteem**e**no*
θέλω να στείλω αυτό το γράμμα συστημένο

how much is it to send this parcel?
*p**o**so kost**ee**zee na st**ee**lo aft**o** to pak**e**to*
πόσο κοστίζει να στείλω αυτό το πακέτο;

by air
*aeroporeek**o**s*
αεροπορικώς

◀ Many photographers develop and print in their shops

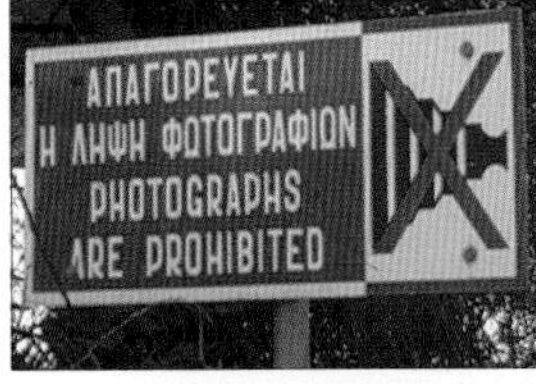

◀ Pay attention to prohibitions: photography is not allowed in some areas and laws may be strictly enforced.

◀ Photo booths can be found in airports, some railway stations and larger shopping centres.

keywords

φίλμ
feelm
film

μπαταρία
*batar**ee**a*
battery

ματ
mat
mat

γυαλιστερό
*waleester**o***
glossy

εμφάνιση
*emf**a**neesee*
developing

φωτογραφίες
*fotograf**ee**es*
photographs

βιντεοκάμερα
*videok**a**mera*
camcorder

κασσέτες
*kas**e**tes*
tapes

talking

where can I buy...?
*poo bor**o** na aghor**a**so...*
πού μπορώ να αγοράσω...;

film
film
φιλμ

tapes for a camcorder?
*kas**e**tes ya videocamera*
κασέτες για βιντεοκάμερα;

a colour film
***e**na **e**nkhromo film*
ένα έγχρωμο φιλμ

24
*eekoseetes**a**ree*
εικοσιτεσσάρι

36
*treeantaeks**a**ree*
τριανταεξάρι

have you batteries for this camcorder?
***e**khete batar**ee**es yaft**ee** tee videoc**a**mera*
έχετε μπαταρίες γι'αυτή τη βιντεοκάμερα;

is it OK to take pictures here?
*peer**a**zee an trav**ee**kso fotoghraf**ee**es edh**o***
πειράζει αν τραβήξω φωτογραφίες εδώ;

would you take a picture of us, please?
*bor**ee**te na mas trav**ee**ksete m**ee**a fotoghraf**ee**a parakal**o***
μπορείτε να μας τραβήξετε μία φωτογραφία, παρακαλώ;

PHONES

*Payphones abound in Greece – just look for the blue sign. The instructions are easy to follow. Cards are easier to use than coins – ask for **teelekarta**. The cheapest of these cost 3 euros. You can get cards from supermarkets, kiosks, newsagents and Post Offices. To phone direct from a hotel phone will cost you a lot more than if you use a phonecard. Some kiosks have a small payphone on the counter – the card goes in at the side. The telephone offices (OTE) have cardphones too, and it may be possible to have someone call you back on a phone in the OTE office.*

◀ Public phones take coins and cards.

A Greek pay-phone ▶ Pictograms show you how to use the phone. The easiest way to phone is by using a phonecard, available at kiosks, newsagents and some supermarkets.

a phonecard
*m**ee**a teelek**a**rta*
μία τηλεκάρτα

do you have phonecards?
***e**khete teeleek**a**rtes*
έχετε τηλεκάρτες

Mr Antoniou, please
*ton k**ee**reeo anton**ee**oo parakal**o***
τον κύριο Αντωνίου, παρακαλώ

extension ..., please
*esotereeko ... parakal**o***
εσωτερικό ... παρακαλώ

can I speak to...?
*bor**o** na meel**ee**so ston / steen...*
μπορώ να μιλήσω στον / στην...;

this is Caroline
eemay ee caroline
είμαι η caroline

can I have an outside line
*bor**o** na **e**kho m**ee**a eksotereek**ee** ghramm**ee***
μπορώ να έχω μία εξωτερική γραμμή

what is your phone number?
*pyos **ee**ne o areethm**o**s too teelef**o**noo soo*
ποιός είναι ο αριθμός του τηλεφώνου σου;

my phone number is...
*o areethm**o**s too teelef**o**noo moo **ee**ne...*
ο αριθμός του τηλεφώνου μου είναι...

▲ Look for this sign if you need a phone-box. OTE is the Greek phone company.

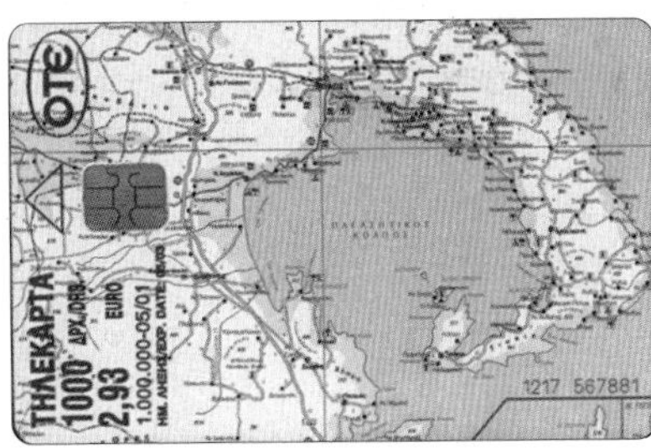

▲ OTE phonecard. The cards are economical and easy to use.

International dialling codes
UK 00 44
USA & Canada 00 1
Australia 00 61
Greece 00 30

τηλ: ◀ Abbreviation for tel:

keywords

τηλέφωνο
*teel**e**fono*
phone

τήλεκαρτα
*t**ee**lekarta*
phonecard

κινητό
*keeneet**o***
mobile

κωδικός
*kodeek**o**s*
code

κατάλογος
*kat**a**logos*
phone book

χρυσός οδηγός
*khrees**o**s odeeg**o**s*
yellow pages

πληροφορίες καταλόγου
*pleerofor**ee**es katal**o**goo*
directory enquiries

YELLOW ▶ PAGES

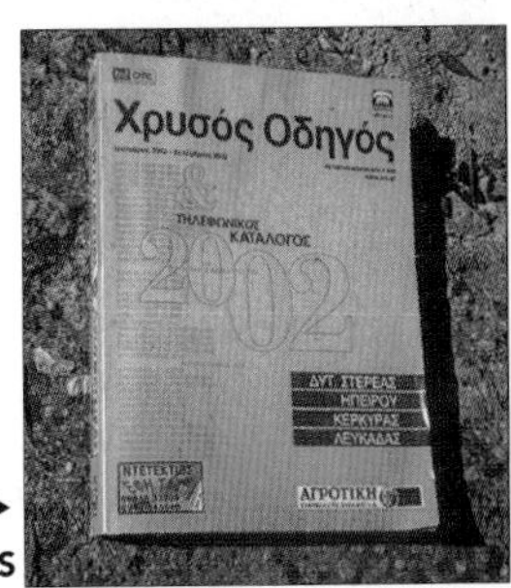

talking

I'll call later
*tha p**a**ro argh**o**tera*
θα πάρω αργότερα

do you have a mobile?
e**khete keeneet**o
έχετε κινητό;

I'll call back tomorrow
*tha ksanap**a**ro **a**vreeo*
θα ξαναπάρω αύριο

what is the number?
*pyo **ee**ne to n**oo**mero*
ποιο είναι το νούμερο;

my mobile number is...
*o areethm**o**s too keeneet**oo** moo (teelef**o**noo) **ee**ne...*
ο αριθμός του κινητού μου (τηλεφώνου) είναι...

E-MAIL, INTERNET, FAX

*It is usually easy to find an Internet cafe to check your e-mail messages etc. National and local tourist information can be accessed via the Internet. Greek web-sites end in **.gr**. Rates at Internet cafes will vary so ask beforehand about the price.*

laminating
stamps
cards
translating
fax (sending & receiving)

• ΠΛΑΣΤΙΚΟΠΟΙΗΣΕΙΣ
• ΣΦΡΑΓΙΔΕΣ
• ΚΑΡΤΕΣ
• ΜΕΤΑΦΡΑΣΕΙΣ
• FAX (ΑΠΟΣΤΟΛΗ & ΛΗΨΗ)
• ΜΕΤΑΞΑ ΧΑΡΑ •

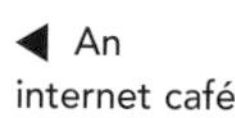
◀ An internet café

The Greek ▶ for 'at' is **παπάκι** *pap**a**kee* (which literally means little duck).

talking talking

I want to send an e-mail
*th**e**lo na st**ee**lo **e**na **e**mail*
θέλω να στείλω ένα e-mail

did you get my e-mail?
*p**ee**rate to e-mail moo*
πήρατε το e-mail μου;

do you have e-mail?
***e**khete e-mail*
έχετε e-mail;

what is your e-mail address?
*tee **ee**ne ee e-mail dhee-**ef**theens**ee** sas*
τι είναι η e-mail διεύθυνσή σας;

how do you spell it?
*pos gr**a**fete*
πώς γράφεται;

my e-mail address is...
*ee e-mail dhee-**ef**theens**ee** moo **ee**ne..*
η e-mail διεύθυνσή μου είναι...

caroline dot zmith@harpercollins dot co dot uk
*caroline tel**ee**a zmith pap**a**kee harpercollins tel**ee**a co tel**ee**a uk*
caroline τελεία zmith παπάκι harpercollins τελεία co τελεία uk

do you have a website?
***e**khete website*
έχετε website;

can I book by e-mail?
*bo**ro** na k**a**no kr**a**teesee me e-mail*
μπορώ να κάνω κράτηση με e-mail;

▲ Internet café interior

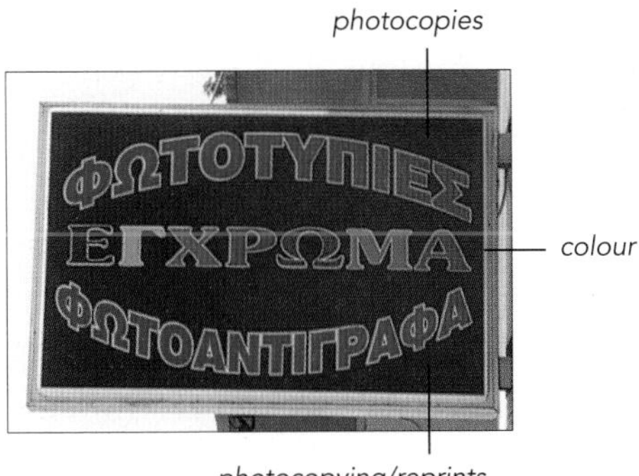

keywords

οθόνη
othonee
screen

πληκτρολόγιο
pleektrologeeo
keyboard

επισύναψη
epeeseenapsee
attachment

κατέβασμα
katevasma
download

ποντίκι
ponteekee
mouse

ιστοσελίδα
eestoseleeda
website

τελεία
teleea
dot

βοήθεια
voeetheea
help

talking

I want to send a fax
thelo na steelo ena fax
θέλω να στείλω ένα φαξ

what's your fax number?
pyo eene to noomero too fax sas
ποιο είναι το νούμερο του φαξ σας;

please resend your fax
parakalo ksanasteelte to fax sas
παρακαλώ ξαναστείλτε το φαξ σας

your fax is constantly engaged
to fax sas eene seenekhos kateeleemeno
το φαξ σας είναι συνεχώς κατειλημένο

where can I send a fax from?
poo boro na steelo ena fax
πού μπορώ να στείλω ένα φαξ;

do you have a fax?
ekhete fax
έχετε φαξ;

did you get my fax?
lavate to fax moo
λάβατε το φαξ μου;

I can't read it
dhen boro na to dheeavaso
δεν μπορώ να το διαβάσω

OUT & ABOUT

Tourist offices will have information on all the local sites and places of interest. Check on the opening times of archaeological sites and museums. Try to avoid walking round sites in the heat of the day in summer, though!

◀ **TOURIST INFORMATION OFFICE**

▲**SWIMMING POOL**

▲ Street signs to places of interest are normally brown.

◀ You can rent motor-bikes and scooters in many places. It's great fun and a good way to explore Greece. Be sure to check out the insurance situation carefully and make sure your bike is roadworthy.

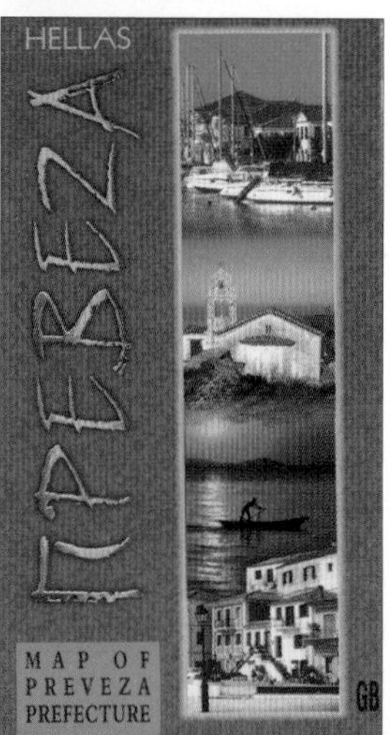

◀ Local tourist information offices have free brochures, leaflets and maps.

▲ Signs on the beach will often be in English

◀ Throughout the summer you can see Greek plays and other shows performed in the ancient theatres.

Tickets for museums and visitor attractions often have English translations, as in this ticket for the Acropolis. ▼

keywords

βόλτα
v**o**lta
walk, trek

ορειβασία
oreevas**ee**a
mountaineering

εκκλησία
eklees**ee**a
church

ναός
na**o**s
temple

παλάτι
pal**a**tee
palace

θέατρο
th**a**yatro
theatre

σινεμά
seenem**a**
cinema

δημαρχείο
deemarh**ee**o
town hall

talking

where is the tourist office?
poo ***ee****ne to tooreesteek****o*** *ghraf****ee****o*
πού είναι το τουριστικό γραφείο;

we want to visit...
*th****e****loome na epeeskeft****oo****me...*
θέλουμε να επισκεφτούμε...

have you any leaflets?
e*khete odheey****ee****-es*
έχετε οδηγίες;

are there any excursions?
*eep****a****rkhoon orghaneesm****e****nes ekdhrom****e****s*
υπάρχουν οργανομένες εκδρομές;

when does it leave?
*p****o****te f****e****vyee*
πότε φεύγει;

where does it leave from?
*ap****o*** *poo f****e****vyee*
από που φεύγει;

how much is it to get in?
*p****o****so kost****ee****zee ee seemetokh****ee***
πόσο κοστίζει η συμμετοχή;

is it open to the public?
ee*ne aneekt****o*** *sto keen****o***
είναι ανοικτό στο κοινό;

There is plenty of excellent walking and mountaineering to be done all over Greece, with clearly marked walking trails and refuge huts. The highest and most spectacular mountain is Mount Olympus, but there are many other scenic walks and climbs. Maps are available, showing you the National Parks and other areas where you can walk or drive.

▲ Panathenaikos football ground

◀ ▲ Greek dancing is popular

talking talking

where can we...?
*poo bor**oo**me na...*
πού μπορούμε να...;

play tennis
*p**e**ksoome t**e**nnis*
παίξουμε τέννις

play golf
*p**e**ksoome golf*
παίξουμε γκολφ

hire bikes
*neeky**a**soome podh**ee**lata*
νοικιάσουμε ποδήλατα

how much is it...?
*p**o**so kost**ee**zee...*
πόσο κοστίζει...;

per hour
*teen **o**ra*
την ώρα

per day
*tee m**e**ra*
τη μέρα

is there a swimming pool?
*eep**a**rkhee pees**ee**na*
υπάρχει πισίνα;

can you recommend a quiet beach?
*ks**e**rete k**a**pya **ee**seekhee paral**ee**a*
ξέρετε κάποια ήσυχη παραλία;

is there a pool?
***e**khee pees**ee**na*
έχει πισίνα;

are there strong currents?
*eep**a**rkhoon dheenat**a** r**e**vmata*
υπάρχουν δυνατά ρεύματα;

is it a nudist beach?
***ee**ne paral**ee**a yeemneest**o**n*
είναι παραλία γυμνιστών;

*There are many ferries to the islands and the high-speed 'flying dolphins' (**ιπτάμενο δελφίνι** eeptameno dhelfeenee) provide a fast service. You can visit their website **www.dolphins.gr.***

◀ Prices are listed for various ticket types to different destinations. There are many day-trips available.

You can buy ferry tickets from travel agents or at the quayside. ▼

High-speed boats provide a fast route to the islands. ▼

is there a hydrofoil to...?
eeparkhee eeptameno dhelfeenee ya...
υπάρχει ιπτάμενο δελφίνι για...;

when is the next boat?
pote fevyee to epomeno pleeo
πότε φεύγει το επόμενο πλοίο;

when does the ferry leave?
pote fevyee to fereebot
πότε φεύγει το φεριμπότ;

can we hire a boat?
boroome na neekyasoome meea varka
μπορούμε να νοικιάσουμε μία βάρκα;

is there a boat to...?
eeparkhee pleeo ya...
υπάρχει πλοίο για...;

ACCOMMODATION

In major cities there are hotels classified by the star system. In general you are more likely to find hotels categorized in the Greek way: **α Α** *(alpha) = 1st class;* **β Β** *(veeta) = 2nd class;* **γ Γ** *(gamma) = 3rd class. Most of these will also provide breakfast if you require it. The Tourist Offices will advise you about hotels and other accommodation. You can also stay in rooms, small guest-houses and self-catering apartments.*

▲ Large hotels use the star system, but the traditional Greek categories are **Α, Β, Γ** classes, for accommodation.

◀ **ΞΕΝΟΔΟΧΕΙΟ** *hotel*
ΔΩΜΑΤΙΑ *rooms*
ΔΙΑΜΕΡΙΣΜΑΤΑ *apartments*
ΚΛΙΜΑΤΙΣΜΟΣ *air conditioning*
ΠΙΣΙΝΑ *swimming pool*
ΜΠΑΡ *bar*
ΠΑΡΚΙΝΚ *parking*
100m ΑΠΟ ΤΗΝ ΑΚΤΗ *100m from the beach*

Booking in advance

The tourist office can help booking hotels and rooms.

I want to book a room...
*th**e**lo na kl**ee**so **e**na dhom**a**teeo...*
θέλω να κλείσω ένα δωμάτιο...

double
*dh**ee**kleeno*
δίκλινο

single
*mon**o**kleeno*
μονόκλινο

a family room
***e**na dhom**a**teeo ya eekoy**e**nya*
ένα δωμάτιο για οικογένεια

with bathroom
*me b**a**nyo*
με μπάνιο

with shower
me doos
με ντους

with a double bed
*me dheepl**o** krev**a**tee*
με διπλό κρεβάτι

twin-bedded
*me dh**ee**o krev**a**teea*
με δύο κρεβάτια

we'd like to stay ... nights
*tha th**e**lame na m**ee**noome ... vr**a**dheea*
θα θέλαμε να μείνουμε ... βράδυα

from ... till...
*ap**o** ... m**e**khree...*
από ... μέχρι...

I booked a room
***e**kho k**a**nee m**ee**a kr**a**teesee*
έχω κάνει μία κράτηση

my name is...
*to **o**nom**a** moo **ee**ne...*
το όνομά μου είναι...

HOTEL ΑΘΩΣ

▲ *Hotel Athos*

▲ The word 'Reception' always appears in English in Greek hotels.

Hotels have to post information about their services on bedroom doors. ▼

ΠΙΝΑΚΙΔΑ ΕΝΗΜΕΡΩΣΗΣ ΤΟΥ ΠΕΛΑΤΗ - GUEST INFORMATION

have you a room for tonight?
__e__khete __e__na dhom__a__teeo ya ap__o__pse
έχετε ένα δωμάτιο για απόψε;

for ... nights
ya ... n__ee__khtes
για ... νύχτες

a single room
__e__na mon__o__kleeno dhom__a__teeo
ένα μονόκλινο δωμάτιο

a double room
__e__na dh__ee__kleeno dhom__a__teeo
ένα δίκλινο δωμάτιο

a room for three people
__e__na tr__ee__kleeno dhom__a__teeo
ένα τρίκλινο δωμάτιο

with bathroom
me b__a__nyo
με μπάνιο

with shower
me doos
με ντους

how much is it...?
p__o__so k__a__nee...
πόσο κάνει...;

per night
to vr__a__dhee
το βράδυ

per week
tee vdhom__a__dha
τη βδομάδα

I'd like to see the room
tha __ee__thela na dho to dhom__a__teeo
θα ήθελα να δω το δωμάτιο

is there anything cheaper?
__e__khete t__ee__pota ftheen__o__tero
έχετε τίποτα φθηνότερο;

is breakfast included?
to proeen__o__ __ee__ne steen teem__ee__
το πρωινό είναι στην τιμή;

can you suggest somewhere else?
bor__ee__te na prot__ee__nete k__a__poo al__oo__
μπορείτε να προτείνετε κάπου αλλού;

*A 'garsony**e**ra' or a 'st**oo**deeo' is a small apartment. A 'deeam**e**reesma' is a medium-sized apartment. A 'dhom**a**teeo' is a room, usually without a kitchen. You will see signs for all types of accommodation, but if you are in a small place and there is no sign, just ask instead.*

▲ Apartments for rent

▼ Pension or guest house

Guest House Olga
For rent : rooms and small apartments

◀ Not all areas have facilities for recycling.

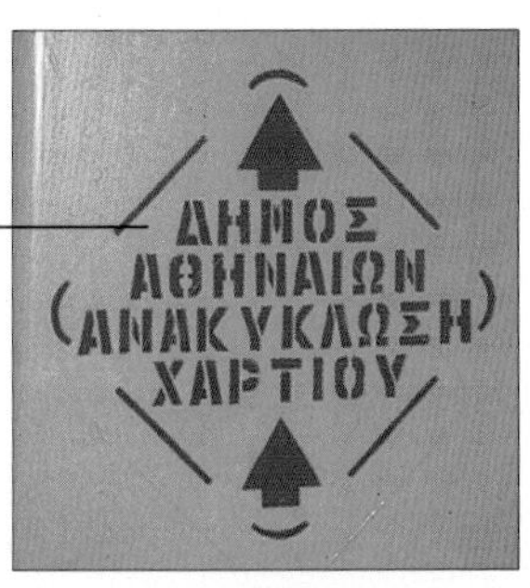

Paper-recycling bin ▶

▲ Logo of the Hostelling International organisation at the YHA hostel in Athens. The Greek Youth Hostel Asociation is the other hostelling organisation. There are also private hostels with economical rates, especially in cities.

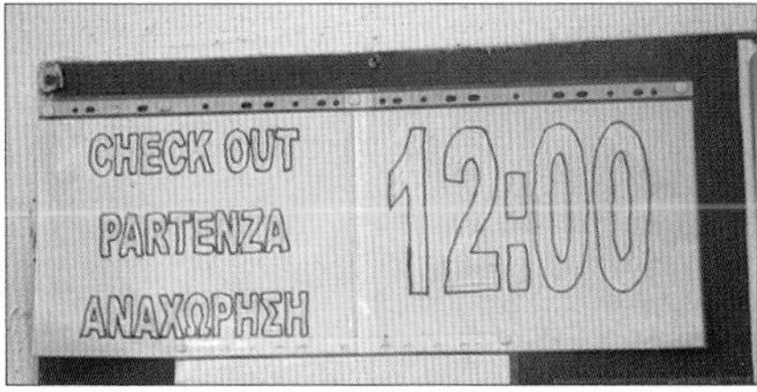

▲ Check out times vary according to where you are staying.

keywords

υγρό πλυσίματος
eegro pleeseematos
washing-up liquid

σκόνη πλυσίματος
skonee pleeseematos
washing powder

σαπούνι
sapoonee
soap

ανοικτήρι
aneekteeree
tin-opener

κεριά
kereea
candles

σπίρτα
speerta
matches

φυάλη αεριού
feealee a-ereeoo
gas cylinder *(large)*

γκαζάκι
gazakee
camping gas

talking

can we have an extra set of keys?
boroome na ekhoome ena extra set kleedheea
μπορούμε να έχουμε ένα έξτρα σετ κλειδιά;

when does the cleaner come?
pote erkhete ee kathareestreea
πότε έρχεται η καθαρίστρια;

is there always hot water?
ekhee panta zesto nero
έχει πάντα ζεστό νερό;

who do we contact if there are problems?
se pee-on thape-ftheenthoome an eeparksoon provleemata
σε ποιόν θ' απευθυνθούμε αν υπάρξουν προβλήματα;

where is the nearest supermarket?
poo eene to kondeenotero supermarket
πού είναι το κοντινότερο supermarket;

where do we leave rubbish?
poo petame ta skoopeedheea
που πετάμε τα σκουπίδια;

when is the rubbish collected?
pote eene ee seeloghee skoopeedhee-on
πότε είναι η συλλογή σκουπιδιών;

what are the neighbours called?
pos leghonte ee gheetones
πώς λέγονται οι γείτονες;

CAMPING

There is no shortage of well-equipped campsites in Greece. Look for the tent/caravan sign, with CAMPING written in English. Prices are reasonable and facilities are good. Most campsites have hot showers (generally heated by solar power).

▲ Road sign for campsite

◀ Campsite sign

▲ In smaller places you can have clothes washed or dry-cleaned at small laundries like this, where they charge per item. In towns there are bigger versions of the same thing. Self-service launderettes do not exist.

talking talking talking

we're looking for a campsite
*psakhnoome ya th**e**see k**a**mping*
ψάχνουμε για θέση κάμπινγκ

have you a list of campsites?
***e**khete l**ee**sta me ta k**a**mping*
έχετε λίστα με τα κάμπινγκ;

have you any vacancies?
***e**khete th**e**sees*
έχετε θέσεις;

we'd like to stay for ... nights
*th**e**loome na m**ee**noome ... vr**a**dya*
θέλουμε να μείνουμε ... βράδυα

how much is it per night...?
*p**o**so kost**ee**zee tee n**ee**khta...*
πόσο κοστίζει τη νύχτα...;

for a tent
*ee skeen**ee***
η σκηνή

per person
*to **a**tomo*
το άτομο

is there a restaurant on the campsite?
*eep**a**rkhee esteeat**o**reeo sto camping*
υπάρχει εστιατόριο στό κάμπινγκ;

how far is the beach?
*p**o**so makree**a** **ee**ne ee paral**ee**a*
πόσο μακριά είναι η παραλία;

can we camp here overnight?
*bor**oo**me na per**a**soome edh**o** tee n**ee**khta*
μπορούμε να περάσουμε εδώ τη νύχτα;

Typical pricelist for campsite ▶
Tariffs can be listed in English as well as Greek.

▲ Most sites have at least basic laundry facilities.

On-site laundrette ▼ washing machines ▼

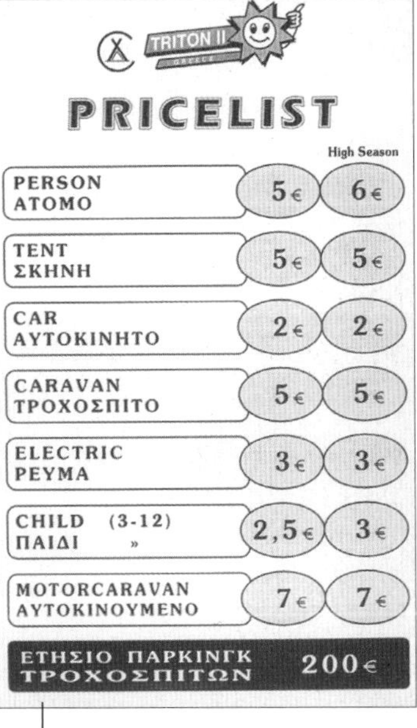

PRICELIST

		High Season
PERSON ΑΤΟΜΟ	5€	6€
TENT ΣΚΗΝΗ	5€	5€
CAR ΑΥΤΟΚΙΝΗΤΟ	2€	2€
CARAVAN ΤΡΟΧΟΣΠΙΤΟ	5€	5€
ELECTRIC ΡΕΥΜΑ	3€	3€
CHILD (3-12) ΠΑΙΔΙ »	2,5€	3€
MOTORCARAVAN ΑΥΤΟΚΙΝΟΥΜΕΝΟ	7€	7€
ΕΤΗΣΙΟ ΠΑΡΚΙΝΓΚ ΤΡΟΧΟΣΠΙΤΩΝ	200€	

annual parking fee for mobile homes

◀ **DRY CLEANERS** are often open only in the morning

where can I do some washing?
poo boro na pleeno mereeka rookha
που μπορώ να πλύνω μερικά ρούχα;

do you have a laundry service?
ekhete eepeereseea pleendeereeoo
έχετε υπηρεσία πλυντηρίου;

when will my things be ready?
pote tha eene eteema ta praghmata moo
πότε θα είναι έτοιμα τα πράγματά μου;

is there a dry-cleaner's near here?
eeparkhee kathareesteereeo edho konda
υπάρχει καθαριστήριο εδώ κοντά;

can I borrow an iron?
boro na dhaneesto ena seedhero
μπορώ να δανειστώ ένα σίδερο;

where can I dry clothes?
poo boro na steghnoso rookha
πού μπορώ να στεγνώσω ρούχα;

SPECIAL NEEDS

Recent new facilities on the Metro and at the Venizelos Airport are superb. Elsewhere they are gradually improving, but it is still difficult to get around on public transport.

▲ Disabled parking sign

Disabled lift access sign in the metro station ▶

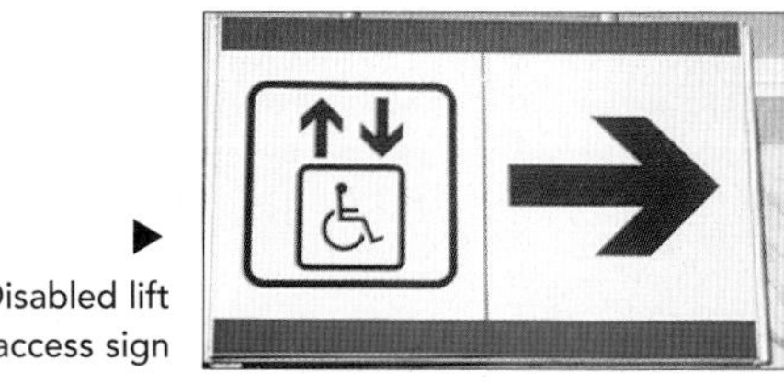

▶ Disabled lift access sign

are there any toilets for the disabled?
eeparkhoon tooaletes ya atoma me eedheekes ananges
υπάρχουν τουαλέτες για άτομα με ειδικές ανάγκες;

do you have any bedrooms on the ground floor?
ekhete eepnodhomateea sto eesoyeeo
έχετε υπνοδωμάτια στο ισόγειο;

is there a lift?
eeparkhee asanser
υπάρχει ασανσέρ;

where is the lift?
poo eene to asanser
πού είναι το ασανσέρ;

how many stairs are there?
poses skales eeparkhoon
πόσες σκάλες υπάρχουν;

do you have wheelchairs?
ekhete karotseea
έχετε καρότσια;

can you visit ... in a wheelchair?
boree kanees na episkeftee ... me karotsee
μπορεί κανείς να επισκεφτεί ... με καρότσι;

where is the wheelchair-accessible entrance?
poo eene ee eesodhos me prosvasee ya ta karotseea
πού είναι η είσοδος με πρόσβαση για τα καρότσια;

is there a reduction for disabled people?
yeenete ekptosee sta atoma me eedheekes ananges
γίνεται έκπτωση στα άτομα με ειδικές ανάγκες;

WITH KIDS

Greek people make a fuss of children and always make them welcome. Greek children are generally polite and well-behaved. Greeks tend to eat altogether as a family, so you don't usually find special menus designed for children, except in the national/international fast-food eateries such as MacDonalds, Pizza Hut, Goody's etc. In the summer (schools close from mid-June to mid-September) children stay up late with their parents and most families have a 'siesta' in the afternoon.

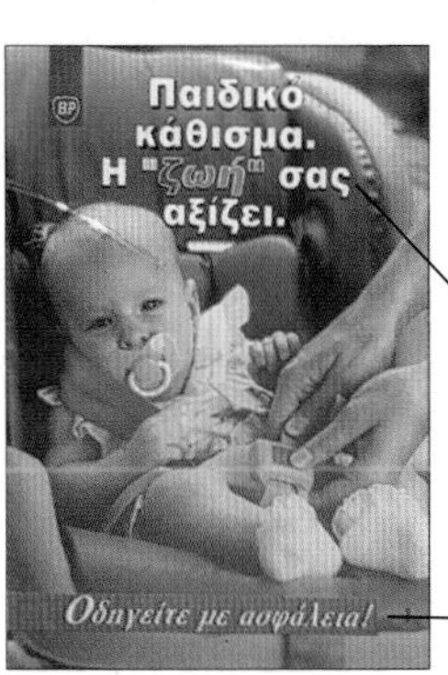

◀ Children should be securely strapped in the car.

your child deserves it

drive safely!

keywords

παιδί
*ped**ee***
child

παιδικό κάθισμα
*pedeek**o** k**a**theesma*
high-chair

κούνια
*k**oo**nya*
cot

παιδική χαρά
*pedeek**ee** har**a***
play park

πάνες
*p**a**nes*
nappies

talking

a child's ticket
***e**na pedheek**o** eeseet**ee**reeo*
ένα παιδικό εισητήριο

he/she is ... years old
***ee**ne ... khron**o**n*
είναι ... χρονών

is there a reduction for children?
*eep**a**rkhee eedheek**ee** teem**ee** ya pedy**a***
υπάρχει ειδική τιμή για παιδιά;

is there a children's menu?
*eep**a**rkhee pedheek**o** men**oo***
υπάρχει παιδικό μενού;

have you...?
***e**khete...*
έχετε...;

a high chair
*m**ee**a pedheek**ee** kar**e**kla*
μία παιδική καρέκλα

a child's bed
***e**na pedheek**o** krev**a**tee*
ένα παιδικό κρεββάτι;

is it safe for children?
ee**ne asfal**e**s ya ta pedhy**a
είναι ασφαλές για τα παιδιά;

what is there for children to do?
*tee bor**oo**n na k**a**noon ta pedhy**a***
τι μπορούν να κάνουν τα παιδιά;

where is there a play park?
*poo **ee**ne ee pedheek**ee** khar**a***
πού είναι η παιδική χαρά;

HEALTH

Make sure you take your stamped E111 form with you (available from post offices). This will be a safeguard against any medical problems or emergencies. There will be a health-centre nearby and there are many private doctors, too. Specialists are also easy to find. For minor ailments, ask the pharmacist for advice.

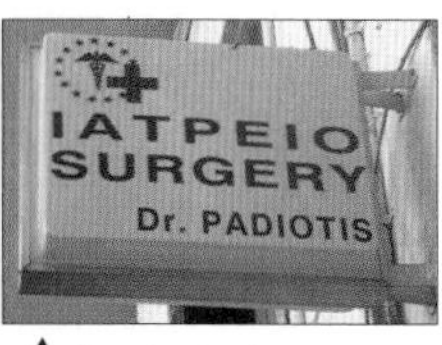

▲ Doctor's sign
You can often see a doctor right away, or at least on the same day.

pharmacy — ΦΑΡΜΑΚΕΙΟ

(name of pharmacist) — ΔΗΜΗΤΡΙΟΣ Β. ΛΕΝΑΣ

▶ *Parga Health Centre*

ΕΘΝΙΚΟ ΣΥΣΤΗΜΑ ΥΓΕΙΑΣ
Πε.Σ.Υ. ΗΠΕΙΡΟΥ
ΚΕΝΤΡΟ ΥΓΕΙΑΣ
ΠΑΡΓΑΣ
EMERGENCY & HEALTH CENTER
PRONTO SOCCORSO

Chemists work on a rota basis, so there is always one open. ▼

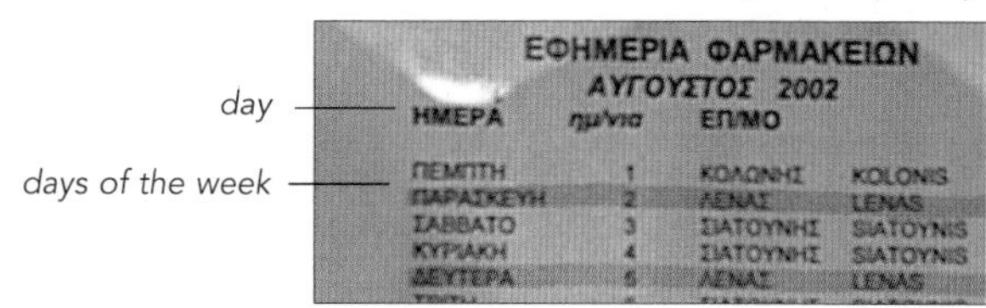

where is there a chemist?
*poo **ee**ne **e**na farmak**ee**o*
πού είναι ένα φαρμακείο;

I don't feel well
*dhen esth**a**nome kal**a***
δεν αισθάνομαι καλά

have you something for...?
***e**khete t**ee**pote ya...*
έχετε τίποτε για...;

sunburn
*ta eng**a**vmata*
τα εγκαύματα

mosquito bites
*tseeb**ee**mata koonoopee**o**n*
τσιμπήματα κουνουπιών

diarrhoea
*tee dhee**a**reea*
τη διάρροια

sunstroke
*teen eel**ee**asee*
την ηλίαση

toothache
*ton pon**o**dhonto*
τον πονόδοντο

I have a rash
***e**kho **e**na eks**a**ntheema*
Έχω ένα εξάνθημα

is it safe to give children?
ee**ne asfal**e**s ya ta pedhy**a
είναι ασφαλές για τα παιδιά;

visiting times ▼

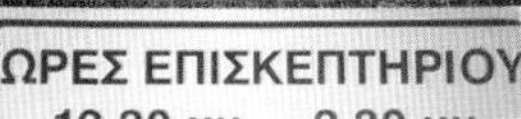

ΩΡΕΣ ΕΠΙΣΚΕΠΤΗΡΙΟΥ
12.30 μμ - 2.30 μμ
17.30 μμ - 19.30 μμ

▶ The dental system is reliable and efficient.

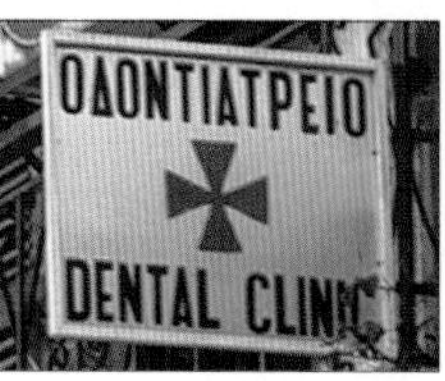

I feel ill
*dhen esth**a**nome kal**a***
δεν αισθάνομαι καλά

I need a doctor
*khree**a**zome yatr**o***
χρειάζομαι γιατρό

my son is ill
*o yos moo **ee**ne **a**rostos*
ο γιος μου είναι άρρωστος

my daughter is ill
*ee k**o**ree moo **ee**ne **a**rostee*
η κόρη μου είναι άρρωστη

I'm on this medication
*p**e**rno aft**a** ta f**a**rmaka*
παίρνω αυτά τα φάρμακα

I have high blood pressure
***e**kho eep**e**rtasee*
έχω υπέρταση

I'm diabetic *(m/f)*
ee**me dheeaveeteek**o**s/**ee
είμαι διαβητικός/ή

I'm pregnant
***ee**me **e**ngeeos*
είμαι έγγυος

I'm on the pill
*p**e**rno anteeseeleepteek**a***
παίρνω αντισυλληπτικά

I'm allergic to penicillin
***e**kho aleryee**a** steen peneekeel**ee**nee*
έχω αλλεργία στην πενικιλλίνη

I'm breastfeeding
*theel**a**zo to mor**o** moo*
θηλάζω το μωρό μου

is it safe to take while breastfeeding?
***ee**ne asfal**e**s kat**a** teen ghalookh**ee**a*
είναι ασφαλές κατά την γαλουχία;

I need a dentist
*khree**a**zome odhond**y**atro*
χρειάζομαι οδοντίατρο

I have toothache
***e**kho pon**o**dhondo*
έχω πονόδοντο

the filling has come out
*moo **e**feeye to sfr**a**yeesma*
μου έφυγε το σφράγισμα

I have an abscess in the tooth
***e**kho **e**na ap**o**steema sto d**o**ndee*
έχω ένα απόστημα στο δόντι

it hurts
*me pon**a**ee*
με πονάει

can you repair my dentures?
*bor**ee**te na moo epeedheeorth**o**sete teen odhondosteekh**ee**a*
μπορείτε να μου επιδιορθώσετε την οδοντοστοιχία;

do I have to pay now?
*pr**e**pee na pleer**o**so t**o**ra*
πρέπει να πληρώσω τώρα;

If you require hospital treatment, take your E111 form and your passport with you. A proportion of the cost will be covered, depending on the type of hospital and the treatment.

GENERAL HOSPITAL (OF PREVEZA) ▲

ΑΠΑΓΟΡΕΥΕΤΑΙ
ΤΟ ΚΑΠΝΙΣΜΑ

SMOKING ▲ PROHIBITED

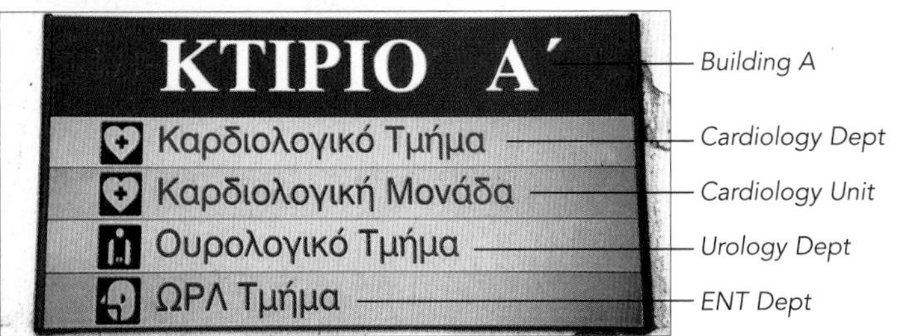

If you need to go to hospital

will he/she have to go to hospital?
*pr**e**pee na bee sto nosokom**ee**o*
πρέπει να μπει στο νοσοκομείο;

where is the hospital?
*poo **ee**ne to nosokom**ee**o*
πού είναι το νοσοκομείο;

to the hospital, please
*sto nosokom**ee**o parakal**o***
στο νοσοκομείο παρακαλώ

I need to go to casualty
*pr**e**pee na p**a**o sta ep**ee**ghonda pereestateek**a***
πρέπει να πάω στα επείγοντα περιστατικά

when are visiting hours?
*p**o**te **e**khee epeeskept**ee**reeo*
πότε έχει επισκεπτήριο;

which ward?
*pya kleeneek**ee***
ποια κλινική;

can you tell me what is the matter?
*bor**ee**te na moo p**ee**te tee seemv**e**nee*
μπορείτε να μου πείτε τί συμβαίνει;

is it serious?
ee**ne sovar**o
είναι σοβαρό;

I need a receipt for the insurance
*khree**a**zome ap**o**dheeksee ya teen asfaleesteek**ee** moo eter**ee**a*
χρειάζομαι απόδειξη για την ασφαλιστική μου εταιρεία

EMERGENCY

*If you experience a theft or other crime, you must go to the police (asteenom**ee**a) and make a report. You will need the report for any related insurance claim. Emergency phone numbers: Police – 100, Medical emergency – 166, Fire Brigade – 199.*

An ▶ ambulance. Vehicles connected with the council or government have orange number-plates.

There are often bush-fires in Greece in summer, so the fire-brigade has to be on the alert. ▲

help!
*vo**ee**theea*
βοήθεια

can you help me?
*bor**ee**te na me voeeth**ee**sete*
μπορείτε να με βοηθήσετε;

there's been an accident
***e**khee y**ee**nee at**ee**kheema*
έχει γίνει ατύχημα

someone is injured
*eeparkhoon travmat**ee**-es*
υπάρχουν τραυματίες

please call...
*parakal**o** kal**e**ste...*
παρακαλώ καλέστε...

the police
*teen asteenom**ee**a*
την αστυνομία

an ambulance
***e**na asthenof**o**ro*
ένα ασθενοφόρο

he was going too fast
***e**trekhe me megh**a**lee takh**ee**teeta*
έτρεχε με μεγάλη ταχύτητα

where's the police station?
*poo **ee**ne to asteenomeek**o** tm**ee**ma*
πού είναι το αστυνομικό τμήμα;

I've been raped
*me v**ee**asan*
με βίασαν

I want to report a theft
*th**e**lo na dheel**o**so m**ee**a klop**ee***
θέλω να δηλώσω μία κλοπή

I've been robbed
***e**kho p**e**see th**ee**ma klop**ee**s*
έχω πέσει θύμα κλοπής

my car's been broken into
*parav**ee**asan to aftok**ee**neet**o** moo*
παραβίασαν το αυτοκίνητό μου

I've been attacked
***e**kho p**e**see th**ee**ma ef**o**dhoo klept**o**n*
έχω πέσει θύμα εφόδου κλεπτών

I need a report for my insurance
*khree**a**zome khart**ee** pereeghraf**ee**s seemv**a**ndon ya teen asf**a**leea moo*
χρειάζομαι χαρτί περιγραφής συμβάντων για την ασφάλεια μου

how much is the fine?
*p**o**so **ee**ne to pr**o**steemo*
πόσο είναι το πρόστιμο;

where do I pay it?
*poo bor**o** na to pleer**o**so*
πού μπορώ να το πληρώσω;

FOOD AND DRINK

ΡΕΤΣΙΝΑ
ΟΝΟΜΑΣΙΑ ΚΑΤΑ ΠΑΡΑΔΟΣΗ
BOUTARI
ΕΜΦΙΑΛΩΣΗ Δ.Κ.Μ./09-0014/99
Ι. ΜΠΟΥΤΑΡΗΣ & ΥΙΟΣ ΟΙΝΟΠΟΙΗΤΙΚΗ Α.Ε., ΘΕΣΣΑΛΟΝΙΚΗ-ΕΛΛΑΣ
750 ml
ΕΛΛΗΝΙΚΟ ΠΡΟΪΟΝ
11.5 % vol.

GREEK FOOD

Greek food is not only tasty but healthy, interesting, and reasonably priced. Greece's long and diverse history, along with its varied geography, is reflected in the wide range of dishes on offer. Unlike the UK, regional traditions are very much alive. The unifying theme is simplicity: unfussy, nutritious food with the emphasis on seasonality and fresh local produce.

Fish is of course well represented, as you would expect from a maritime nation. Other mainstays are lamb, goat and pork, cheese (including feta and halloumi), yoghurt, olive oil and salads, with lemon to pep up savoury dishes and honey to sweeten the desserts. Typical vegetables include aubergine/eggplant, courgettes/zucchini, cucumbers, tomatoes, peppers and vine leaves. This is the classic Mediterranean diet, credited with so many medical benefits, including lowering your risk of cancer and heart disease. Wine, whether red, white or rosé, is abundant, often with the famous resinous flavours traditionally associated with Greece. Greeks tend to drink a little and often; being visibly drunk is considered shameful.

*It is often just as cheap to eat out as to cook for yourself, and there is no shortage of places to eat. Restaurants are informal, friendly places, where children are welcome. In the less grand places you can often see the food being prepared, and even go into the kitchen to see what's in the pot (***tapsee***), so you can choose by pointing at what you want. Ideal for those who are not confident of their Greek culinary vocabulary!*

▲ Fried squid *(kalam***a***reea)*, stuffed tomatoes *(dom***a***tes yemeest***e***s)*, green beans *(fasol***a***keea)* and yogurt and garlic dip *(tsats***ee***kee)*.

◀ *steef***a***dho* Beef in a rich sauce with onions, tomatoes, wine, peppercorns and spices.

▶ Kebabs are great for a cheap, tasty meal. You will often spot the big doner kebabs from afar, and the little 'souvlakis' (pieces of meat on small skewers) lined up on the charcoal grill.

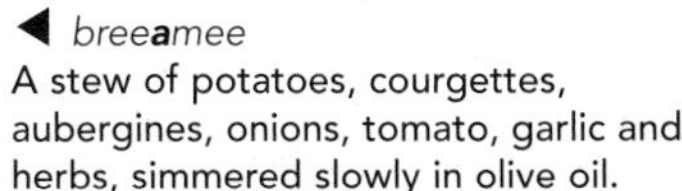

◀ *breeamee*
A stew of potatoes, courgettes, aubergines, onions, tomato, garlic and herbs, simmered slowly in olive oil.

baklava and *kataeefee* ▶
Cakes made with nuts and honey

▲ Stuffed tomatoes (*tomates yemeestes*), oven-baked. The filling is usually rice, garlic, tomato and herbs, sometimes with mince. There are also stuffed peppers (*peepereees*) courgettes (*kolookeethakeea*) and aubergines (*meleetzanes*).

Moussaka, made with mince, aubergines and ▼ béchamel sauce

talking talking

where can we have a snack?
poo boroome na fame katee prokheera
πού μπορούμε να φάμε κάτι πρόχειρα;

is there a good local restaurant?
eeparkhee ena kalo topeeko esteeatoreeo
υπάρχει ένα καλό τοπικό εστιατόριο;

not too expensive
okhee polee akreevo
όχι πολύ ακριβό

are there any vegetarian restaurants here?
eeparkhoon katholoo esteeatoreea ya khortofaghoos edho
υπάρχουν καθόλου εστιατόρια για χορτοφάγους εδώ;

can you recommend a local dish?
boreete na moo seesteesete ena topeeko fayeeto
μπορείτε να μου συστήσετε ένα τοπικό φαγητό;

what is this?
tee eene afto
τι είναι αυτό;

I'll have this
tha paro afto
θα πάρω αυτό

excuse me!
me seengkhoreete
με συγχωρείτε!

*Snacking is easy and convenient, with food available on every street corner: cheese, spinach or sausage pies (**teeropeetes**, **spanakopeetes**, **lookaneekopeetes**), toasted sandwiches (**sandveets**), pitta bread (**peeta**), bread rolls (**kooloorakeeya**) and so on, or for the sweet-toothed, **lookoomee** (Turkish delight) and such honey-based treats as **baklava** and **kataeefee**.*

keywords

κρέας
kreas
meat

ψάρι
psaree
fish

λαχανικά
lakhaneeka
vegetables

φρούτα
froota
fruit

κέικ
cake
cakes

γλυκά
gleeka
cakes

all with the most pure ingredients

▲ Pop-corn stands are popular.

talking talking

I'd like a white cofee
tha eethela ena kafe me ghala
θα ήθελα ένα καφέ με γάλα

a decaffeinated coffee
ena dekafeeene
ένα ντεκαφεϊνέ

a tea...
ena tsaee...
ένα τσάι...

with milk
me ghala
με γάλα

with lemon
me lemonee
με λεμόνι

without sugar
khorees zakharee
χωρις ζάχαρη

an orange juice please
ena kheemo portokalee parakalo
ένα χυμό πορτοκάλι παρακαλώ

an iced coffee
ena frape
ένα φραπέ

for me
ya mena
για μένα

for her
yafteen
γι' αυτήν

for him
yafton
γι' αυτόν

for us
ya mas
για μας

with ice please
me paghakeea parakalo
με παγάκια παρακαλώ

I'm very thirsty
dheepsao polee
διψάω πολύ

a bottle of mineral water
ena bookalee emfeealomeno nero
ένα μπουκάλι εμφιαλωμένο νερό

sparkling
aereeookho
αεριούχο

still
aplo
απλό

Snack and take-away van ◀

Take-away ▶

Quick and easy sit-down or take-away place for a snack (doner kebab with slices of pork or chicken), wrapped up in a pitta bread with tomatoes, onions, chips and plain yogurt.

- buffet
- coffee
- soft drinks
- cheese & ham toasties
- sandwiches

keywords

σοκολάτα
*sokol**a**ta*
chocolate

παγωτό
*paghot**o***
ice cream

πάστες
*p**a**stes*
slices of gateau

λεμόνι
*lem**o**nee*
lemon

ροδάκινο
*rodh**a**keeno*
peach

φράουλα
*fr**a**oola*
strawberry

τυρόπιτα
*teer**o**peeta*
cheese pie

πατάτες
*pat**a**tes*
chips

φραπέ
*frap**e***
iced coffee

talking

I'd like a toasted sandwich
*tha **ee**thela **e**na tost*
θα ήθελα ένα τοστ

what sandwiches do you have?
*tee s**a**ndwich **e**khete*
τι σάντουϊτς έχετε;

a cheese pie
*m**ee**a teer**o**peeta*
μία τυρόπιτα

I'd like an ice cream
*tha **ee**thela **e**na paghot**o***
θα ήθελα ένα παγωτό

with chips
*me pat**a**tes*
με πατάτες

with cheese
*me teer**ee***
με τυρί

with ham
*me zamb**o**n*
με ζαμπόν

what cakes do you have?
*tee ghleek**a** **e**khete*
τι γλυκά έχετε;

what flavours do you have?
*tee gh**e**fsees **e**khete*
τι γεύσεις έχετε;

Particularly convenient for the visitor is the Greek tradition of ordering a selection of different dishes: ***mezedhes****. This is a wonderful way of discovering Greek food without committing yourself to one dish.*

◀ You are never far from a taverna

traditional cuisine

everything chargrilled

views over the Ionian Sea

▼ Seaside taverna

talking talking

I'd like to book a table
*tha **ee**thela na krat**ee**so **e**na trap**e**zee*
θα ήθελα να κρατήσω ένα τραπέζι

for tonight
*ya ap**o**pse*
για απόψε

for tomorrow night
*ya **a**vreeo to vr**a**dhee*
για αύριο το βράδυ

I booked a table
*ekl**ee**sa **e**na trap**e**zee*
έκλεισα ένα τραπέζι

in a non-smoking area
*stoos mee kapn**ee**zontes*
στους μη καπνίζοντες

for ... people
*ya ... **a**toma*
για ... άτομα

at 8 o'clock
*ya tees okt**o** to vr**a**dhee*
για τις οκτώ το βράδυ

for 5th August
*ya tees 5 avgh**oo**stoo*
για τις 5 Αυγούστου

in the name of...
*sto **o**noma...*
στο όνομα...

◀ Grill/Bar

Specialities:
ΚΟΚΟΡΕΤΣΙ *spit-roasted liver and spleen, wrapped in intestines*

ΤΥΡΟΣΟΥΦΛΕ *cheese soufflé*

Some restaurants have Greek dancing, as shown by the illustration. ▼

charcoal/grill house
restaurant
café-bar

a table for two
ena trapezee ya deeo
ένα τραπέζι για δύο

the menu, please
ton katalogho parakalo
τον κατάλογο παρακαλώ

what is the dish of the day?
pyo eene to pyato tees eemeras
ποιο είναι το πιάτο της ημέρας;

can we see what you have?
boroome na dhoome tee ekhete
μπορούμε να δούμε τι έχετε;

what is this?
tee eene afto
τι είναι αυτό;

I'll have this
tha paro afto
θα πάρω αυτό

do you have any vegetarian dishes?
ekhete fayeeta ya khortofaghoos
έχετε φαγητά για χορτοφάγους;

please bring...
parakalo ferte...
παρακαλώ, φέρτε...

some more bread
kee alo psomee
κι άλλο ψωμί

some more water
kee alo nero
κι άλλο νερό

another bottle
alo ena bookalee
άλλο ένα μπουκάλι

the bill
to loghareeasmo
το λογαριασμό

*Breakfast for many Greeks is simply coffee, perhaps with a bowl of yoghurt and honey. If you prefer something substantial to start the day, fresh bread (***psomee***) with cheese (***teeree***), olives (***elyes***) or jam (***marmeladha***) is a common choice. You can buy it yourself from the bakery (***foorno***), which will also sell* ***teeropeetee*** *(cheese pies).*

▲ Menu of the day ▼

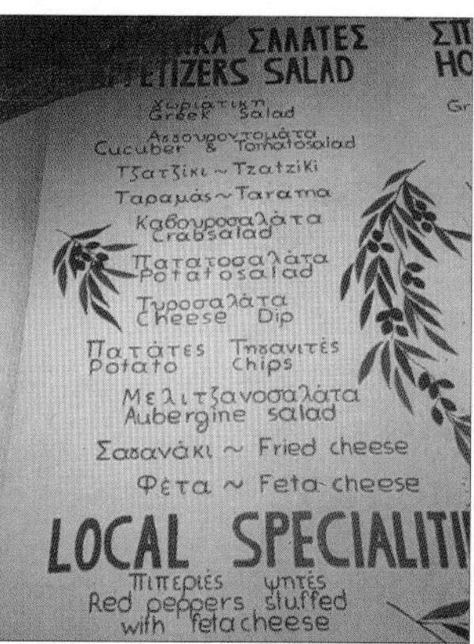

▲ Many restaurants have bilingual menus, like this one.

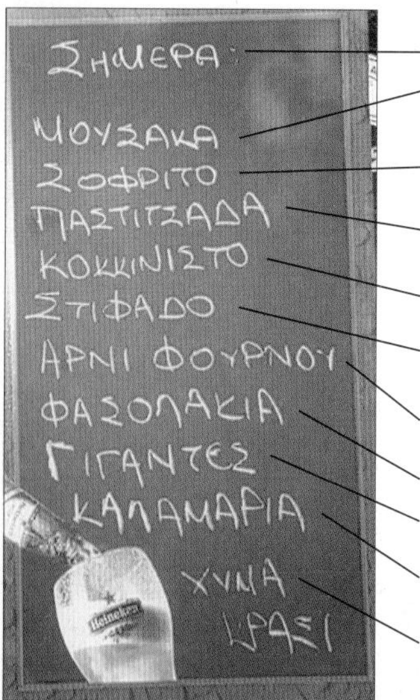

ΣΗΜΕΡΑ today

ΜΟΥΣΑΚΑΣ *moosak**a**s* moussaka with mince, aubergine/eggplant and béchamel sauce

ΣΟΦΡΙΤΟ *sofr**ee**to* tender beef in a creamy garlic sauce.

ΠΑΣΤΙΤΣΑΔΑ *pasteets**a**da* beef and pasta in tomato sauce

ΚΟΚΚΙΝΙΣΤΟ *kokeeneest**o*** braised beef in red wine sauce

ΣΤΙΦΑΔΟ *steef**a**do* braised beef in onion and peppercorn sauce

ΑΡΝΙ ΦΟΥΡΝΟΥ *arn**ee** f**oo**rnoo* lamb cooked slowly in the oven

ΦΑΣΟΛΑΚΙΑ *fasol**a**keea* green beans

ΓΙΓΑΝΤΕΣ *g**ee**gantes* large butter beans

ΚΑΛΑΜΑΡΙΑ *kalam**a**reea* rings of squid (calamari) in batter

ΧΥΜΑ ΚΡΑΣΙ *heem**a** kras**ee*** draft wine from the barrel

*Lunch is taken between 1 and 3pm, and is usually a cooked meal, though fairly light: typically one main dish, with salad or chips, followed by a simple dessert such as fruit or yoghurt. The evening meal, which is the main one of the day, might be any time from about six until very late. It's accompanied by side-dishes and bread. Classic Greek dishes include moosak***a** *(layers of aubergine, meat and béchamel sauce);* **soovlakeea** *(pieces of pork grilled on a skewer like a shish kebab);* **klefteeko** *(lamb casserole); and* **keftedhes** *(herbed meat patties). These might be accompanied by Greek salad (***khoreeateekee salata***), including chunks of tomato, cucumber, onions and feta cheese;* **tzatzeekee** *(yoghurt, cucumber, garlic and mint); or* **taramosalata** *(a purée of fish roes).*

ΟΡΕΚΤΙΚΑ

APPETISERS

ΛΑΔΕΡΑ

COOKED IN OIL

ΚΥΡΙΑ ΦΑΓΗΤΑ

MAIN DISHES

ΣΑΛΑΤΕΣ

SALADS

ΖΥΜΑΡΙΚΑ

PASTA

ΤΗΣ ΩΡΑΣ

DISHES OF THE DAY

usually fresh meat or fish, barbecued to order

ΤΥΡΙΑ

CHEESE

ΚΙΜΑΔΕΣ

MINCEMEAT

FISH

▲ Typical headings you will come across on restaurant menus.

Whole pigs roasting on spits. You buy the roast pork by the kilo. ▶

Beer, though not native to Greece, is popular. The major international lager brands are widely available, usually brewed in Greece under licence.

Greek coffee (**eleeneekos kafes**), is small, strong and sweet, like that of Turkey and the Arab countries. Instead of being filtered, it's ground very fine and brewed in a pot with the sugar included, rather than added afterwards. If you prefer yours without sugar, you will need to ask for a 'plain' coffee (**sketo kafe**). Sweet is **gleeko**, and medium is **metreeo**. If you want it white, specify **me ghala** (with milk). The usual alternative to Greek coffee is instant, known by the name Nescafe regardless of brand, which can be served cold as a **frape**. Coffee is often served with a glass of water as a preliminary thirst-quencher, a welcome addition in a hot country. It is not common practice to finish a meal with coffee: in fact some restaurants do not serve it.

Tea (**tsaee**) is not quite so popular, but easily available. It will tend to be in the form of a teabag to dip in a glass of (fairly) hot water, which may be a disappointment to a British tea-drinker!

Bars, café-bars and bistros ▶ all serve beer and wine.

keywords keywords

ΟΥΖΕΡΙ
oozeree
ouzeria

μεζέδες
mezedes
snacks to go with ouzo

ΚΑΦΕ
café
café-bar

ΚΟΝΙΑΚ
konyak
brandy

ΜΠΥΡΑ ΕΛΛΑΣ
beera hellas
'Hellas' beer

ΜΠΥΡΑ ΚΟΡΩΝΑ
beera corona
'Corona' beer

International and Greek beers are available. Retsina is also popular, and is sold chilled.

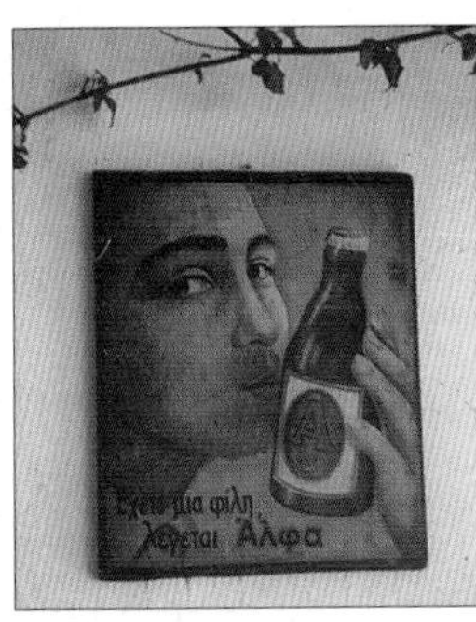

keywords

red
κόκκινο
k**o**keeno

white
άσπρο
aspro

rosé
ροζέ
roz**e**

dry
ξηρό
xeer**o**

sweet
γλυκό
gleek**o**

bottle
μπουκάλι
book**a**lee

glass
ποτήρι
pot**ee**ree

litre
λίτρο
l**ee**tro

half litre
μισό λίτρο
mees**o** l**ee**tro

house wine
σπιτικό κρασί
speeteek**o** kras**ee**

carafe
καράφα
kar**a**fa

from the barrel
από το βαρέλι
ap**o** to var**e**lee

talking

a beer please
*m**ee**a b**ee**ra parakal**o***
μία μπύρα παρακαλώ

a small beer
*m**ee**a mekr**ee** b**ee**ra*
μία μικρή μπίρα

a glass of wine please
e**na pot**ee**ree kras**ee** parakal**o
ένα ποτήρι κρασί παρακαλώ

a large beer
*m**ee**a megh**a**lee b**ee**ra*
μία μεγάλη μπίρα

Wine in Greece is plentiful and cheap. It tends to be served by the glass, carafe or jug, straight from the barrel. Rosé is popular, more so than in Britain. You may be sceptical about the famous retsina (white wine flavoured with pine resin) but it is very refreshing, and can be diluted with soda, coke or iced water to quench your thirst. Those looking for fine wines may be disappointed, at least in more basic or traditional establishments. However, new wine-making techniques are finding their way into Greece, and a good restaurant will often have a selection of bottled vintages. Brand names to look out for include Boutari and Kourtaki.

*Perhaps the best-known Greek spirits are ouzo (**oo**zo, flavoured with aniseed, a little like French pastis) and Metaxa (Greek brandy). Ouzo is usually served with ice, and diluted to taste by the drinker, which makes the clear spirit turn cloudy. It can be found in ordinary bars or specialist ouzerias. Other famous Greek spirits include raki, from Crete, and **tseepooro**, an eau-de-vie distilled from the skins, stems, and pips of crushed grapes.*

There are many types of the aniseed-flavoured spirit, ouzo. Metaxa brandy has three categories – 3-, 5- and 7-star.

talking

enjoy your meal!
*kal**ee** **o**reksee*
καλή όρεξη!

cheers!
***ya** mas*
γειά μας!

your health!
*steen eey**a** sas*
στην υγειά σας!

would you like a drink?
*tha th**e**late **e**na pot**o***
θα θέλατε ένα ποτό;

it's my round!
***ee**ne ee seer**a** moo*
είναι η σειρά μου!

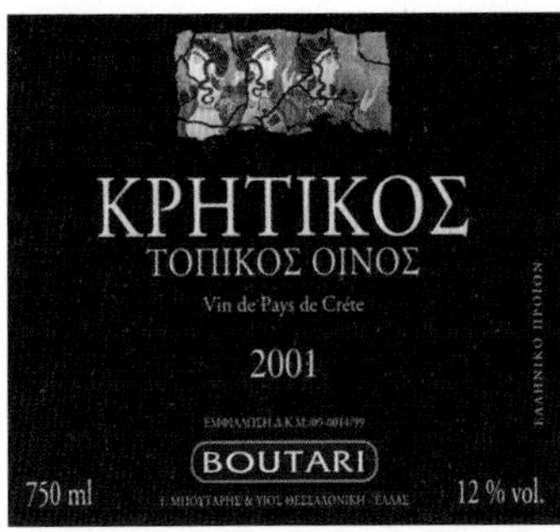

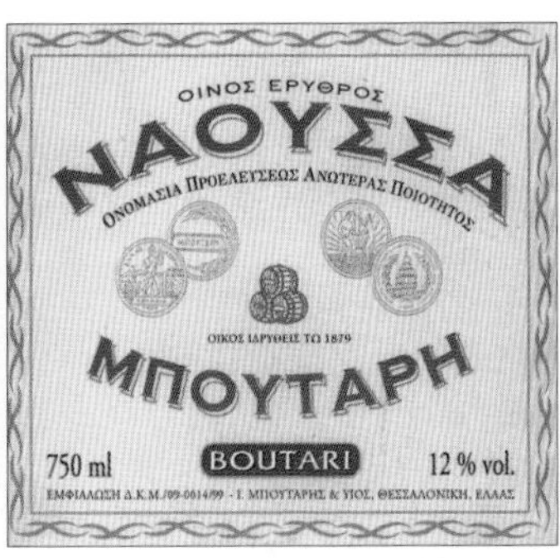

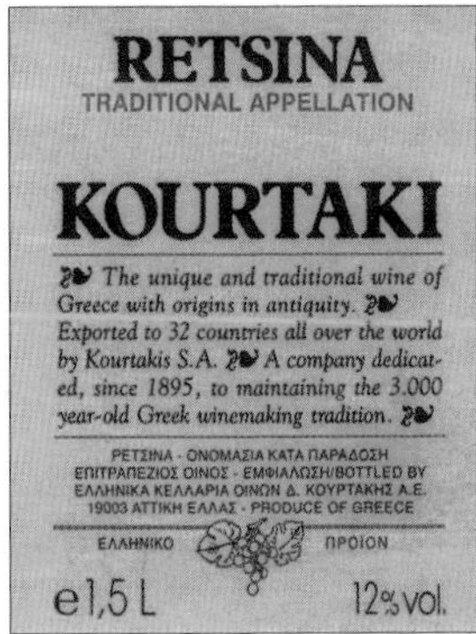

the wine list, please
ton katalogho krasyon parakalo
τον κατάλογο κρασιών, παρακαλώ

a carafe of wine
meea karafa krasee
μία καράφα κρασί

a glass of wine
ena poteeree krasee
ένα ποτήρι κρασί

a bottle of wine
ena bookalee krasee
ένα μπουκάλι κρασί

red
kokeeno
κόκκινο

white
lefko
λευκό

a bottle...
ena bookalee...
ένα μπουκάλι...

a carafe...
meea karafa...
μία καράφα...

of wine
krasee
κρασί

of dry wine
kseero krasee
ξηρό κρασί

of sweet wine
ghleeko krasee
γλυκό κρασί

of a local wine
topeeko krasee
τοπικό κρασί

FLAVOURS OF GREECE

Πηλιορίτικο μπουμπάρι (peeleeoree-teeko boob**a**ree) spicy sausage
Μακαρονόπιτα (makar**o**nopeeta) macaroni pie
Χαλβάς (halv**a**s) fudge-like sweet made from sesame seeds and hone
Μεζέδες (mez**e**dhes) traditional snacks
Εξοχικό (exokheek**o**) beef or pork stuffed with vegetables and cheese

Παστιτσάδα (pasteets**a**dha) braised beef in spicy red sauce with pasta
Σοφρίτο (sofr**ee**to) beef casseroled in a creamy sauce with onions, garlic and herbs

Πίτα (p**ee**ta) various pies; you may buy a large one to share, for a main course.
Γίδα βραστή (y**ee**dha vrast**ee**) goat-meat soup, eaten with the juice of fresh lemon
Κυνήγι (keen**ee**ghee) game
Φασολάδα (fasol**a**da) a thick soup with haricot beans and vegetables, served with lemon
Ψάρια φρέσκα (ps**a**reea fr**e**ska) fresh fish
Γραβιέρα (gravee**er**a) gruyère-like cheese
Μπουγάτσα (boog**a**tsa) vanilla custard pie with cinnamon and icing-sugar
Μπακλαβάς (baklav**a**s) filo pastries with honey, nuts and syrup
Χαλβάς (halv**a**s) soft, gelatinous cake, garnished with almonds
WINES
Ζίτσα (z**ee**tsa); **Αβέρωφ** (av**e**rof)

GREECE
MACEDO
Kastoria
Véroia
NORTHERN GREECE
CORFU
Ioánnina
THESSALY
Tríkala
Lári
EPIRUS
CENTRAL WESTERN GREECE
Arta
Lamía
IONIAN ISLANDS
STEREA ELLADA
Mesólongi
Pátra
PELOPONNESE
Pýrgos
Náfplio
Trípoli
Kalámata
Spár

Στην σούβλα (steen s**oo**vla) on the spit
Γουρουνόπουλο (gooroon**o**poolo) suckling pig roasted slowly with herbs
Χυλοπίτες με κοτόπουλο κρασάτο (kheelop**ee**tes me kot**o**poolo kras**a**to) Pie containing chicken marinated in wine
Τουρλού (toorl**oo**) ratatouille with aubergines, courgettes, potatoes, onions and sometimes cheese
Σπανακόπιτα (spanak**o**peeta) spinach pie
Ελιές Καλαμάτας (ely**e**s kalam**a**tas) Kalamata olives
Μηλόπιτα (meel**o**peeta) apple pie with cinnamon
Δίπλες (dh**ee**ples) pastries with honey and walnuts
Μελιτζανάκι γλυκό (meleetzan**a**kee gleek**o**) sweet crystallized aubergine in syrup
Σύκα μαυροδάφνη (s**ee**ka mavrodh**a**fnee) figs in wine syrup
Σταφιδόπιτα (stafeedh**o**peeta) raisin pie
WINES
Νεμέας (nem**e**as); **Αχαία Κλάους** (akheya kl**a**oos); **Καμπάς** (kamp**a**s)

Χοιρινό κρήτικο (heereen**o** kr**ee**teeko) pork chops baked with vegetables i a spicy sauce
Σοφρίτο (sofr**ee**to) beef braised in a creamy garlic sauc with herbs and spices
Σαλιγκάρια (saleeng**a**reea) snails, prepared in different dishes
Ψάρια φρέσκα (ps**a**reea fr**e**ska) fresh fish and shellfish of all kinds

Κοντοσούβλι *(kontosoovlee)* *lamb, pork or beef, spit-roasted with herbs and spices*
μέλι θυμαρίσιο *(melee theemareesio) thyme-flavoured honey*
Ούζο *(oozo) aniseed-flavour spirit*
Τσίπουρο *(tseepooro) spirit*
WINES
Τσάνταλη *(tsantalee)*; **Μπουτάρη** *(bootaree)*; **Κουρτάκη** *(koortakee)*; **Καμπάς** *(kampas)*; **Χατζημιχάλη** *(khadzeemeehalee)*

THRACE
•Dráma
•Komotiní
Kavála•
Alexandroúpoli
THASSOS
NE AEGEAN ISLANDS
SPORADES
EVIA
Athens
CYCLADES
RHODES
DODECANESE
CRETE

Σουτζουκάκια *(sootzookakya)* *meat balls in tomato sauce*
Τας κεμπάμπ *(tash kebab) lamb, goat, pork or beef in spicy sauce*
Ντολμάδες *(dolmadhes) spicy, rice-stuffed vine-leaves*
Τυροκαυτερή *(teerokafteree)* *feta cheese and red pepper dip*
Τυρί Μετσόβου *(teeree metsovoo)* *smoked cheese from Metsovo*
Τουρσί *(toorsee)* *vegetables pickled in vinegar*
Μπακλαβάς *(baklavas)* and **καταίφι** *(kataeefee) pastries of filo, with honey, nuts and syrup*
WINES
Μακεδονικός *(makedhoneekos)*; **Τσάνταλη** *(tsantalee)*; **Μπουτάρη** *(bootaree)*; **Αγιορείτικο** *(ayoreeteeko (made by monks on Mt Athos)*

Aegean Islands

Αρνάκι ψητό *(arnakee pseeto)* *grilled lamb cutlets*
Παστίτσιο *(pasteetsyo)* *pie made of spiced macaroni and mince (similar to moussaka)*
Κακαβιά *(kakaveea) fish soup*
Χταπόδι κρασάτο *(khtapodhee krasato)* *octopus in wine sauce*
Μυδοπίλαφο *(meedopeelafo)* *mussels and seafood cooked with rice*
Στρείδια *(streedheea) oysters*
Κάβουρας *(kavooras) crab*
Καλαμάρια *(kalamareea) squid*
Γλυκά κουταλιού *(gleeka kootalyoo)* *fruit preserved and crystallized in syrup*
Σύκα στο φούρνο με μαυποδάφνη *(seeka sto foorno me mavrodhafnee)* *figs cooked in Mavrodafni red-wine sauce with spices; from Chios and Lesvos islands*
WINES
Σάμος *(samos)*; **Σαντορίνη** *(santoreenee)*; **Πάρος** *(paros)*

Γραβιέρα *(graveeera)* *graviera cheese*
Μανούρι *(manooree)* *soft cheese, similar to feta*
Σύκα *(seeka) figs*
Καρπούζι *(karpoozee) watermelon*
Ρακί *(rakee) raki, traditional spirit*
WINES
Κοκκινέλι *(kokeenelee) (red only)*; **Κρητικός** *(kreeteekos)*

There are times when you cannot eat some things. It is as well warning the waiter before making your choice.

talking talking talking talking talking

I'm vegetarian
eeme khortofaghos
είμαι χορτοφάγος

do you have any vegetarian dishes?
ekhete katee ya khortofaghoos
έχετε κάτι για χορτοφάγους;

I don't eat meat
dhen tro-o kreas
δεν τρώω κρέας

I don't eat pork
dhen tro-o kheereeno
δεν τρώω χοιρινό

I don't eat fish / shellfish
dhen tro-o psaree / ostraka
δεν τρώω ψάρι / όστρακα

which dishes have no meat / fish?
pya fayeeta dhen ekhoon kreas / psaree
ποια φαγητά δεν έχουν κρέας / ψάρι;

I have an allergy to peanuts
ekho aleryeea sta feesteekeea
έχω αλλεργία στα φυστίκια

what do you recommend?
tee proteenete
τι προτείνετε;

what is this made with?
me tee eene fteeaghmeno afto
με τι είναι φτιαγμένο αυτό;

I'm on a diet
kano dheeeta
κάνω δίαιτα

is it raw?
eene omo
είναι ωμό;

I don't drink alcohol
dhen peeno alko-ol
δεν πίνω αλκοόλ

enjoy your meal!
kalee oreksee
καλή όρεξη

τηγανιτό
teeganeeto
fried

βραστό
vrasto
boiled

ψητό
pseeto
roast

γεμιστό
yemeesto
stuffed

στο φούρνο
sto foorno
baked in the oven

στη σούβλα
stee soovla
on the spit

λαδερά
ladera
braised in olive oil

στη σχάρα
stee skhara
on the grill

στα κάρβουνα
sta karvoona
barbecued on charcoal

μαγειρευτά
mayeerefta
ready cooked (in casserole pots)

της ώρας
tees oras
while you wait

καπνιστό
kapneesto
smoked

μαγειρεμένο
mayeeremeno
cooked

ωμό
omo
raw

MENU READER

α Α

αγγούρι *ang**oo**ree* cucumber

αγκινάρες *ankeen**a**res* artichokes

αγκινάρες άλα πολίτα *ankeen**a**res **a**la pol**ee**ta* artichokes with lemon juice and olive oil

αγριογούρουνο *agreeog**oo**roono* wild boar

αεριούχο *aereе**oo**kho* fizzy, sparkling

αθερίνα *ather**ee**na* whitebait, usually fried

αλάτι *al**a**tee* salt

αλεύρι *al**e**vree* flour

αλευρόπιτα *alevr**o**peeta* pie made with cheese, milk and eggs

αμύγδαλα *am**ee**gdala* almonds

άνηθος ***a**neethos* dill

αρακάς *arak**a**s* peas

αρνάκι ψητό *arn**a**kee pseet**o*** lamb chop grilled with herbs

αρνί *arn**ee*** lamb

αρνί γκιοβετσι *arn**ee** gyoov**e**tsee* roast lamb with small pasta

αρνί λεμονάτο *arn**ee** lemon**a**to* lamb braised in sauce with herbs and lemon juice

αρνί με βότανα *arn**ee** me v**o**tana* lamb stewed with vegetables and herbs

αρνίσιες μπριζόλες *arn**ee**see-es breez**o**les* lamb chops

αρνί ψητό *arn**ee** pseet**o*** roast lamb

αστακός *astak**o**s* lobster (often served with lemon juice and olive oil)

άσπρο ***a**spro* white

άσπρο κρασί ***a**spro kras**ee*** white wine

αυγά *avgh**a*** eggs

αυγολέμονο *avghol**e**mono* egg and lemon soup

αυγοτάραχο *avghot**a**rakho* mullet roe (smoked)

αφελία *afel**ee**a* pork in red wine with seasonings (Cyprus)

αχινοί *akheen**ee*** sea urchin roes

αχλάδι *akhl**a**dhee* pear

αχλάδι στο φούρνο *akhl**a**dhee sto f**oo**rno* baked pear in syrup sauce

αχνιστό *akhneest**o*** steamed

β Β

βασιλικός *vaseeleek**o**s* basil

βερίκοκο *ver**ee**koko* apricot

βισινό κασέρι *veeseen**o** kas**e**ree* sheep's cheese served with cherry preserve

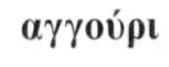

αγγούρι

βερίκοκο

βλίτα *vl**ee**ta* wild greens (like spinach, eaten with olive oil and lemon)

βότκα *v**o**tka* vodka

βοδινό *vodheen**o*** beef

βουτήματα *voot**ee**mata* biscuits to dip in coffee

βούτυρο *v**oo**teero* butter

βραδινό *vradeen**o*** evening meal

βραστό *vrast**o*** boiled

γ Γ

γάλα *gh**a**la* milk

γαλακτομπούρικο *ghalaktob**oo**reeko* custard tart

γαλακτοπωλείο *ghalaktopol**ee**o* café/patisserie

γαρίδες *ghar**ee**dhes* shrimps; prawns

γαρίδες γιουβέτσι *ghar**ee**dhes yoov**e**tsee* prawns in tomato sauce with feta

γαρύφαλλο *gar**ee**falo* clove (spice)

γαύρος *g**a**vros* sardine-type fish (if salted: anchovy)

γίδα βραστή *y**ee**da vrast**ee*** goat soup

γεμιστά *yemeest**a*** stuffed vegetables

γιαούρτι *ya**oo**rtee* yoghurt

γιαούρτι με μέλι *ya**oo**rtee me m**e**lee* yoghurt with honey

γιαχνί *yakhn**ee*** cooked in tomato sauce and olive oil

γίγαντες *y**ee**ghantes* large butter beans

γιουβαρλάκια *yoovarl**a**kya* meatballs in lemon sauce

γκαζόζα *ghaz**o**za* fizzy drink

γλυκά *ghlyk**a*** dessert

γλυκά κουταλιού *ghlyk**a** kootaly**oo*** crystalized fruit

γλώσσα *ghl**o**sa* sole

γόπες *gh**o**pes* bogue, a type of fish

γραβιέρα *ghravy**e**ra* cheese resembling gruyère

γύρος *y**ee**ros* doner kebab

δεντρολίβανο

δ Δ

δάφνη *d**a**fnee* bay leaf

δάκτυλα *dh**a**kteela* almond cakes

δαμάσκηνα *dham**a**skeena* prunes with cream in wine sauce

δείπνο *dh**ee**pno* dinner

δεντρολίβανο *dendrol**ee**vano* rosemary

δίπλες *dh**ee**ples* pastry with honey and walnuts

δολμάδες *dholm**a**dhes* vine leaves, rolled up and stuffed with minced meat and rice

ελιές

ε Ε

ελάχιστα ψημένο *elakheesta pseemeno* rare (meat)

ελαιόλαδο *eleoladho* olive oil

ελιές *elyes* olives

ελιές τσακιστές *elyes tsakeestes* cracked green olives with coriander seeds and garlic (Cyprus)

ελιοτή *elyotee* olive bread

εξοχικό *eksokheeko* stuffed pork or beef with vegetables and cheese

εστιατόριο *esteeatoreeo* restaurant

ζ Ζ

ζαμπόν *zambon* ham

ζαχαροπλαστείο *zakharoplasteeo* cake shop

ζάχαρη *zakharee* sugar

ζελατίνα *zelateena* brawn

ζεστή σοκολάτα *zestee sokolata* hot chocolate

ζεστό *zesto* hot, warm

θ Θ

Θαλασσινά *thalaseena* seafood

Θυμάρι *theemaree* thyme

ι Ι

Ιμάμ μπαϊλντί *eemam baeeldee* stuffed aubergines (eggplants)

κακαβιά fish soup

κ Κ

κάβα *kava* wine shop

κάβουρας *kavooras* boiled crab

καγιανάς με παστό κρέας *kayanas me pasto kreyas* salted pork with cheese, tomatoes and eggs

κακαβιά *kakaveea* fish soup

κακάο *kakow* hot chocolate

καλαμάκια *kalamakya* small skewers

καλαμάρια *kalamareea* squid

καλαμάρια τηγανιτά *kalamareea teeghaneeta* fried squid

καλαμπόκι

καλαμπόκι *kalambokee* corn on the cob

καλαμποκόπιτα *kalambokopeeta* corn bread

καλοψημένο *kalopseemeno* well done (meat)

κανέλα *kanella* cinnamon

κάπαρι *kaparee* pickled capers

καπνιστό *kapneesto* smoked

καραβίδα *karaveedha* crayfish

καράφα *karafa* carafe

καρέκλα *karekla* chair

καρότο *karoto* carrot

καρπούζι *karpoozee* watermelon

καρύδι *kareedhee* walnut

καρυδόπιτα *kareedhopeeta* walnut cake

καρυδόπιτα walnut cake

καρύδα *kar**ee**dha* coconut

κασέρι *kas**e**ree* sheep's milk cheese, often served fried

κάστανα *k**a**stana* chestnuts

καταΐφι *kata**ee**fee* small shredded pastry drenched in syrup

κατάλογος *kat**a**loghos* menu

κατάλογος κρασιών *kat**a**loghos krasy**o**n* wine list

καταψυγμένο *katapseeghm**e**no* frozen

κατσίκι *kats**ee**kee* roast kid

καφενείο *kafen**ee**o* café

καφές *kaf**e**s* coffee (Greek-style)
καφέδες *kaf**e**des* coffees (plural)

κεράσια

καφές γλυκύς *kaf**e**s ghleek**ee**s* very sweet coffee
καφές με γάλα *kaf**e**s me gh**a**la* milky coffee
καφές μέτριος *kaf**e**s m**e**treeos* medium-sweet coffee
καφές σκέτος *kaf**e**s sk**e**tos* coffee without sugar
καφές φραπέ *kaf**e**s frapp**e*** iced coffee

κεράσια *ker**a**seea* cherries

φασολάκια green beans

κεφαλοτύρι *kefalot**ee**ree* type of cheese, often served fried in olive oil

κεφτέδες *keft**e**dhes* meat balls

κιδώνι *keedh**o**nee* quince

κιδώνι στο φούρνο *keedh**o**nee sto f**oo**rno* baked quince

κιμάς *keem**a**s* mince

κλέφτικο *kl**e**fteeko* casserole with lamb, potatoes and vegetables

κοκορέτσι *kokor**e**tsee* traditional spit-roasted dish of spiced liver and other offal

κοκτέιλ *kokt**ey**l* cocktail

κολατσιό *kolatsy**o*** brunch, elevenses

κολοκότες *kolok**o**tes* pastries with pumpkins and raisins

κολοκυθάκια *kolokeeth**a**keea* courgettes, zucchini

κουνουπίδι

κολοκυθόπιτα *kolokeeth**o**peeta* courgette/zucchini pie

κολοκυθόπιτα γλυκιά *kolokeeth**o**peeta gleeky**a*** sweet courgette/zucchini pie

κονιάκ *kony**a**k* brandy, cognac

κοντοσούβλι *kontos**oo**vlee* spicy pieces of lamb, pork or beef, spit-roasted

κοτόπουλο *kot**o**poolo* chicken

κοτόπουλο ριγανάτο *kot**o**poolo reeghan**a**to* grilled basted chicken with herbs

κοτόπουλο καπαμά *kot**o**poolo kapam**a*** chicken casseroled with red peppers, onions, cinnamon and raisins

κουκιά *kooky**a*** broad beans

κουλούρια *kool**oo**reea* bread rings

κουνέλι *koon**e**lee* rabbit

κουπέπια stuffed vine leaves

κουνουπίδι *koonoop**ee**dhee* cauliflower

κουπέπια *koop**e**peea* stuffed vine leaves (Cyprus)

κουπές *koop**e**s* meat pasties

κουραμπιέδες *koorambу**e**dhes* small almond cakes eaten at Christmas

κρασί *kras**ee*** wine

κρέας *kr**e**as* meat

κρέμα *kr**e**ma* cream

κρεμμύδια *krem**ee**dheea* onions

κρητική σαλάτα *kreeteek**ee** sal**a**ta* watercress salad

κρύο *kr**ee**o* cold

κυδώνια *keedh**o**neea* type of clams, cockles

κυνήγι *keen**ee**yee* game

κύριο πιάτο *k**ee**reeo py**a**to* main course

λεμόνι

λ Λ

λαβράκι *lavr**a**kee* baked sea-bass

λαγός *lag**o**s* hare

λαδερά *ladher**a*** vegetable casserole

λάδι *l**a**dhee* oil

λαδότυρο *lad**o**teero* soft cheese with olive oil

λάχανα *l**a**khana* green vegetables

λαχανικά *lakhaneek**a*** vegetables (menu heading)

λάχανο *l**a**khano* cabbage, greens

λεμονάδα *lemon**a**dha* lemon drink

λεμόνι *lem**o**nee* lemon

λευκό *lefk**o*** white (used for wine as well as **άσπρο**)

λίγο ***lee**go* a little, a bit

λουκάνικα *look**a**neeka* type of highly seasoned sausage

λουκουμάδες *lookoom**a**dhes* small fried dough balls in syrup

λουκούμι *look**oo**mee* Turkish delight

λουκούμια *look**oo**meea* shortbread served at weddings

λούντζα ***loo**ndza* loin of pork, marinated and smoked

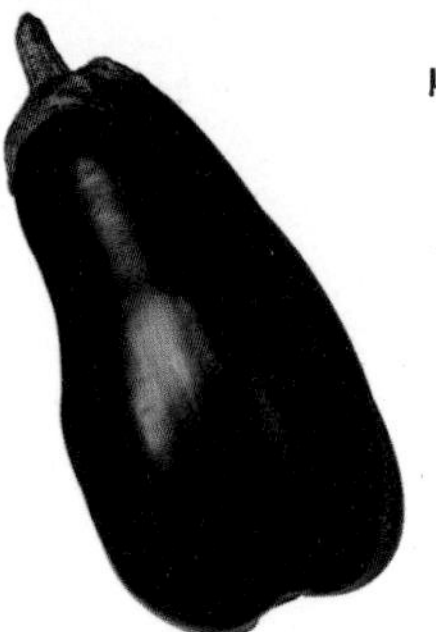

μελιτζάνα

μ Μ

μαγειρίτσα *mayeer**ee**tsa* soup made of lamb offal, special Easter dish

μαϊντανός *maeedan**o**s* parsley

μακαρόνια *makar**o**nya* spaghetti

μακαρόνια με κιμά *makar**o**nya me keem**a*** spaghetti bolognese

μαρίδες *mar**ee**dhes* small fish like sprats, served fried

μαρούλι *mar**oo**lee* lettuce

μαρτίνι *marteenee* martini

μαύρο κρασί *m**a**vro kras**ee*** red wine (although you'll hear *k**o**keeno kras**ee*** more often)

μανιτάρια *maneed**a**reea* mushrooms

μαυρομάτικα *mavrom**a**teeka* black-eyed peas

μεγάλο *meg**a**lo* large, big

μανιτάρια

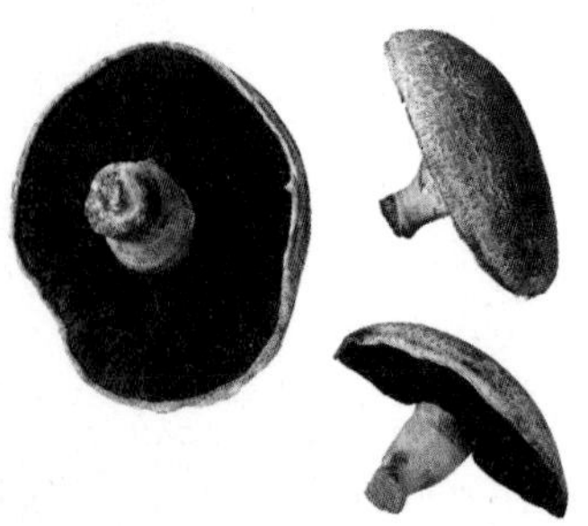

μεζές *mez**e**s* mezedhes, selection of starters (served free of charge with ouzo or retsina)

μεζέδες *mez**e**dhes* mezedhes, selection of starters

μεζεδοπωλείο *mezedhopol**ee**o* mezés shop

μέλι *m**e**lee* honey

μελιτζάνα *meleetz**a**na* aubergine (eggplant)

μελιτζάνες ιμάμ *meleetz**a**nes eem**a**m* aubergines (eggplants) stuffed with tomato and onion

μελιτζανοσαλάτα *meleetzanosal**a**ta* aubergine (eggplant) mousse (dip)

μελιτζανάκι γλυκό *meleetzan**a**kee gleek**o*** crystalized sweet in syrup, made from aubergine/ eggplant

μεσημεριανό *meseemereean**o*** lunch

μεταλλικό νερό *metaleek**o** ner**o*** mineral water

μεταξά *meta**xa*** Metaxa (Greek brandy-type spirit)

μέτρια ψημένο *m**e**treea pseem**e**no* medium (meat)

μη αεριούχο *mee aeree**oo**kho* still, not fizzy

μήλα *m**ee**la* apples

μηλόπιτα *meel**o**peeta* apple pie

μίλκο *m**ee**lko* milky chocolate drink

μήλα

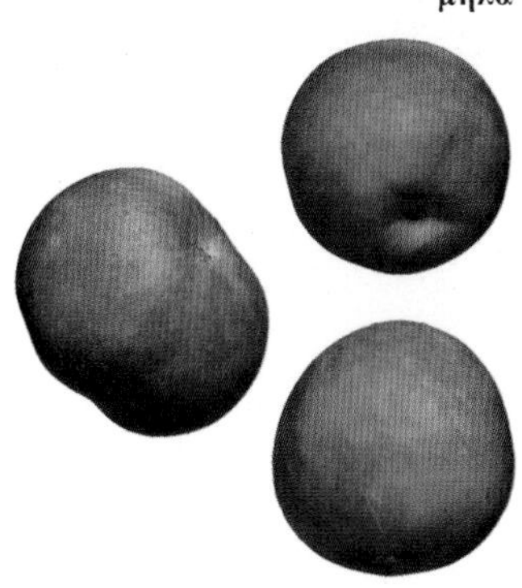

μιλκσέικ *meelkseik* milkshake

μικρό *meekro* small, little

μοσχάρι *moskharee* beef

μοσχάρι κοκινιστό *moskharee kokeeneesto* beef in wine sauce with tomatoes and onions

μουσακάς *moosakas* moussaka, layers of aubergine (eggplant), minced meat and potato, with white sauce

μπακαλιάρος *bakaleearos* cod

μπακαλιάρος παστός *bakaleearos pastos* salt cod

μπακλαβάς *baklavas* filo-pastry with nuts soaked in syrup

μπάμιες *bameeyes* okra, ladies' fingers (vegetable)

μουσακάς moussaka

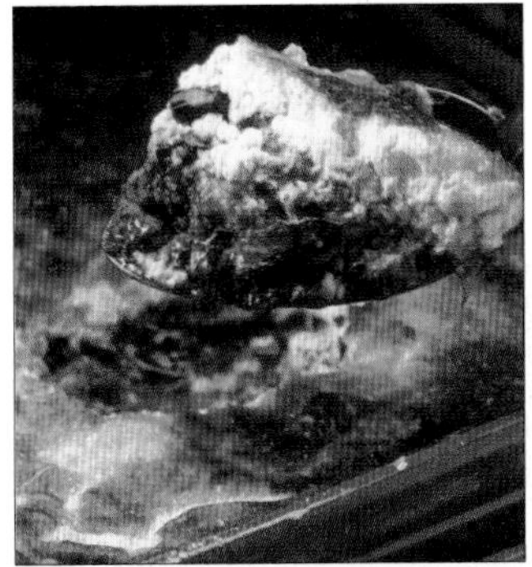

μπαράκι *barakee* bar

μπαρμπούνι *barboonee* red mullet

μπέικον *baykon* bacon

μπίρα, μπύρα *beera* beer (lager-type)

μπιφτέκια *beeftekya* meat rissole/burger

μπουγάτσα *bougatsa* cheese or custard pastry sprinkled with sugar and cinnamon

μπουκάλι *bookalee* bottle

μπουρέκι *boorekee* cheese potato and courgette pie

μπουρέκια *boorekeea* puff pastry filled with meat and cheese (Cyprus)

μπακλαβάς *baklavas*

μπουρδέτο *boordeto* fish or meat in a thick sauce of onions, tomatoes and red peppers

μπριάμ *breeam* ratatouille

μπριζόλα *breezola* steak/chop (beef/pork)

μπριζόλα αρνίσια *breezola arneeseea* lamb chop

μπριζόλα μοσχαρίσια *breezola moskhareeseea* beef steak/chop

μύδια *meedheea* mussels

ν N

νες, νεσκαφέ *nes, nescafe* instant coffee (of any brand)

νερό *nero* water

ντολμάδες *dolmadhes* vine leaves, rolled up and stuffed with mincemeat and rice

ντομάτες *domates* tomatoes

ντομάτες γεμιστές *domates yemeestes* tomatoes stuffed with rice and herbs, and sometimes with mince

ξ Ξ

ξιφίας *kseefeeas* swordfish

ξύδι *kseedhee* vinegar

ο Ο

οβελιστήριο *oveleesteereeo* shop selling souvlakia and doner kebabs

οβελιστήριο

οινοπωλείο *eenopoleeo* wine shop

ομελέτα *omeletta* omelette

ορεκτικά *orekteeka* first course/starter

ούζερι *oozeree* small bar selling ouzo and other drinks, maybe with mezedhes (**μεζέδες**)

ούζο *oozo* ouzo (traditional aniseed-flavoured spirit)

ουίσκι *weeskee* whisky

οχταπόδι *okhtapodhee* octopus (see also **χταπόδι**)

οχταπόδι κρασάτο *okhtapodhee krasato* octopus in red wine sauce

π Π

παγάκια *pagakya* ice-cubes

παγωτό *paghoto* ice-cream

παϊδάκια *paeedhakeea* grilled lamb chops

παντζάρια *pandzareea* beetroot with seasonings

παξιμάδια *pakseemadheea* crispy bread (baked twice)

παξιμαδοκούλουρα *pakseemadhokooloora* tomato and cheese bread

παπουτσάκια *papootsakeea* stuffed aubergines (eggplants)

πασατέμπο *pasatempo* pumpkin seeds

πάστα *pasta* cake, pastry

παστό *pasto* salted

παστιτσάδα *pasteetsada* beef with tomatoes, onions, red wine, herbs, spices and pasta

παστίτσιο *pasteetseeo* baked pasta dish with a middle layer of meat and white sauce

πατσάς *patsas* tripe soup

πατάτες *patates* potatoes

πατάτες τηγανιτές *patates teeghaneetes* chips, fries

πεπόνι *peponee* melon

πέστροφα *pestrofa* trout

πηλιορίτικο μπουμπάρι *peeleeoreeteeko boobaree* spicy sausage

πεπόνι

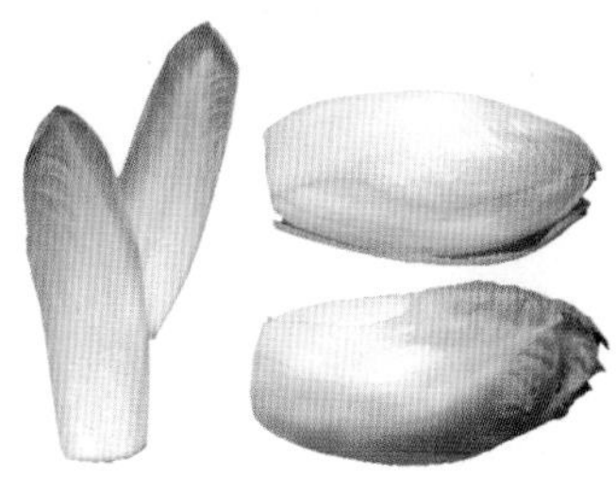

ραδίκια
ρίγανη

πιάτο της ημέρας *pyato tees eemeras* dish of the day

πιλάφι *peelafee* rice

πιπέρι *peeperee* pepper

πιπεριές *peeperyes* peppers

πιπεριές γεμιστές *peeperyes yemeestes* stuffed peppers with rice and meat

πίτα or **πίττα** *peeta* pitta (flat envelope of unleavened bread); pie with different fillings, such as meat, cheese, vegetables

πίττες or **πίττες** *peetes* pittas; pies with different fillings, such as meat, vegetables or cheese

πλακί *plakee* fish in tomato sauce

πορτοκαλάδα *portokaladha* orange drink

πορτοκάλια *portokalya* oranges

πουργούρι *poorghooree* cracked wheat (Cyprus)

πουργούρι πιλάφι *poorghooree peelafee* salad made of cracked wheat (Cyprus)

πράσα με σησάμι *prasa me seesamee* leeks baked and sprinkled with sesame seeds

πρωινό *proeeno* breakfast

ρ Ρ

ραβιόλι *raveeolee* pastry stuffed with cheese (Cyprus)

ραδίκια *radheekeea* chicory

ρακή, ρακί *rakee* raki, strong spirit a bit like schnapps

ρεβίθια *reveetheea* chickpeas

ρέγγα *renga* herring

ρέγγα καπνιστή *renga kapneestee* smoked herring, kipper

ρετσίνα *retseena* retsina, traditional resinated white wine

ρίγανη *reeghanee* oregano

ροδάκινο *rodakeeno* peach

ροζέ κρασί *roze krasee* rosé wine

ρολό με κιμά *rolo me keema* meatloaf

ρύζι *reezee* rice

ρυζόγαλο *reezoghalo* rice pudding

ρώσσικη σαλάτα *roseekee salata* Russian salad (pieces of egg, potatoes, gherkins, peas and carrots in mayonnaise)

σ ς Σ

σαγανάκι *saghanakee* mezedhes dish of fried cheese

σαλάτα *salata* salad

σαλατικά *salateeka* salads (menu heading)

σαλάχι *salakhee* ray

σαλιγκάρια *saleengareea* snails

σαρδέλλες

σαλιγκάρια γιαχνί *saleengareea yakhnee* snails in tomato sauce

σάντουιτς *sandweets* sandwich (sometimes a filled roll, sometimes a toasted sandwich with your own chosen combination of fillings)

σαραγλί *saranglee* pastry with walnuts, sesame seeds and syrup; sometimes chocolate too

σαρδέλλες *sardheles* sardines

σέλινο *seleeno* celery

σεφταλιά *seftalya* minced pork pasty

σικαλέσιο ψωμί *seekaleseeo psomee* rye bread

σικώτι *seekotee* liver

σκορδαλιά *skordhalya* garlic and potato mash

σκορδαλιά με ψάρι τηγανιτό *skordhalya me psaree teeghaneeto* fried fish served with garlic and potato mash

σκόρδο *skordho* garlic

σόδα *soda* soda

σουβλάκι *soovlakee* meat kebab

σουβλατζίδικο *soovlatseedeeko* shop selling souvlakia, doner kebabs, etc

σκόρδο

σούπα *soopa* soup

σουπιά *soopya* cuttlefish

σουτζουκάκια *sootzookakeea* highly seasoned meat balls

σπανακόπιτα spinach pie

σοφρίτο *sofreeto* meat stew with creamy garlic sauce (Corfu)

σπανάκι *spanakee* spinach

σπανακόπιτα *spanakopeeta* spinach pie

σπαράγγι *sparangee* asparagus

σπαράγγια και αγγινάρες *sparangeea ke angeenares* artichokes and asparagus in lemon juice

σπαράγγια σαλάτα *sparangeea salata* asparagus salad

σταφύλια *stafeeleea* grapes

στη σούβλα *stee soovla* spit-roasted

στιφάδο *steefadho* braised meat in spicy onion and tomato sauce

στο φούρνο *sto foorno* baked in the oven

σπαράγγι

φασολάδα bean soup

στρείδια *str**ee**dheea* oysters

σύκα *s**ee**ka* figs

σύκα στο φούρνο με μαυροδάφνη *s**ee**ka sto f**oo**rno me mavrod**a**fnee* figs cooked in red wine sauce with spices

σχάρας *skh**a**ras* grilled

τ Τ

ταραμοσαλάτα *taramosal**a**ta* mousse of cod roe

ταχίνι *takh**ee**nee* sesame seed paste

τζατζίκι *tzatz**ee**kee* yoghurt, garlic and cucumber dip

τζατζίκι *tzatz**ee**kee*

τόννος ψητός *t**o**nos pseet**o**s* grilled tuna with vegetables

τραπανός *trapan**o**s* soup made of cracked wheat and yoghurt (Cyprus)

τσάι *ts**a**ee* tea

τσιπούρα *tseep**oo**ra* type of sea bream

τσουρέκι *tsoor**e**kee* festive bread

τυρί *teer**ee*** cheese

τυροκαυτερή *teerokafter**ee*** spicy dip made of cheese and peppers

τυρόπιτα *teer**o**peeta* cheese pie

τυροσαλάτα *teerosal**a**ta* starter made of cheese and herbs

φέτα *f**e**ta*

φ Φ

φάβα *f**a**va* yellow split peas or lentils, served in a purée with olive oil and capers

φαγγρί *fangr**ee*** sea bream

φακές *fak**e**s* lentils

φασολάδα *fasol**a**dha* very popular soup made with white beans

φασολάκια *fasol**a**keea* green beans

φασόλια *fas**o**leea* haricot bean casserole

φέτα *f**e**ta* feta cheese, tangy white cheese used in salads and other dishes

φλαούνες *flaoones* Easter cheese cake (Cyprus)

φράουλες *fraooles* strawberries

φρέσκα φρούτα *freska froota* fresh fruit

φρούτα *froota* fruit

φυστίκια *feesteekya* peanuts

φυστίκια Αιγίνης *feesteekya eyeenees* pistacchios

χ Χ

χαλβάς *khalvas* sesame seed sweet

χαλούμι *khaloomee* ewe's- or goat's-milk cheese, often grilled

χέλι καπνιστό *khelee kapneesto* smoked eel

χοιρινό *kheereeno* pork

χοιρινό κρητικό *kheereeno kreeteeko* baked pork chops (Crete)

χοιρομέρι *kheeromeree* marinated, smoked ham

χόρτα *khorta* wild greens

χορτοφάγος *khortofaghos* vegetarian

χούμους *khoomoos* dip made with puréed chickpeas, hummus

χταπόδι *khtapodhee* octopus, often grilled

χωριάτικη σαλάτα *khoreeateekee salata* salad, Greek-style, with tomatoes, feta cheese, cucumber, onions, olives and oregano

ψ Ψ

ψάρι *psaree* fish

ψάρια καπνιστά *psareea kapneesta* smoked fish

ψάρια πλακί *psareea plakee* baked whole fish with vegetables and tomatoes

ψάρι fish

ψαρόσουπα *psarosoopa* seafood soup

ψαροταβέρνα *psarotaverna* fish taverna

ψησταριά *pseestareea* grill house

ψητό *pseeto* roast

ψωμάκι *psomakee* bread roll, bread bun

ψωμί *psomee* bread

ψωμι ολικής αλέσεως *psomee oleekees aleseos* wholemeal bread

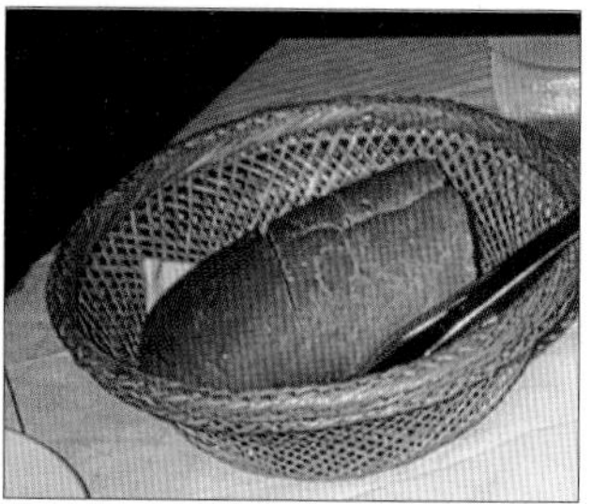

ψωμί

PHONETIC MENU READER

A

aereeookho fizzy, sparkling

afeleea pork in red wine with seasonings (Cyprus)

agreeogooroono wild boar

akheenee sea urchin roes

akhladhee pear
akhladhee sto foorno baked pear with syrup sauce

akhneesto steamed

alatee salt

alevree flour

alevropeeta pie made with cheese, milk and eggs

ameegdala almonds

aneethos dill

angeenares artichokes

angeenares ala poleeta artichokes with lemon juice and olive oil

angooree cucumber

arakadhes peas

arnakee pseeto lamb chop grilled with herbs

arnee lamb
arnee gyoovetsee roast lamb with small pasta
arnee lemonato lamb braised in sauce with herbs and lemon juice
arnee me votana lamb stewed with vegetables and herbs
arneeseeo lamb chops
arnee pseeto roast lamb

aspro white

aspro krasee white wine

astakos lobster (often served with lemon juice and olive oil)

athereena whitebait, usually fried

avgha eggs

avgholemono egg and lemon soup

avghotarakho mullet roe (smoked)

avrakee baked sea-bass

B

bakaleearos cod

bakaleearos pastos salt cod

baklavas filo-pastry with nuts soaked in syrup

bameeyes okra (vegetable)

barakee bar

barboonee red mullet

baykon bacon

beeftekya meat rissole/burger

beera beer (lager-type)

bookalee bottle

boordeto fish or meat in a thick sauce of onions, tomatoes and red peppers

boorekee cheese potato and courgette pie

boorekeea puff pastry filled with meat and cheese (Cyprus)

bougatsa cheese or custard pastry sprinkled with sugar and cinnamon

breeam ratatouille

breezola steak (beef/pork)

breezola arneeseea lamb chop

breezola moskhareeseea veal chop

D

dafnee bay leaf

dhakteela almond cakes

*dham**a**skeena* prunes with cream in wine sauce

*dh**ee**pno* dinner

*dendrol**ee**vano* rosemary

*dh**ee**ples* pastry with honey and walnuts

*dolm**a**dhes* vine leaves, rolled up and stuffed with mincemeat and rice

*dom**a**tes* tomatoes
  *dom**a**tes yemeest**e**s* tomatoes stuffed with rice and herbs, and sometimes with mince

E

*eem**a**m baeeld**ee*** stuffed aubergines (eggplants)

*eenopol**ee**o* wine shop

*el**a**kheesta pseem**e**no* rare (meat)

*ele**o**ladho* olive oil

*ely**e**s* olives

*ely**e**s tsakeest**e**s* cracked green olives with coriander seeds and garlic (Cyprus)

*elyot**ee*** olive bread

*esteeat**o**reeo* restaurant

*exokheek**o*** stuffed pork or beef with vegetables and cheese

F

*fak**e**s* lentils

*fangr**ee*** sea bream

*fasol**a**dha* very popular dish made with large white beans and herbs

*fasol**a**keea* green beans

*fas**o**leea* haricot bean casserole

*f**a**va* yellow split peas or lentils, served in a purée with olive oil and capers

*feest**ee**kya* peanuts

*feest**ee**kya ey**ee**nees* pistacchios

*f**e**ta* feta cheese, used in salads and other dishes

*fla**oo**nes* Easter cheese cake (Cyprus)

*fr**a**ooles* strawberries

*fr**e**ska fr**oo**ta* fresh fruit

*fr**oo**ta* fruit

G

*gar**ee**falo* clove (spice)

*g**a**vros* sardine-type fish (if salted: anchovy)

*gh**a**la* milk

*ghalaktob**oo**reko* custard tart

*galaktopol**ee**o* café/patisserie

*ghar**ee**dhes* shrimps; prawns
  *ghar**ee**dhes yoov**e**tsee* prawns in tomato sauce with feta

*ghaz**o**za* fizzy drink

*ghl**o**sa* sole

*ghlyk**a*** dessert

*ghlyk**a** kootaly**oo*** dessert

*gh**o**pes* bogue, a type of fish

*ghravy**e**ra* cheese resembling gruyère

K

*kafen**ee**o* café

*kaf**e**des* coffees (plural)

*kaf**e**s* coffee (Greek-style)

*kaf**e**s frapp**é*** iced coffee

*kaf**e**s ghleek**ee**s* very sweet coffee

*kaf**e**s me gh**a**la* milky coffee

*kaf**e**s m**e**treeos* medium-sweet coffee

*kaf**e**s sk**e**tos* coffee without sugar

*kakavee**a***fish soup

ka-kow hot chocolate

*kalam**a**kya* small skewers

*kalam**a**reea* squid

*kalam**a**reea teeghaneet**a*** fried squid

*kalamb**o**kee* corn on the cob

kalambok**o**peeta corn bread

kalopseem**e**no well done (meat)

kan**e**lla cinnamon

k**a**paree pickled capers

kapneest**o** smoked

kar**a**fa carafe

karav**ee**dha crayfish

kar**ee**dhee walnut

kareedh**o**peeta walnut cake

kar**ee**dha coconut

kar**e**kla chair

kar**o**to carrot

karp**oo**zee watermelon

kas**e**ree sheep's milk cheese, often served fried

k**a**stana chestnuts

kata**ee**fee small pastry drenched in syrup

kat**a**loghos menu

kat**a**loghos krasy**o**n wine list

katapseegm**e**no frozen

kats**ee**kee roast kid

k**a**vawine shop

k**a**vooras boiled crab

kayan**a**s me past**o** kr**e**yas salted pork with cheese, tomatoes and eggs

keedh**o**nee quince

keedh**o**neea type of clams

keedh**o**nee sto f**oo**rno baked quince

keem**a**s mince

keen**ee**yee game

keer**ee**o py**a**to main course

kefal**o**teeree type of cheese, often served fried in olive oil

keft**e**dhes meat balls

ker**a**seea cherries

khalv**a**s sesame seed sweet, halva

khal**oo**mee ewe's or goat's milk cheese, often grilled

kheereen**o** pork

kheereen**o** kreeteek**o** baked pork chops (Crete)

kheerom**e**ree marinated, smoked ham

kh**e**lee kapneest**o** smoked eel

kh**oo**moos dip made with puréed chickpeas

kh**o**rta wild greens

khoree**a**teekee sal**a**ta salad, Greek style, with tomatoes, feta cheese, cucumber and onions

khortof**a**ghos vegetarian

kl**e**fteeko casserole with meat, potatoes and vegetables

kokor**e**tsee stewed offal or liver, a special Easter dish

kokt**e**eel cocktail

kolatsy**o** brunch, elevenses

kolokeeth**a**keea courgettes, zucchini

kolokeeth**o**peeta courgette/zucchini pie

kolokeeth**o**peeta gleeky**a** sweet courgette/zucchini pie

kolok**o**tes pastries with pumpkins and raisins

kontos**oo**vlee spicy pieces of lamb, pork or beef, spit-roasted

kony**a**k brandy, cognac

kooky**a** broad beans

kool**oo**reea bread rings

koon**e**lee rabbit

koonoop**ee**dhee cauliflower

koop**e**peea stuffed vine leaves (Cyprus)

koop**e**s meat pasties

koorambye**e**dhes small almond cakes eaten at Christmas

kot**o**poolo chicken

kot**o**poolo reeghan**a**to grilled basted chicken with herbs

kot**o**poolo kapam**a** chicken casseroled with red peppers, onions, cinnamon and raisins

krasee wine
kreas meat
kreeo cold
kreeteekee salata watercress salad
krema cream
kremeedheea onions
kseedhee vinegar
kseefeeas swordfish
khtapodhee octopus, often grilled

L

ladhee oil
ladhera vegetable casserole
ladoteero soft cheese with olive oil
lagos hare
lakhana vegetables
lakhaneeka vegetables (menu heading)
lakhano cabbage
leego a little, a bit
lemonadha lemon drink
lemonee lemon
lefko white
lookaneeka type of highly seasoned sausage
lookoomadhes small fried dough balls in syrup
lookoomee Turkish delight
lookoomeea shortbread served at weddings
loondza loin of pork, marinated and smoked

M

maeedanos parsley
makaronya spaghetti
makaronya me keema spaghetti bolognese
maneedareea mushrooms
mareedhes small fish like sprats, served fried
mareezoles meat cooked in olive oil and lemon juice
maroolee lettuce
marteenee martini
mavro red wine
mavro krasee red wine (although you'll hear *kokeeno krasee* more often)
mavromateeka black-eyed peas
mayeereetsa soup made of lamb offal, special Easter dish
mee aereeookho still, not fizzy
meedheea mussels
meekro small, little
meela apples
meelopeeta apple pie
meelko milky chocolate drink
megalo large, big
melee honey
meleetzana aubergine
meleetzanakee gleeko crystalized sweet in syrup, made from aubergine (eggplant)
meleetzanes eemam aubergines stuffed with tomato and onion
meleetzanosalata aubergine mousse (dip)
meseemereeano lunch
metaleeko nero mineral water
metaxa Metaxa (Greek brandy-type spirit)
metreea pseemeno medium (meat)
mezedhes mezedhes, selection of starters
mezedhopoleeo mezés shop
mezes mezedhes, selection of starters (served free of charge with ouzo or retsina)
moskharee veal
moskharee beef
moskharee kokeeneesto beef in wine sauce with tomatoes and onions
moosakas moussaka, layered aubergine, meat and potato, with white sauce

N

nes, nescafé instant coffee (of any brand)

*ner**o*** water

O

*okhtap**o**dheea* octopus

*okhtap**o**dhee kras**a**to* octopus in red wine sauce

*omel**e**tta* omelette

*oozer**ee*** small bar selling ouzo and other drinks, maybe with mezedhes

***oo**zo* ouzo (traditional aniseed-flavoured spirit)

*orekteek**a*** first course/starter

*oveleest**ee**reeo* shop selling souvlakia and doner kebabs

P

*pag**a**kya* ice-cubes

*paghot**o*** ice-cream

*paeedh**a**keea* grilled lamb chops

*pakseem**a**dheea* crispy bread (baked twice)

*pandz**a**reea* beetroot with seasonings

*papoots**a**keea* stuffed aubergines

*pasat**e**mpo* pumpkin seeds

*p**a**sta* cake, pastry

*past**o*** salted

*pasteets**a**da* beef with tomatoes, onions, red wine, herbs, spices and pasta

*past**ee**tseeo* baked pasta dish with a middle layer of meat and white sauce

*pats**a**s* tripe soup

*pat**a**tes* potatoes

*pat**a**tes teeghaneet**e**s* chips, fries

*paxeemadhok**oo**looa* tomato and cheese bread

*peel**a**fee* pilau rice

*peeleeor**ee**teeko boob**a**ree* spicy sausage

*peep**e**ree* pepper

*peepery**e**s* peppers

*peepery**e**s yemeest**e**s* stuffed peppers with rice and meat

*p**ee**ta* pitta (flat envelope of unleavened bread)

*p**ee**tes* meaning pies, but they have different fillings, such as meat, vegetables or cheese

*pep**o**nee* melon

*p**e**strofa* trout

*plak**ee*** fish in tomato sauce

*poorgh**oo**ree* cracked wheat (Cyprus)

*poorgh**oo**ree peel**a**fee* salad made of cracked wheat (Cyprus)

*portokal**a**dha* orange drink

*portok**a**lya* oranges

*pr**a**sa me sees**a**mee* leeks baked and sprinkled with sesame seeds

*proeen**o*** breakfast

*ps**a**ree* fish

*ps**a**reea kapneest**a*** smoked fish

*ps**a**reea plak**ee*** baked whole fish with vegetables and tomatoes

*psar**o**soopa* seafood soup

*psarotav**e**rna* fish taverna

*pseestar**ee**a* grill house

*pseet**o*** roast

*psom**a**kee* bread roll

*psom**ee*** bread

*psom**ee** oleek**ee**s al**e**seos* wholemeal bread

Q

*py**a**to tees eem**e**ras* dish of the day

R

*radh**ee**keea* chicory

*rak**ee*** raki, strong spirit a bit like schnapps

raveeolee pastry stuffed with cheese (Cyprus)

reeghanee oregano or chicory

renga herring

renga kapneestee smoked herring, kipper

retseena retsina, traditional resinated white wine

reveetheea chickpeas

rolo me keema meatoaf

rodakeeno peach

roze krasee rosé wine

reezee rice

reezoghalo rice pudding

roseekee salata Russian salad (pieces of egg, potatoes, gherkins, peas and carrots in mayonnaise)

S

saghanakee mezedhes dish of fried cheese

salata salad

salakhee ray

salateeka salads (menu heading)

salates salads (on menu)

saleengareea snails

saleengareea yakhnee snails in tomato sauce

sandweets sandwich (sometimes a filled roll, sometimes a toasted sandwich with your own chosen combination of fillings)

saranglee pastry with walnuts, sesame seeds and syrup; sometimes chocolate too

sardhelles sardines

seeka figs

seekaleseeo psomee rye bread

seeka sto foorno me mavrodafnee figs cooked in red wine sauce with spices

seekotee liver

seftalya minced pork pasty

seleeno celery

skharas grilled

skordhalya garlic and potato mash

skordhalya me psaree teeghaneeto fried fish served with garlic and potato mash

skordho garlic

soda soda

sofreeto meat stew, highly seasoned (Corfu)

soopa soup

soopya cuttlefish

soovlakee meat kebab

soovlatseedeeko shop selling souvlakia, doner kebabs, etc

sootzookakeea highly seasoned meat balls

spanakee spinach

spanakopeeta spinach pie

sparangee asparagus

sparangeea ke angeenares mezedhes of artichokes and asparagus in lemon juice

sparangeea salata asparagus salad

stafeeleea grapes

steefadho braised meat in onion and tomato sauce

stee soovla spit-roasted

sto foorno baked in the oven

streedheea oysters

T

takheenee sesame seed paste

taramosalata mousse of cod roe

teeree cheese

teerokafteree spicy dip made of cheese and peppers

teeropeeta cheese pie

teerosalata starter made of cheese and herbs

*thalaseen**a*** seafood

*theem**a**ree* thyme

*t**o**nos pseet**o**s* grilled tuna with vegetables

*trapan**o**s* soup made of cracked wheat and yoghurt (Cyprus)

*ts**a**ee* tea

*tseep**oo**ra* type of sea bream

*tsoor**e**kee* festive bread

*tzatz**ee**kee* cucumber, garlic and yoghurt dip

V

*vaseeleek**o**s* basil

*veeseen**o** kas**e**ree* sheep's cheese served with cherry preserve

*ver**ee**koko* apricot

*vl**ee**ta* wild greens (like spinach, eaten with olive oil and lemon)

*vodheen**o*** beef

*voot**ee**mata* biscuits to dip in coffee

*v**oo**teero* butter

*v**o**tka* vodka

*vradeen**o*** evening meal

*vrast**o*** boiled

W

***wee**skee* whisky

Y

*yakhn**ee*** cooked in tomato sauce and olive oil

*ya**oo**rtee* yoghurt

*ya**oo**rtee me m**e**lee* yoghurt with honey

*y**ee**da vrast**ee*** goat soup

*y**ee**ghantes* large butter beans

*y**ee**ros* doner kebab

*yemeest**a*** stuffed vegetables

*yoovarl**a**kya* meatballs in lemon sauce

Z

*z**a**kharee* sugar

*zakharoplast**ee**o* cake shop

*zelat**ee**na* brawn

*zamb**o**n* ham

*zest**ee** sokol**a**ta* hot chocolate

*zest**o*** hot, warm

DICTIONARY

english-greek

A

a ένας *enas (masculine* ο *words)*
μία *meea (feminine* η *words)*
ένα *ena (neuter* το *words)*

abbey το μοναστήρι *to monasteeree*

abortion η άμβλωση *ee amvlosee*

about: ***a book about Athens*** ένα βιβλίο για την Αθήνα *ena veevleeo ya teen Atheena*
at about ten o'clock περίπου στις δέκα *pereepoo stees dheka*

above πάνω από *pano apo*

abscess το απόστημα *to aposteema*

accident το ατύχημα *to ateekheema*

accommodation το κατάλυμα *to kataleema*

ache ο πόνος *o ponos*

Acropolis η Ακρόπολη *ee Akropolee*

activities οι δραστηριότητες *ee dhrasteereeoteetes*

adaptor ο μετατροπέας *o metatropeas*

address η διεύθυνση *ee dheeeftheensee*
what is your address? ποια είναι η διεύθυνσή σας; *pya eene ee dhee-eftheensee sas*

address book η ατζέντα *ee atzenda*

adhesive tape η συγκολλητική ταινία *ee seengoleeteekee teneea*

admission charge η είσοδος *ee eesodhos*

adult ο ενήλικος *o eneeleekos*

advance: ***in advance*** προκαταβολικώς *prokatavoleekos*

Aegean Sea το Αιγαίο (πέλαγος) *to eyeo (pelaghos)*

after μετά *meta*

afternoon το απόγευμα *to apoyevma*

aftershave το αφτερσέιβ *to aftershave*

afterwards αργότερα *arghotera*

again πάλι *palee*

ago: ***a week ago*** πριν μια βδομάδα *preen meea vdhomadha*

AIDS ΕΙΤΖ *e-eetz*

airbag ο αερόσακος *o aerosakos*

air conditioning ο κλιματισμός *o kleemateesmos*

air freshener το αποσμητικό χώρου *to aposmeeteeko khoroo*

airline η αεροπορική εταιρία *ee aeroporeekee etereea*

air mail αεροπορικώς *aeroporeekos*

air mattress το στρώμα για τη θάλασσα *to stroma ya tee thalasa*

airplane το αεροπλάνο *to aeroplano*

airport το αεροδρόμιο *to aerodhromeeo*

airport bus το λεωφορείο για το αεροδρόμειο *to leoforeeo ya to aerodhromeeo*

air ticket το αεροπορικό εισιτήριο *to aeroporeeko eeseeteereeo*

aisle *(in aircraft)* ο διάδρομος *o dheeadhromos*

alarm *(emergency)* ο συναγερμός *o seenayermos*

alarm clock το ξυπνητήρι *to kseepneeteeree*

alcohol το αλκοόλ *to alko-ol*

alcohol-free χωρίς αλκοόλ *khorees alko-ol*

alcoholic οινοπνευματώδης *eenopnevmatodhees*

all όλος *olos*
all the milk όλο το γάλα *olo to ghala*
all the time όλον τον καιρό *olon ton kero*

allergic to αλλεργικός σε *aleryeekos se*

alley το δρομάκι *to dhromakee*

allowance: *duty-free allowance* η επιτρεπόμενη ποσότητα *ee epeetrepomenee posoteeta*

all right *(agreed)* εντάξει *endaksee*

almond το αμύγδαλο *to ameeghdhalo*

also επίσης *epeesees*

always πάντα *panda*

am *see* **(to be)** GRAMMAR

ambulance το ασθενοφόρο *to asthenoforo*

America η Αμερική *ee amereekee*

American ο Αμερικανός / η Αμερικανίδα *o amereekanos / ee amereekaneedha*

amphitheatre το αμφιθέατρο *to amfeetheatro*

anaesthetic το αναισθητικό *to anestheeteeko*

anchor η άγκυρα *ee ankeera*

anchovy η αντζούγια *ee andzooya*

and και *ke*

angina η στηθάγχη *ee steethangkhee*

angry θυμωμένος *theemomenos*

another άλλος *alos*
another beer άλλη μία μπίρα *alee meea beera*

answer η απάντηση *ee apandeesee*

to answer απαντώ *apando*

answerphone ο αυτόματος τηλεφωνητής *o aftomatos teelefoneetees*

antacid το αντιόξινο *to andeeokseeno*

antibiotics τα αντιβιοτικά *ta andeeveeoteeka*

antihistamine το αντιισταμινικό *to andeestameeneeko*

antiques οι αντίκες *ee anteekes*

antiseptic το αντισηπτικό *to andeeseepteeko*

anywhere οπουδήποτε *opoodheepote*

apartment το διαμέρισμα *to dheeamereesma*

apartment block η πολυκατοικία *ee poleekateekeea*

aperitif το απεριτίφ *to apereeteef*

apple το μήλο *to meelo*

appendicitis η σκωληκοειδίτιδα *ee skoleekoeedheeteedha*

application form η αίτηση *ee eteesee*

appointment το ραντεβού *to randevoo*

apricot το βερίκοκο *to vereekoko*

archaeology η αρχαιολογία *ee arkheoloyeea*

architecture η αρχιτεκτονική *ee arkheetektoneekee*

are *see* **(to be)** GRAMMAR

arm το μπράτσο *to bratso*

armbands *(for swimming)* τα μπρατσάκια *ta bratsakya*

around γύρω *yeero*

to arrest συλλαμβάνω *seelamvano*

arrivals οι αφίξεις *ee afeeksees*

to arrive φτάνω *ftano*

art gallery η πινακοθήκη *ee peenakotheekee*

arthritis η αρθρίτιδα *ee arthreeteedha*

artichoke η αγκινάρα *ee angeenara*

ashtray το τασάκι *to tasakee*

asparagus το σπαράγγι *to sparangee*

aspirin η ασπιρίνη *ee aspeereenee*
soluble aspirin διαλυόμενη ασπιρίνη *dheealeeomenee aspeereenee*

asthma το άσθμα *to asthma*

at σε (στο / στη / στο) *se (sto / stee / sto)*

atlas ο άτλαντας *o atlandas*

attractive *(person)* ελκυστικός *elkeesteekos*

aubergine η μελιτζάνα *ee meleetzana*

aunt η θεία *ee theea*

Australia η Αυστραλία *ee afstraleea*

Australian ο Αυστραλός / η Αυστραλίδα *o afstralos / ee afstraleedha*

automatic αυτόματος *aftomatos*

autoteller το ATM *to ey tee em*

autumn το φθινόπωρο *to ftheenoporo*

avalanche η χιονοστιβάδα *ee khyonosteevadha*

avocado το αβοκάντο *to avokado*

awful φοβερός *foveros*

B

baby το μωρό *to moro*

baby food οι βρεφικές τροφές *ee vrefeekes trofes*

baby milk το βρεφικό γάλα *to vrefeeko ghala*

baby's bottle το μπιμπερό *to beebero*

baby seat *(in car)* το παιδικό κάθισμα *to pedheeko katheesma*

baby-sitter η μπεϊμπισίτερ *ee babysitter*

baby wipes τα υγρά μαντηλάκια για μωρά *ta eeghra mandeelakya ya mora*

back *(of a person)* η πλάτη *ee platee*

backpack το σακκίδιο *to sakeedheeo*

bad *(of food)* χαλασμένος *khalasmenos*
(of weather) κακός *kakos*

bag *(small)* η τσάντα *ee tsanda*
(suitcase) η βαλίτσα *ee valeetsa*

baggage οι αποσκευές *ee aposkeves*

baggage reclaim η παραλαβή αποσκευών *ee paralavee aposkevon*

bait *(for fishing)* το δόλωμα *to dholoma*

baker's ο φούρνος *o foornos*

balcony το μπαλκόνι *to balkonee*

bald *(person, tyre)* φαλακρός *falakros*

ball η μπάλα *ee bala*

banana η μπανάνα *ee banana*

band *(musical)* η ορχήστρα *ee orkheestra*

bandage ο επίδεσμος *o epeedhesmos*

bank η τράπεζα *ee trapeza*

banknote το χαρτονόμισμα *to khartonomeesma*

bar το μπαρ *to bar*

barbecue **η ψησταριά** *ee pseestarya*

barber **ο κουρέας** *o kooreas*

barrel **το βαρέλι** *to varelee*

basil **ο βασιλικός** *o vaseeleekos*

basket **το καλάθι** *to kalathee*

basketball **το μπάσκετ** *to basket*

bath *(tub)* **το μπάνιο** *to banyo*
to take a bath **κάνω μπάνιο** *kano banyo*

bathing cap **ο σκούφος του μπάνιου** *o skoofos too banyoo*

bathroom **το μπάνιο** *to banyo*

battery **η μπαταρία** *ee batareea*

to be *see* **(to be)** GRAMMAR

beach **η πλαζ** *ee plaz* // **η παραλία** *ee paraleea*

bean *(haricot)* **το φασόλι** *to fasolee*
(broad) **το κουκί** *to kookee*
(green) **το φασολάκι** *to fasolakee*
(soya) **η σόγια** *ee soya*

beautiful **όμορφος** *omorfos*

bed **το κρεββάτι** *to krevatee*
double bed **διπλό κρεββάτι** *dheeplo krevatee*
single bed **μονό κρεββάτι** *mono krevatee*
twin beds **δύο μονά κρεββάτια** *dheeo mona krevatya*
sofa bed **καναπές κρεββάτι** *kanapes krevatee*

bedding **τα κλινοσκεπάσματα** *ta kleenoskepasmata*

bedroom **η κρεββατοκάμαρα** *ee krevatokamara*

beef **το βοδινό** *to vodheeno* // **το μοσχάρι** *to moskharee*

beer **η μπίρα** *ee beera*

beetroot **το παντζάρι** *to pandzaree*

before *(time)* **πριν (από)** *preen (apo)*
(place) **μπροστά από** *brosta apo*

to begin **αρχίζω** *arkheezo*

behind **πίσω από** *peeso apo*

to believe **πιστεύω** *peestevo*

bell *(electric)* **το κουδούνι** *to koodhoonee*

below **κάτω από** *kato apo*

belt **η ζώνη** *ee zonee*

beside **δίπλα** *dheepla*

best **ο καλύτερος** *o kaleeteros*

better (than) **καλύτερος (από)** *kaleeteros (apo)*

between **μεταξύ** *metaksee*

bib **η σαλιάρα** *ee salyara*

bicycle **το ποδήλατο** *to podheelato*

big **μεγάλος** *meghalos*

bigger **μεγαλύτερος** *meghaleeteros*

bikini **το μπικίνι** *to beekeenee*

bill **ο λογαριασμός** *o logharyasmos*

bin **το καλάθι των αχρήστων** *to kalathee ton akhreeston*

bin liner **η σακούλα σκουπιδιών** *ee sakoola skoopeedhyon*

binoculars **τα κιάλια** *ta kyalya*

bird **το πουλί** *to poolee*

birth **η γέννηση** *ee yeneesee*

birth certificate **το πιστοποιητικό γεννήσεως** *to peestopyeetiko yeneeseos*

birthday **τα γενέθλια** *ta yenethleea*
happy birthday! **χρόνια πολλά** *khronya pola*

biscuit **το μπισκότο** *to beeskoto*

bit: *a bit (of)* **λίγο** *leegho*

bite *(insect)* **το τσίμπημα** *to tseebeema*

bitten: ***I have been bitten*** **με δάγκωσε** *me dhangose*

bitter **πικρός** *peekros*

black **μαύρος** *mavros*

blackcurrant **το μαύρο φραγκοστάφυλο** *to mavro frangostafeelo*

blanket **η κουβέρτα** *ee kooverta*

bleach **το λευκαντικό** *to lefkandeeko*

to bleed **αιμορραγώ** *emoragho*

blister **η φουσκάλα** *ee fooskala*

blocked *(pipe)* **βουλωμένος** *voolomenos*
(nose) **κλειστή** *kleestee*

blood group **η ομάδα αίματος** *ee omadha ematos*

blood pressure **η πίεση αίματος** *ee peeyesee ematos*

blouse **η μπλούζα** *ee blooza*

blow-dry **στέγνωμα** *steghnoma*

blue **γαλάζιος** *ghalazeeos*

boarding card **το δελτίο επιβιβάσεως** *to dhelteeo epeeveevaseos*

boarding house **η πανσιόν** *ee pansyon*

boat *(small)* **η βάρκα** *ee varka*
(ship) **το πλοίο** *to pleeo*

boat trip **η βαρκάδα** *ee varkadha*

to boil **βράζω** *vrazo*

boiled **βραστός** *vrastos*
boiled water **βραστό νερό** *vrasto nero*

bone **το κόκκαλο** *to kokalo*
(fishbone) **το αγκάθι** *to angkathee*

book *n* **το βιβλίο** *to veevleeo*

to book *(room, tickets)* **κλείνω** *kleeno*

booking: ***to make a booking*** **κλείνω θέση** *kleeno thesee*

booking office *(railways, airlines, etc.)* **το εκδοτήριο** *to ekdhoteereeo*
(theatre) **το ταμείο** *to tameeo*

bookshop **το βιβλιοπωλείο** *to veevleeopoleeo*

boots **οι μπότες** *ee botes*

border *(frontier)* **τα σύνορα** *ta seenora*

boring **βαρετός** *varetos*

boss **ο / η προϊστάμενος** *o / ee proeestamenos*

both **και οι δυο** *ke ee dheeo*

bottle **το μπουκάλι** *to bookalee*

bottle-opener **το ανοιχτήρι** *to aneekhteeree*

bowl **το μπωλ** *to bol*

box *(container)* **το κιβώτιο** *to keevotyo*
(cardboard) **το κουτί** *to kootee*

box office **το ταμείο** *to tameeo*

boy **το αγόρι** *to aghoree*

boyfriend **ο φίλος** *o feelos*

bra **το σουτιέν** *to sootyen*

bracelet **το βραχιόλι** *to vrakheeolee*

to brake **φρενάρω** *frenaro*

brake fluid **το υγρό των φρένων** *to eeghro ton frenon*

brake light **τα φώτα πεδήσεως** *ta fota pedheeseos*

brakes **τα φρένα** *ta frena*

brandy **το κονιάκ** *to konyak*

bread **το ψωμί** *to psomee*
(wholemeal) **ψωμί ολικής αλέσεως** *psomee oleekees aleseos*

to break **σπάζω** *spazo*

breakdown **η βλάβη** *ee vlavee*

breakdown van **το συνεργείο διασώσεως** *to seeneryeeo dheeasoseos*

breakfast **το πρωινό** *to proeeno*

breast **το στήθος** *to steethos*

to breathe **αναπνέω** *anapneo*

bride **η νύφη** *ee neefee*

bridegroom **ο γαμπρός** *o ghambros*

briefcase **ο χαρτοφύλακας** *o khartofeelakas*

to bring **φέρνω** *ferno*

Britain **η Βρετανία** *ee vretaneea*

British **ο Βρετανός / η Βρετανίδα** *o vretanos / ee vretaneedha*

brochure **η μπροσούρα** *ee brosoora*

broken **σπασμένος** *spasmenos*
broken down **χαλασμένος** *khalasmenos*

bronze **μπρούντζινος** *broondzeenos*

brooch **η καρφίτσα** *ee karfeetsa*

brother **ο αδελφός** *o adhelfos*

brown **καφέ** *kafe*

bruise **η μελανιά** *ee melaneea*

brush **η βούρτσα** *ee voortsa*

bucket **ο κουβάς** *o koovas*

buffet **ο μπουφές** *o boofes*

buffet car **το βαγόνι εστιατόριο** *to vaghonee esteeatoreeo*

bulb *(light)* **ο γλόμπος** *o ghlobos*

bumbag **η τσαντάκι μέσης** *ee tsantakee mesees*

buoy **η σημαδούρα** *ee seemadhoora*

bureau de change *(bank)* **ξένο συνάλλαγμα** *kseno seenalaghma*

to burn **καίω** *keo*

burnt **καμένος** *kamenos*

to burst **σκάζω** *skazo*

bus **το λεωφορείο** *to leoforeeo*

business **η δουλειά** *ee dhoolya*

bus station **ο σταθμός του λεωφορείου** *o stathmos too leoforeeoo*

bus stop **η στάση του λεωφορείου** *ee stasee too leoforeeoo*

bus terminal **το τέρμα του λεωφορείου** *to terma too leoforeeoo*

bus tour **η εκδρομή με λεωφορείο** *ee ekdhromee me leoforeeo*

busy **απασχολημένος** *apaskholeemenos*

but **αλλά** *ala*

butcher's **το κρεοπωλείο** *to kreopoleeo*

butter **το βούτυρο** *to vooteero*

button **το κουμπί** *to koombee*

to buy **αγοράζω** *aghorazo*

bypass **η παρακάμψη** *ee parakampsee*

C

cab **το ταξί** *to taksee*

cabbage **το καμπρολάχανο** *to kambrolakhano*

cabin **η καμπίνα** *ee kabeena*

cable car **το τελεφερίκ** *to telefereek*

cable TV **η δορυφορική τηλεώραση** *ee dhoreeforeekee teeleorasee*

café **το καφενείο** *to kafeneeo*

cake **το γλύκισμα** *o ghleekeesma*

cake shop **το ζαχαροπλαστείο** *to zakharoplasteeo*

calculator **ο υπολογιστής** *o eepoloyeestees*

calendar το ημερολόγιο *to eemeroloyo*

to call φωνάζω *fonazo*

call *n (telephone)* η κλήση *ee kleesee*
long-distance call η υπεραστική κλήση *ee eeperasteekee kleesee*

calm ήσυχος *eeseekhos*

camcorder η βιντεοκάμερα *ee veedeokamera*

camera η φωτογραφική μηχανή *ee fotoghrafeekee meekhanee*

to camp κατασκηνώνω *kataskeenono*

camping gas το γκαζάκι *to gazakee*

camping stove το πετρογκάζ *to petrogas*

campsite το κάμπινγκ *to camping*

can *(to be able)* : *I can* μπορώ *boro*
you can μπορείς *borees*
he can μπορεί *boree*
we can μπορούμε *boroome*

can *(of food)* η κονσέρβα *ee konserva*
(for oil) ο τενεκές *o tenekes*

Canada ο Καναδάς *o kanadhas*

Canadian ο Καναδός / η Καναδή *o Kanadhos / ee Kanadhee*

candle το κερί *to keree*

to cancel ακυρώνω *akeerono*

canoe το κανό *to kano*

can-opener το ανοιχτήρι *to aneekhteeree*

cappuccino το καπουτσίνο *to kapootseeno*

car το αυτοκίνητο *to aftokeeneeto*

car alarm ο συναγερμός *o seenayermos*

car ferry το φεριμπότ *to fereebot*

car keys τα κλειδιά αυτοκινήτου *ta kleedhya aftokeeneetoo*

car park το πάρκινγκ *to parking*

car radio το ραδιόφωνο αυτοκινήτου *to radhyofono aftokeeneetoo*

car seat *(for children)* το παιδικό κάθισμα αυτοκινήτου *to pedheeko katheesma aftokeeneetoo*

car wash το πλυντήριο αυτοκινήτων *to pleenteereeo aftokeeneeton*

carafe η καράφα *ee karafa*

caravan το τροχόσπιτο *to trokhospeeto*

card η κάρτα *ee karta*

cardigan η ζακέτα *ee zaketa*

careful προσεκτικός *prosekteekos*

carpet το χαλί *to khalee*

carriage *(railway)* το βαγόνι *to vaghonee*

carrot το καρότο *to karoto*

to carry κουβαλώ *koovalo*

case *(matter)* η υπόθεση *ee eepothesee*
(suitcase) η βαλίτσα *ee valeetsa*

to cash *(cheque)* εξαργυρώνω *eksaryeerono*

cash τα μετρητά *ta metreeta*

cash desk το ταμείο *to tameeo*

cash dispenser το ATM *to ey tee em*

cashier ο ταμίας *o tameeas*

casino το καζίνο *to kazeeno*

cassette η κασέτα *ee kaseta*

castle το κάστρο *to kastro*

casualty department τα επείγοντα περιστατικά *ta epeeghonda pereestateeka*

cat η γάτα *ee ghata*

catalogue ο κατάλογος *o kataloghos*

to catch πιάνω *pyano* (bus, train, etc.) παίρνω *perno*

Catholic καθολικός *katholikos*

cauliflower το κουνουπίδι *to koonoopeedhee*

cave η σπηλιά *ee speelya*

CD το CD *to see dee*

celery το σέλινο *to seleeno*

cemetery το νεκροταφείο *to nekrotafeeo*

cents (euro) λεπτά *lepta*

centimetre το εκατοστό *to ekastosto*

central κεντρικός *kendreekos*

central locking (car) η αυτόματη κλειδαριά *ee aftomatee kleedharya*

centre το κέντρο *to kendro*

century ο αιώνας *o eonas*

certificate το πιστοποιητικό *to peestopyeeteeko*

chain η αλυσίδα *ee aleeseedha*

chair η καρέκλα *ee karekla*

champagne η σαμπάνια *ee sambanya*

change η αλλαγή *ee alayee* (money) τα ρέστα *ta resta*

to change αλλάζω *alazo*

changing room (beach, sports) το αποδυτήριο *to apodheeteereeo*

chapel το παρεκκλήσι *to parekleesee*

charcoal το ξυλοκάρβουνο *to kseelokarvoono*

charge η τιμή *ee teemee*

charter flight το τσάρτερ *to tsarter*

cheap φτηνός *fteenos*

cheap rate (for phone, etc) η φτηνή ταρίφα *ee fteenee tareefa*

cheaper φτηνότερος *fteenoteros*

to check ελέγχω *elenkho*

check in περνώ από τον έλεγχο εισιτηρίων *perno apo ton elenkho eeseeteereeon*

check-in desk ο έλεγχος εισιτηρίων *o elenkhos eeseeteereeon*

cheek το μάγουλο *to maghoolo*

cheerio! γεια *ya*

cheers! γεια μας! *ya mas*

cheese το τυρί *to teeree*

chemist's το φαρμακείο *to farmakeeo*

cheque η επιταγή *ee epeetayee*

cheque card η κάρτα επιταγών *ee karta epeetaghon*

cherry το κεράσι *to kerasee*

chestnut το κάστανο *to kastano*

chewing gum η τσίχλα *ee tseekhla*

chicken το κοτόπουλο *to kotopoolo*

chickenpox η ανεμοβλογιά *ee anemovloya*

chickpeas τα ρεβίθια *ta reveetheea*

child το παιδί *to pedhee*

children τα παιδιά *ta pedhya*

chilli το τσίλλι *to tseelee*

chilled: *is the wine chilled?* είναι κρύο το κρασί; *eene kreeo to krasee*

chips πατάτες τηγανητές *patates teeghaneetes*

chocolate η σοκολάτα *ee sokolata*

Christmas **τα Χριστούγεννα** *ta khreestooyena*
merry Christmas! **καλά Χριστούγεννα** *kala khreestooyena*

church **η εκκλησία** *ee ekleeseea*

cigar **το πούρο** *to pooro*

cigarette **το τσιγάρο** *to tseegharo*

cigarette paper **το τσιγαρόχαρτο** *to tseegharokharto*

cinema **ο κινηματογράφος** *o keeneematoghrafos*

cistern **το καζανάκι** *to kazanakee*

city **η πόλη** *ee polee*

clean **καθαρός** *katharos*

to clean **καθαρίζω** *kathareezo*

cleansing cream **η κρέμα καθαρισμού** *ee krema kathareesmoo*

client **ο πελάτης / η πελάτισσα** *o pelatees / ee pelateesa*

cliffs **οι γκρεμοί** *ee gremee*

climbing **η ορειβασία** *ee oreevaseea*

climbing boots **οι μπότες ορειβασίας** *ee botes oreevaseeas*

clingfilm **το σελαφάν** *to selofan*

cloakroom **η γκαρνταρόμπα** *ee gardaroba*

clock **το ρολόι** *to roloee*

to close **κλείνω** *kleeno*

close *adj (near)* **κοντινός** *kondeenos*
(weather) **αποπνιχτικός** *apopneekhteekos*

closed **κλειστός** *kleestos*

cloth **το πανί** *to panee*
(for floor) **το σφουγγαρόπανο** *to sfoongaropano*

clothes **τα ρούχα** *ta rookha*

clothes line **το σκοινί για τα ρούχα** *to skeenee ya ta rookha*

clothes peg **το μανταλάκι** *to mandalakee*

cloudy **συννεφιασμένος** *seenefyasmenos*

clove *(spice)* **το γαρίφαλο** *to ghareefalo*

club **η λέσχη** *ee leskhee*

coach *(railway)* **το βαγόνι** *to vaghonee*
(bus) **το πούλμαν** *to poolman*
(instructor) **ο προπονητής** *o proponeetees*

coach station **ο σταθμός λεωφορείων** *o stathmos leoforeeon*

coach trip **το ταξίδι με πούλμαν** *to takseedhee me poolman*

coast **η ακτή** *ee aktee*

coastguard **η ακτοφυλακή** *ee aktofeelakee*

coat **το παλτό** *to palto*

coat hanger **η κρεμάστρα** *ee kremastra*

cockroach **η κατσαρίδα** *ee katsareedha*

cocoa **το κακάο** *to kakao*

coffee **ο καφές** *o kafes*
black coffee **σκέτος καφές** *sketos kafes*
white coffee **καφές με γάλα** *kafes me ghala*

coin **το νόμισμα** *to nomeesma*

colander **το σουρωτήρι** *to sooroteeree*

cold **κρύος** *kreeos*
I have a cold **είμαι κρυωμένος** *eeme kreeomenos*
I'm cold **κρυώνω** *kreeono*

cold sore **ο έρπητας** *o erpeetas*

colour **το χρώμα** *to khroma*

colour blind **δαλτωνικός** *dhaltoneekos*

colour film το έγχρωμο φιλμ *to enkhromo feelm*

comb η χτένα *ee khtena*

to come έρχομαι *erkhome*

to come back γυρίζω *yeereezo*

to come in μπαίνω *beno*

comfortable αναπαυτικός *anapafteekos*

communion *(holy)* η θεία κοινωνία *ee theea keenoneea*

company *(firm)* η εταιρία *ee etereea*

compartment *(train)* το διαμέρισμα *to dheeamereesma*

compass η πυξίδα *ee peekseedha*

to complain παραπονούμαι *paraponoome*

compulsory υποχρεωτικός *eepokhreoteekos*

computer ο κομπιούτερ *o computer*

computer software το software *to software*

concert η συναυλία *ee seenavleea*

concert hall το μέγαρο μουσικής *to megharo mooseekees*

condition η κατάσταση *ee katastasee*

condom το προφυλακτικό *to profeelakteeko*

conductor *(bus)* ο εισπράκτορας *o eespraktoras*
(train) ο ελεγκτής *o elenktees*

conference η διάσκεψη *ee dheeaskepsee*

to confirm επιβεβαιώνω *epeeveveono*

congratulations! συγχαρητήρια *seenkhareeteereea*

connection *(trains, etc)* η σύνδεση *ee seendhesee*

to be constipated έχω δυσκοιλιότητα *ekho dheeskeeleeoteeta*

consulate το προξενείο *to prokseneeo*

to contact επικοινωνώ *epeekeenono*

contact lenses οι φακοί επαφής *ee fakee epafees*

contact lens cleaner το καθαριστικό διάλυμα *to kathareesteeko dheealeema*

contraceptives τα αντισυλληπτικά *ta andeeseeleepteeka*

contract το συμβόλαιο *to seemvoleo*

to cook μαγειρεύω *mayeerevo*

cooker η κουζίνα *ee koozeena*

cool δροσερός *dhroseros*

cool box *(for picnics)* το ψυγειάκι *to pseeyeeakee*

copper ο χάλκος *o khalkos*

to copy *(photocopy)* φωτοτυπώ *fototeepo*

copy *n* το αντίγραφο *to andeeghrafo*

coral το κοράλλι *to koralee*

corkscrew το τιρμπουσόν *to teerbooson*

corn *(sweet corn)* το καλαμπόκι *to kalambokee*

corner η γωνία *ee ghoneea*

cornflakes τα κορνφλέικς *ta cornflakes*

cortisone η κορτιζόνη *ee korteezonee*

cosmetics τα καλλυντικά *ta kaleendeeka*

to cost κοστίζω *kosteezo*
how much does it cost?
πόσο κάνει; *poso kanee*

cotton **το βαμβάκι** *to vamvakee*
cotton buds **οι μπατουέτες** *ee batooetes*
cotton wool **το βαμβάκι** *to vamvakee*
couchette **η κουκέτα** *ee kooketa*
cough **ο βήχας** *o veekhas*
country **η χώρα** *ee khora*
(not town) **η εξοχή** *ee eksokhee*
couple *(two people)* **το ζευγάρι** *to zevgharee*
courgette **το κολοκυθάκι** *to kolokeethakee*
courier *(for tourists)* **ο / η συνοδός** *o / ee seenodhos*
course *(meal)* **το πιάτο** *to pyato*
cousin **ο εξάδελφος / η εξαδέλφη** *o eksadhelfos / ee eksadhelfee*
cover charge **το κουβέρ** *to koover*
crab **το καβούρι** *to kavooree*
cramp **η κράμπα** *o krampa*
to crash **συγκρούομαι** *seengkrooome*
crash **η σύγκρουση** *ee seengroosee*
crash helmet **το κράνος** *to kranos*
cream **η κρέμα** *ee krema*
credit card **η πιστωτική κάρτα** *ee peestoteekee karta*
crime **το έγκλημα** *to engkleema*
crisps **τα πατατάκια** *ta patatakya*
croquette **η κροκέτα** *ee kroketa*
cross **ο σταυρός** *o stavros*
to cross **διασχίζω** *dheeaskheezo*
crossroads **το σταυροδρόμι** *to stavrodhromee*
crowded **γεμάτος** *yematos*
cruise **η κρουαζιέρα** *ee krooazyera*
crutches **οι πατερίτσες** *ee patereetses*
cucumber **το αγγούρι** *to angooree*
cup **το φλυτζάνι** *to fleedzanee*
cupboard **το ντουλάπι** *to doolapee*
currant **η σταφίδα** *ee stafeedha*
current *(electric)* **το ρεύμα** *to revma*
cushion **το μαξιλάρι** *to makseelaree*
custard **η κρέμα** *ee krema*
customer **ο πελάτης** *o pelatees*
customs **το τελωνείο** *to teloneeo*
to cut **κόβω** *kovo*
cut **το κόψιμο** *to kopseemo*
cutlery **τα μαχαιροπήρουνα** *ta makheropeeroona*
to cycle **ποδηλατώ** *podheelato*
cyst **η κύστη** *ee keestee*
cystitis **η κυστίτιδα** *ee keesteeteedha*

D

daily **ημερήσιος** *eemereeseeos*
dairy products **τα γαλακτοκομικά προϊόντα** *ta ghalaktokomeeka proeeonda*
damage **η ζημιά** *ee zeemya*
damp **υγρός** *eeghros*
dance *n* **ο χορός** *o khoros*
to dance **χορεύω** *khorevo*
danger **ο κίνδυνος** *o keendheenos*
dangerous **επικίνδυνος** *epeekeendheenos*
dark *(colour)* **σκούρο** *skooro*
it's dark **είναι σκοτεινά** *eene skoteena*
date **η ημερομηνία** *ee eemeromeeneea*

what's the date? **τι ημερομηνία είναι;** *tee eemeromeeneea eene*

date of birth η ημερομηνία γεννήσεως *ee eemeromeeneea yeneeseos*

daughter η κόρη *ee koree*

day η μέρα *ee mera*

dead νεκρός *nekros*

dear αγαπητός *aghapeetos* *(expensive)* **ακριβός** *akreevos*

decaffeinated χωρίς καφεΐνη *khorees kafe-eenee*

deck chair η ξαπλώστρα *ee ksaplostra*

to declare δηλώνω *dheelono*

deep βαθύς *vathees*

deep freeze η κατάψυξη *ee katapseeksee*

to defrost ξεπαγώνω *ksepaghono*

delay η καθυστέρηση *ee katheestereesee*

delayed καθυστερισμένος *katheestereesmenos*

delicious νόστιμος *nosteemos*

dentist ο / η οδοντίατρος *o / ee odhondeeatros*

dentures η οδοντοστοιχία *ee odhondosteekheea*

deodorant το αποσμητικό *to aposmeeteeko*

department store το πολυκατάστημα *to poleekatasteema*

departure η αναχώρηση *ee anakhoreesee*

departure lounge η αίθουσα αναχωρήσεων *ee ethoosa anakhoreeseon*

deposit *(part payment)* **η προκαταβολή** *ee prokatavolee*

dessert το επιδόρπιο *to epeedhorpeeo*

details οι λεπτομέρειες *ee leptomereeyes*

detergent το απορρυπαντικό *to aporeepandeeko*

detour: ***to make a detour*** **βγαίνω από το δρόμο** *vyeno apo to dhromo*

to develop αναπτύσσω *anapteeso*

diabetic διαβητικός *dheeaveeteekos*

to dial παίρνω αριθμό *perno areethmo*

dialling code ο τηλεφωνικός κώδικας *o teelefoneekos kodheekas*

diamond το διαμάντι *to dheeamandee*

diapers οι πάνες *ee panes*

diarrhoea η διάρροια *ee dheeareea*

diary το ημερολόγιο *to eemeroloyo*

dictionary το λεξικό *to lekseeko*

diesel το ντίζελ *to deezel*

diet η δίαιτα *ee dhee-eta* ***I'm on a diet*** **κάνω δίαιτα** *kano dhee-eta*

different διαφορετικός *dheeaforeteekos*

difficult δύσκολος *dheeskolos*

digital camera η ψηφιακή φωτογραφική μηχανή *ee pseefeeakee fotografeekee meekhanee*

dinghy η μικρή βάρκα *ee meekree varka*

dining room η τραπεζαρία *ee trapezareea*

dinner το δείπνο *to dheepno*

direct **άμεσος** *amesos*

directory *(telephone)* **ο τηλεφωνικός κατάλογος** *o teelefoneekos kataloghos*

directory enquiries **οι πληροφορίες καταλόγου** *ee pleeroforeeyes kataloghoo*

dirty **βρώμικος** *vromeekos*

disabled **ανάπηρος** *anapeeros*

disco **η ντισκοτέκ** *ee deeskotek*

discount **η έκπτωση** *ee ekptosee*

dish **το πιάτο** *to pyato*

dish towel **η πετσέτα πιάτων** *ee petseta pyaton*

dishwasher **το πλυντήριο πιάτων** *to pleenteereeo pyaton*

disinfectant **το απολυμαντικό** *to apoleemandeeko*

disk *(floppy)* **η δισκέτα** *ee dheesketa*

distilled water **το απεσταγμένο νερό** *to apestaghmeno nero*

divorced **ο χωρισμένος / η χωρισμένη** *o khoreesmenos / ee khoreesmenee*

dizzy **ζαλισμένος** *zaleesmenos*

to do: ***I do*** **κάνω** *kano*
you do **κάνεις** *kanees*

doctor **ο / η γιατρός** *o / ee yatros*

documents **τα έγγραφα** *ta engrafa*

dog **το σκυλί** *to skeelee*

doll **η κούκλα** *ee kookla*

dollar **το δολάριο** *to dholareeo*

door **η πόρτα** *ee porta*

donkey **το γαϊδούρι** *to ghaeedhooree*

donor card **η κάρτα δότη** *ee karta dhotee*

double **διπλός** *dheeplos*

double bed **το διπλό κρεββάτι** *to dheeplo krevatee*

double room **το δίκλινο δωμάτιο** *to dheekleeno dhomateeo*

down: ***to go down*** **κατεβαίνω** *kateveno*

downstairs **κάτω** *kato*

drachmas **δραχμές** *dhrakhmes*

drain **η αποχέτευση** *ee apokhetefsee*

draught *(of air)* **το ρεύμα** *to revma*

draught lager **η μπίρα από βαρέλι** *ee beera apo varelee*

drawer **το συρτάρι** *to seertaree*

drawing **το σχέδιο** *to skhedheeo*

dress **το φόρεμα** *to forema*

to dress **ντύνομαι** *deenome*

dressing *(for salad)* **το λαδολέμονο** *to ladholemono*

dressing gown **η ρόμπα** *ee roba*

drill **τρυπώ** *treepo*

drink *n* **το ποτό** *to poto*
to have a drink **παίρνω ένα ποτό** *perno ena poto*

to drink **πίνω** *peeno*

drinking water **το πόσιμο νερό** *to poseemo nero*

to drive **οδηγώ** *odheegho*

driver **ο οδηγός** *o odheeghos*

driving licence **η άδεια οδήγησης** *ee adheea odheeyeesees*

to drown **πνίγομαι** *pneeghome*

drug *(illegal)* **το ναρκωτικό** *to narkoteeko*
(medicine) **το φάρμακο** *to farmako*

drunk **μεθυσμένος** *metheesmenos*

dry *n* **στεγνός** *steghnos*

to dry **στεγνώνω** *steghnono*

dry-cleaners το καθαριστήριο *to kathareesteereeo*

duck η πάπια *ee papya*

due: ***when is the train due?*** πότε θα φτάσει το τραίνο; *pote tha ftasee to treno*

dummy η πιπίλα *ee peepeela*

during κατά τη διάρκεια *kata tee dheearkeea*

dust η σκόνη *ee skonee*

duvet το πάπλωμα *to paploma*

duvet cover η παπλωματοθήκη *ee paplomatotheekee*

E

each κάθε *kathe*
100 cents each εκατό ευρώ ο καθένας *ekato evro o kathenas*

ear το αυτί *to aftee*

earache: ***I have earache*** με πονάει το αυτί μου *me ponaee to aftee moo*

earlier νωρίτερα *noreetera*

early νωρίς *norees*

earrings τα σκουλαρίκια *ta skoolareekya*

earthquake ο σεισμός *o seesmos*

east η ανατολή *ee anatolee*

Easter το Πάσχα *to paskha*

easy εύκολος *efkolos*

to eat τρώω *tro-o*

eel το χέλι *to khelee*

egg το αβγό *to avgho*
fried eggs αβγά τηγανητά *avgha teeghaneeta*
boiled eggs αβγά βραστά *avgha vrasta*
poached eggs αβγά ποσέ *avgha pose*

either ... or ή ... ή *ee ... ee* // είτε ... είτε *eete ... eete*

elastic το λάστιχο *to lasteekho*

elastic band το λαστιχάκι *to lasteekhakee*

electrician ο ηλεκτρολόγος *o eelektrologhos*

electricity meter ο μετρητής ηλεκτρισμού *o metreetees eelektreesmoo*

electric razor η ξυριστική μηχανή *ee kseereesteekee meekhanee*

e-mail το e-mail *to e-mail*

e-mail address η e-mail διεύθυνση *ee e-mail dheeeftheensee*

embassy η πρεσβεία *ee presveea*

emergency: ***it's an emergency*** είναι επείγον περιστατικό *eene epeeghon pereestateeko*

empty άδειος *adheeos*

end το τέλος *to telos*

engaged (*to marry*) αρραβωνιασμένος / η *aravonyasmenos / ee*
(*toilet*) κατειλημμένη *kateeleemenee*
(*phone*) μιλάει *meelaee*

engine η μηχανή *ee meekhanee*

England η Αγγλία *ee angleea*

English (*thing*) αγγλικός *angleekos*

Englishman / woman ο Άγγλος / η Αγγλίδα *o anglos / ee angleedha*

to enjoy oneself διασκεδάζω *dheeaskedhazo*

enough αρκετά *arketa*
enough bread αρκετό ψωμί *arketo psomee*

enquiry desk / office το γραφείο πληροφοριών *to ghrafeeo pleeroforeeon*

to enter μπαίνω *beno*

entertainment **η ψυχαγωγία** *ee pseekhaghoyeea*

entrance **η είσοδος** *ee eesodhos*

entrance fee **η τιμή εισόδου** *ee teemee eesodhoo*

envelope **ο φάκελος** *o fakelos*

equipment **ο εξοπλισμός** *o eksopleesmos*

escalator **η κυλιόμενη σκάλα** *ee keelyomenee skala*

especially **ειδικά** *eedheeka*

essential **απαραίτητος** *apareteetos*

euro **ευρώ** *evro*

Europe **η Ευρώπη** *ee evropee*

even number **ο ζυγός αριθμός** *o zeeghos areethmos*

evening **το βράδυ** *to vradhee*
this evening **απόψε** *apopse*
in the evening **το βράδυ** *to vradhee*

every **κάθε** *kathe*

everyone **όλοι** *olee*

everything **όλα** *ola*

exact **ακριβής** *akreevees*

examination **η εξέταση** *ee eksetasee*

excellent **εξαιρετικός** *eksereteekos*

except **εκτός από** *ektos apo*

excess luggage **επί πλέον αποσκευές** *epee pleon aposkeves*

exchange rate **η τιμή του συναλλάγματος** *ee teemee too seenalaghmatos*

excursion **η εκδρομή** *ee ekdhromee*

excuse me **με συγχωρείτε** *me seenkhoreete*

exhaust pipe **η εξάτμιση** *ee eksatmeesee*

exhibition **η έκθεση** *ee ekthesee*

exit **η έξοδος** *ee eksodhos*

expensive **ακριβός** *akreevos*

expert **ο / η ειδικός** *o / ee eedheekos*

to expire **λήγω** *leegho*

expired **έχει λήξει** *ekhee leeksee*

to explain **εξηγώ** *ekseegho*

express *(train)* **η ταχεία** *ee takheea*

express letter **το κατεπείγον γράμμα** *to katepeeghon ghrama*

extra: ***it costs extra*** **κοστίζει επιπλέον** *kosteezee epeepleon*
extra money **περισσότερα χρήματα** *pereesotera khreemata*

eyes **τα μάτια** *ta matya*

F

fabric **το ύφασμα** *to eefasma*

face **το πρόσωπο** *to prosopo*

facilities **οι ευκολίες** *ee efkoleeyes*

factory **το εργοστάσιο** *to erghostaseeo*

to faint **λιποθυμώ** *leepotheemo*

fainted **λιποθύμησε** *leepotheemeese*

fair *adj (hair)* **ξανθός** *ksanthos*

fair *n (commercial)* **η έκθεση** *ee ekthesee*
(fun fair) **το λουνα-πάρκ** *to loonapark*

to fall **πέφτω** *pefto*
he / she has fallen **έπεσε** *epese*

family **η οικογένεια** *ee eekoyenya*

famous **διάσημος** *dheeaseemos*

fan *(electric)* **ο ανεμιστήρας** *o anemeesteeras*

fan belt **το λουρί του ψυγείου** *to looree too pseeyeeoo*

far **μακριά** *makreea*

fare *(bus, train)* **το εισιτήριο** *to eeseeteereeo*

farm **το αγρόκτημα** *to aghrokteema*

fast **γρήγορα** *ghreeghora*

fat *adj* **χοντρός** *khondros*

fat *n* **το λίπος** *to leepos*

father **ο πατέρας** *o pateras*

father-in-law **ο πεθερός** *o petheros*

fault *(mistake)* **το λάθος** *to lathos*
it is not my fault
δε φταίω εγώ *dhe fteo egho*

favourite **ο πιο αγαπημένος** *o pyo aghapeemenos*

fax **το φαξ** *fax*

feather *(of bird)* **το φτερό** *to ftero*

to feed **ταΐζω** *taeezo*

to feel **αισθάνομαι** *esthanome*
I feel sick **θέλω να κάνω εμετό** *thelo na kano emeto*

female **θηλυκός** *theeleekos*

ferry **το φεριμπότ** *to fereebot*

festival **το φεστιβάλ** *to festeeval*

to fetch **φέρνω** *ferno*

fever **ο πυρετός** *o peeretos*

few: a few **μερικοί / μερικές / μερικά** *mereekee (masculine) / mereekes (feminine) / mereeka (neuter)*

fiancé(e) **ο αρραβωνιαστικός / η αρραβωνιαστικιά** *o aravonyasteekos / ee aravonyasteekya*

field **το χωράφι** *to khorafee*

file *(nail)* **η λίμα** *ee leema*
(computer) **το αρχείο** *to arkheeo*

to fill **γεμίζω** *yemeezo*
fill it up! *(car)* **γεμίστε το** *yemeeste to*

fillet **το φιλέτο** *to feeleto*

filling *(in cake, etc.)* **η γέμιση** *ee yemeesee*
(in tooth) **το σφράγισμα** *to sfrayeesma*

film *(for camera)* **το φιλμ** *to feelm*
(in cinema) **η ταινία** *ee teneea*

filter **το φίλτρο** *to feeltro*

to finish **τελειώνω** *teleeono*

fire *(heater)* **η θερμάστρα** *ee thermastra*
fire! **φωτιά!** *fotya!*
fire brigade **η πυροσβεστική** *ee peerosvesteekee*
fire extinguisher **ο πυροσβεστήρας** *o peerosvesteeras*

fireworks **τα πυροτεχνήματα** *ta peerotekhneemata*

first **πρώτος** *protos*

first aid **οι πρώτες βοήθειες** *ee protes voeetheeyes*

first class *(seat, etc.)* **η πρώτη θέση** *ee protee thesee*

first floor **ο πρώτος όροφος** *o protos orofos*

first name **το όνομα** *to onoma*

fish **το ψάρι** *to psaree*

to fish **ψαρεύω** *psarevo*

fishing rod **το καλάμι ψαρέματος** *to kalamee psarematos*

fit *(healthy)* **υγιής** *eeyee-ees*

to fix **φτιάχνω** *fteeakhno*
(arrange) **κανονίζω** *kanoneezo*

fizzy *(drink)* **αεριούχο** *aeryookho*

flash *(on camera)* **το φλας** *to flas*

flask **το θερμός** *to thermos*

flat *(apartment)* **το διαμέρισμα** *to dheeamereesma*

flat tyre: ***I have a flat tyre*** **έχω σκασμένο λάστιχο** *ekho skasmeno lasteekho*

flea ο ψύλλος *o pseelos*

flight η πτήση *ee pteesee*

flippers *(swimming)* τα βατραχοπέδιλα *ta vatrakhopedheela*

flood η πλημμύρα *ee pleemeera*

floor το πάτωμα *to patoma* *(storey)* ο όροφος *o orofos*

flour το αλεύρι *to alevree*

flower το λουλούδι *to looloodhee*

flu η γρίππη *ee ghreepee*

to fly πετώ *peto*

fly η μύγα *ee meegha*

to follow ακολουθώ *akolootho*

food το φαγητό *to fa-yeeto*

food poisoning η τροφική δηλητηρίαση *ee trofeekee dheeleeteereeasee*

foot το πόδι *to podhee*

football το ποδόσφαιρο *to podhosfero*

for για *ya*

foreign ξένος *ksenos*

forest το δάσος *to dhasos*

to forget ξεχνώ *ksekhno*

fork το πηρούνι *to peeroonee* *(in road)* η διακλάδωση *ee dheeakladhosee*

fortnight το δεκαπενθήμερο *to dhekapentheemero*

fountain το σιντριβάνι *to seendreevanee*

fracture *(of bone)* το κάταγμα *to kataghma*

France η Γαλλία *ee ghaleea*

free ελεύθερος *eleftheros* *(costing nothing)* δωρεάν *dhorean*

to freeze *(food)* ψύχω *pseekho*

freezer ο καταψύκτης *o katapseektees*

French *(thing)* γαλλικός *ghaleekos*

French beans τα φασολάκια *ta fasolakya*

frequent συχνός *seekhnos*

fresh φρέσκος *freskos*

fridge το ψυγείο *to pseeyeeo*

fried τηγανητός *teeghaneetos*

friend ο φίλος / η φίλη *o feelos / ee feelee*

from από *apo*

front *(part)* το μπροστινό (μέρος) *to brosteeno (meros)* ***in front*** μπροστά *brosta*

frozen *(water)* παγωμένος *paghomenos* *(food)* κατεψυγμένος *katepseeghmenos*

fruit τα φρούτα *ta froota*

fruit juice ο χυμός φρούτων *o kheemos frooton*

fruit salad η φρουτοσαλάτα *ee frootosalata*

frying pan το τηγάνι *to teeghanee*

fuel τα καύσιμα *ta kafseema*

fuel pump η αντλία καυσίμων *ee andleea kafseemon*

full γεμάτος *yematos*

full board (η) πλήρης διατροφή *(ee) pleerees dheeatrofee*

fumes *(of car)* τα καυσαέρια *ta kafsaereea*

funeral η κηδεία *ee keedheea*

funny αστείος *asteeos*

fur η γούνα *ee ghoona*

furniture τα έπιπλα *ta epeepla*

fuse η ασφάλεια *ee asfaleea*

fuse box ο ηλεκτρικός πίνακας *o eelektreekos peenakas*

G

gallery *(art)* **η πινακοθήκη** *ee peenakotheekee*

game το παιγνίδι *to peghneedhee*
(to eat) **το κυνήγι** *to keeneeyee*

garage *(for parking car)* **το γκαράζ** *to garaz*

garden ο κήπος *o keepos*

garlic το σκόρδο *to skordho*

gas το γκάζι *to gazee*

gas cooker η γκαζιέρα *ee ghazyera*

gas cylinder η φιάλη γκαζιού *ee feealee gazyoo*

gate *(at airport)* **η έξοδος** *ee eksodhos*

gears οι ταχύτητες *ee takheeteetes*
first gear **πρώτη** *protee*
second gear **δεύτερη** *dhefteree*
third gear **τρίτη** *treetee*
fourth gear **τετάρτη** *tetartee*
neutral **νεκρή** *nekree*
reverse **όπισθεν** *opeesthen*

gearbox το κιβώτιο ταχυτήτων *to keevotyo takheeteeton*

gents *(toilet)* **Ανδρών** *andhron*

genuine γνήσιος *ghneeseeos*

germs τα μικρόβια *ta meekroveea*

German measles η ερυθρά *ee ereethra*

to get παίρνω *perno*
(fetch) **φέρνω** *ferno*

to get in *(car, etc.)* **μπαίνω** *beno*

to get off *(from bus)* **κατεβαίνω από** *kateveno apo*

to get on *(bus)* **ανεβαίνω στο λεωφορείο** *aneveno sto leoforeeo*

to get through *(on the phone)* **συνδέομαι** *seendheome*

gift το δώρο *to dhoro*

gift shop το κατάστημα δώρον *to katasteema dhoron*

gin το τζιν *to gin*

ginger το τζίντζερ *to dzeendzer*

girl το κορίτσι *to koreetsee*

girlfriend η φίλη *ee feelee*

to give δίνω *dheeno*

to give back επιστρέφω *epeestrefo*

glass *(to drink from)* **το ποτήρι** *to poteeree*
a glass of water **ένα ποτήρι νερό** *ena poteeree nero*

glasses *(spectacles)* **τα γυαλιά** *ta yalya*

gloves τα γάντια *ta ghandeea*

glucose η γλυκόζη *ee ghleekozee*

glue *n* **η κόλλα** *ee kola*

to glue κολλώ *kolo*

to go πηγαίνω *peeyeno*
I go / I am going **πηγαίνω** *peeyeno*
you go / you are going **πηγαίνεις** *peeyenees*
we go / we are going **πηγαίνουμε** *peeyenoome*

to go back γυρίζω πίσω *yeereezo peeso*

to go down κατεβαίνω *kateveno*

to go in μπαίνω *beno*

to go out βγαίνω *vyeno*

to go up ανεβαίνω *aneveno*

goat η κατσίκα *ee katseeka*

goggles τα γυαλιά *ta yalya*

gold ο χρυσός *o khreesos*
(made of gold) **χρυσός** *khreesos*

golf το γκολφ *to golf*

golf course το γήπεδο του γκολφ *to yeepedho too golf*

good καλός *kalos*

good afternoon **χαίρετε** *kherete*
goodbye **αντίο** *adeeo*
good day **καλημέρα** *kaleemera*
good evening **καλησπέρα** *kaleespera*
good morning **καλημέρα** *kaleemera*
good night **καληνύχτα** *kaleeneekhta*
goose **η χήνα** *ee kheena*
gram **το γραμμάριο** *to ghramareeo*
grandfather **ο παππούς** *o papoos*
grandmother **η γιαγιά** *ee yaya*
grandparents **ο παππούς και η γιαγιά** *o papoos ke ee yaya*
grapefruit **το γκρέιπ-φρουτ** *to grapefruit*
grapes **τα σταφύλια** *ta stafeelya*
grated cheese **το τυρί τριμένο** *to teeree treemeno*
grater **ο τρίφτης** *o treeftees*
greasy **λιπαρός** *leeparos*
great **μεγάλος** *meghalos*
Greece **η Ελλάδα** *ee eladha*
Greek (person) **ο Έλληνας / η Ελληνίδα** *o eleenas / ee eleeneedha*
Greek *adj* **ελληνικός** *eleeneekos*
green **πράσινος** *praseenos*
grey **γκρίζος** *greezos*
grilled **της σχάρας** *tees skharas*
grocer's **το μπακάλικο** *to bakaleeko* // **το παντοπωλείο** *to pandopoleeo*
ground *n* **το έδαφος** *to edhafos*
ground *adj* (coffee, etc.) **αλεσμένος** *alesmenos*
ground floor **το ισόγειο** *to eesoyeeo*
groundsheet **ο μουσαμάς εδάφους** *o moosamas edhafoos*
group **η ομάδα** *ee omadha*
to grow **μεγαλώνω** *meghalono*
guarantee **η εγγύηση** *ee engeeyeesee*
guard (on train) **ο υπεύθυνος τρένου** *o eepeftheenos trenoo*
guest **ο φιλοξενούμενος** *o feeloksenoomenos*
guesthouse **ο ξενώνας** *o ksenonas*
guide **ο / η ξεναγός** *o / ee ksenaghos*
to guide **ξεναγώ** *ksenagho*
guidebook **ο οδηγός** *o odheeghos*
guided tour **η περιήγηση με ξεναγό** *ee peree-eeyeesee me ksenagho*
gym shoes **τα αθλητικά παπούτσια** *ta athleeteeka papootsya*

H

haemorrhoids **οι αιμορροΐδες** *ee emoroeedhes*
hair **τα μαλλιά** *ta malya*
hairbrush **η βούρτσα** *ee voortsa*
haircut **το κούρεμα** *to koorema*
hairdresser **ο κομμωτής / η κομμώτρια** *o komotees / ee komotreea*
hairdryer **το πιστολάκι** *to peestolakee*
half **το μισό** *to meeso*
half an hour **μισή ώρα** *meesee ora*
half board **(η) ημιδιατροφή** *(ee) eemeedheeatrofee*
half-bottle **το μικρό μπουκάλι** *to meekro bookalee*

half price **μισή τιμή** *meesee teemee*

ham **το ζαμπόν** *to zambon*

hamburger **το χάμπουργκερ** *to khamboorger*

hammer **το σφυρί** *to sfeeree*

hand **το χέρι** *to kheree*

handbag **η τσάντα** *ee tsanda*

handicapped **ανάπηρος** *anapeeros*

handkerchief **το μαντήλι** *to mandeelee*
(tissue) **το χαρτομάυτηλο** *to khartomandeelo*

hand luggage **οι χειραποσκευή** *ee kheeraposkevee*

hand-made **χειροποίητος** *kheeropee-eetos*

to hang up *(phone)* **κλείνω** *kleeno*

to happen **συμβαίνω** *seemveno*
what happened? **τι συνέβη;** *tee seenevee*

happy **χαρούμενος** *kharoomenos*

harbour **το λιμάνι** *to leemanee*

hard *(difficult)* **δύσκολος** *dheeskolos*

hard-boiled *(egg)* **σφιχτό** *sfeekhto*

hardware shop **το σιδηροπωλείο** *to seedheeropoleeo*

harvest **ο θερισμός** *o thereesmos*

hat **το καπέλο** *to kapelo*

to have see GRAMMAR

hay fever **η αλλεργική ρινίτιδα** *ee aleryeekee reeneeteedha*

hazelnut **το φουντούκι** *to foondookee*

he **αυτός** *aftos*

head **το κεφάλι** *to kefalee*

headache: ***I have a headache*** **έχω πονοκέφαλο** *ekho ponokefalo*

headlights **οι προβολείς του αυτοκινήτου** *ee provolees too aftokeeneetoo*

headphones **τα ακουστικά** *ta akoosteeka*

to hear **ακούω** *akoo-o*

hearing aid **το ακουστικό βαρηκοΐας** *to akoosteeko vareekoeeas*

heart **η καρδιά** *ee kardhya*

heart attack **η καρδιακή προσβολή** *ee kardheeakee prosvolee*

heartburn **η καούρα** *ee kaoora*

heater **η θερμάστρα** *ee thermastra*

heating **η θέρμανση** *ee thermansee*

heavy **βαρύς** *varees*

hello **γεια σας** *ya sas*

helmet **ο κράνος** *o kranos*

to help **βοηθώ** *voeetho*
help! **βοήθεια** *voeetheea*

hepatitis **η ηπατίτιδα** *ee eepateeteedha*

herb **το βότανο** *to votano*

herbal tea **το τσάι του βουνού** *to tsaee too voonoo*

here **εδώ** *edho*

hernia **η κήλη** *ee keelee*

high **ψηλός** *pseelos*

high blood pressure **η ψηλή πίεση** *ee pseelee peeyesee*

high chair **η ψηλή παιδική καρέκλα** *ee pseelee pedheekee karekla*

hill **ο λόφος** *o lofos*
(slope) **η πλαγιά** *ee playa*

hill walking **η ορειβασία** *ee oreevaseea*

to hire **νοικιάζω** *neekyazo*

to hit **χτυπώ** *khteepo*

hitchhiking **το οτοστόπ** *to otostop*

HIV positive **θετικός για ΕΙΤΖ** *theteekos ya aids*

to hold **κρατώ** *krato*

hold-up **η καθυστέρηση** *ee katheestereesee*

hole **η τρύπα** *ee treepa*

holiday **οι διακοπές** *ee dheeakopes*

home **το σπίτι** *to speetee*
at home **στο σπίτι** *sto speetee*

honey **το μέλι** *to melee*

honeymoon **ο μήνας του μέλιτος** *o meenas too meleetos*

hook *(fishing)* **το αγκίστρι** *to angkeestree*

to hope **ελπίζω** *elpeezo*

hors d'œuvre **τα ορεκτικά** *ta orekteeka*

horse **το άλογο** *to alogho*

hospital **το νοσοκομείο** *to nosokomeeo*

hot **ζεστός** *zestos*
I'm hot **ζεσταίνομαι** *zestenome*
it's hot **έχει ζέστη** *ekhee zestee*
hot water **το ζεστό νερό** *to zesto nero*

hotel **το ξενοδοχείο** *to ksenodhokheeo*

hour **η ώρα** *ee ora*

house **το σπίτι** *to speetee*

housewife **η νοικοκυρά** *ee neekokeera*

house wine **το κρασί χύμα** *to krasee kheema*

how **πώς** *pos*
how long? **πόση ώρα;** *posee ora*
how much? **πόσο;** *poso*
how many? **πόσα;** *posa*
how are you? **πώς είστε;** *pos eeste*

hungry : ***I'm hungry*** **πεινώ** *peeno*

to hurry : ***I'm in a hurry*** **βιάζομαι** *vyazome*

to hurt : ***that hurts*** **με πονά** *me pona*

husband **ο σύζυγος** *o seezeeghos*

hydrofoil **το ιπτάμενο δελφίνι** *to eeptameno dhelfeenee*

hypodermic needle **η υποδερμική βελόνα** *ee eepodhermeekee velona*

I

I **εγώ** *egho*

ice **ο πάγος** *o paghos*

ice cream / ice lolly **το παγωτό** *to paghoto*

iced *(drink)* **παγωμένος** *paghomenos*

icon **η εικόνα** *ee eekona*

if **αν** *an*

ignition **η ανάφλεξη** *ee anafleksee*

ignition key **το κλειδί μίζας** *to kleedhee meezas*

ill **άρρωστος** *arostos*

immediately **αμέσως** *amesos*

immunisation **ο εμβολιασμός** *o emvoleeasmos*

important **σπουδαίος** *spoodheos*

impossible **αδύνατο** *adheenato*

in **μέσα** *mesa*
(with countries, towns) **σε (στο / στη / στο)** *se (sto / stee / sto)*

included **συμπεριλαμβάνεται** *seembereelamvanete*

indigestion **η δυσπεψία** *ee dheespepseea*

indoors **εσωτερικά** *esotereeka*

infectious **μεταδοτικός** *metadhoteekos*

information **οι πληροφορίες** *ee pleeroforeeyes*

information office **το γραφείο πληροφοριών** *to ghrafeeo pleeroforeeon*

inhaler **η συσκευή εισπνοής** *ee seeskevee eespnoees*

injection **η ένεση** *ee enesee*

injured **τραυματισμένος** *travmateesmenos*

ink **το μελάνι** *to melanee*

inner tube **η σαμπρέλα** *ee sambrela*

insect **το έντομο** *to endomo*

insect bite **το τσίμπημα** *to tseembeema*

insect repellent **το εντομοαπωθητικό** *to endomoapotheeteeko*

inside *n (interior)* **το εσωτερικό** *to esotereeko*
inside the car **μέσα στο αυτοκίνητο** *mesa sto aftokeeneeto*
it's inside **είναι μέσα** *eene mesa*

instant coffee **στιγμιαίος καφές** *steeghmyeos kafes*

instructor **ο εκπαιδευτής** *o ekpedheftees*

insulin **η ινσουλίνη** *ee eensooleenee*

insurance **η ασφάλεια** *ee asfaleea*

insurance certificate **η βεβαίωση ασφαλίσεως** *ee veveosee asfaleeseos*

insured **ασφαλισμένος** *asfaleesmenos*

interesting **ενδιαφέρων** *endheeaferon*

international **διεθνής** *dhee-ethnees*

internet **το ιντερνέτ** *to eenternet*

interpreter **ο / η διερμηνέας** *o / ee dhee-ermeeneas*

interval *(theatre)* **το διάλειμμα** *to dheealeema*

into **σε (στο / στη / στο)** *se (sto / stee / sto)*

invitation **η πρόσκληση** *ee proskleesee*

to invite **προσκαλώ** *proskalo*

invoice **το τιμολόγιο** *to teemoloyo*

Ireland **η Ιρλανδία** *ee eerlandheea*

Irish *(person)* **ο Ιρλανδός / η Ιρλανδή** *o eerlandhos / ee eerlandhee*

iron *(for clothes)* **το σίδερο** *to seedhero*
(metal) **ο σίδηρος** *o seedheeros*

to iron **σιδερώνω** *seedherono*

ironmonger's **το σιδηροπωλείο** *to seedheeropoleeo*

is see **(to be)** GRAMMAR

island **το νησί** *to neesee*

it **το** *to*

Italy **η Ιταλία** *ee eetaleea*

itch **η φαγούρα** *ee faghoora*

itemised bill **ο αναλυτικός λογαριασμός** *o analeeteekos logharyasmos*

J

jack **ο γρύλος** *o ghreelos*

jacket **το μπουφάν** *to boofan*

jam **η μαρμελάδα** *ee marmeladha*

jammed **στριμωγμένος** *streemoghmenos*

jar **το βάζο** *to vazo*

jaundice **ο ίκτερος** *o eekteros*

jeans **το τζιν** *to jean*

jelly **το ζελέ** *to zele*

jellyfish **η τσούχτρα** *ee tsookhtra*

jersey **το πουλόβερ** *to poolover*

to jetski **το jetski** *to jetski*

jetty **ο μώλος** *o molos*

jeweller's **το κοσμηματοπωλείο** *to kosmeematopoleeo*

jewellery **τα κοσμήματα** *ta kosmeemata*

job **η δουλειά** *ee dhoolya*

to jog **κάνω τζόκινγκ** *kano jogging*

joint **το άρθρώση** *to arthrosee*

joke **το αστείο** *to asteeo*

journey **το ταξίδι** *to takseedhee*

jug **η κανάτα** *ee kanata*

juice **ο χυμός** *o kheemos*

jump leads **τα καλώδια μπαταρίας** *ta kalodheea batareeas*

junction *(crossroads)* **η διασταύρωση** *ee dheeastavrosee*

just: ***just two*** **μόνο δύο** *mono dheeo*
I've just arrived **μόλις έφτασα** *molees eftasa*

K

to keep **κρατώ** *krato*

kettle **ο βραστήρας** *o vrasteeras*

key **το κλειδί** *to kleedhee*

key-ring **το μπρελόκ** *to brelok*

kid *(meat)* **το κατσικάκι** *to katseekakee*

kidneys **τα νεφρά** *ta nefra*

kilo **το κιλό** *to keelo*

kilometre **το χιλιόμετρο** *to kheelyometro*

kind *n (sort)* **το είδος** *to eedhos*

kind *adj* **ευγενικός** *efyeneekos*

king **ο βασιλιάς** *o vaseelyas*

kiosk **το περίπτερο** *to pereeptero*

to kiss **φιλώ** *feelo*

kitchen **η κουζίνα** *ee koozeena*

kitchen paper **το χαρτί κουζίνας** *to khartee koozeenas*

kitten **το γατάκι** *to ghatakee*

kiwi fruit **το ακτινίδιο** *to akteeneedheeo*

knee **το γόνατο** *to ghonato*

knee highs **οι κάλτσες** *ee kaltses*

knickers *(women's)* **η κυλότα** *ee keelota*

knife **το μαχαίρι** *to makheree*

to knock down *(by car)* **χτυπώ με αυτοκίνητο** *khteepo me aftokeeneeto*

to knock over *(vase, glass)* **ρίχνω κάτω** *reekhno kato*

L

label **η ετικέτα** *ee eteeketa*

lace **η δαντέλα** *ee dhandela*

laces *(of shoe)* **τα κορδόνια** *ta kordhoneea*

ladder **η σκάλα** *ee skala*

ladies *(toilet)* **Γυναικών** *yeenekon*

lady **η κυρία** *ee keereea*

lager **η μπίρα** *ee beera*

lake **η λίμνη** *ee leemnee*

lamb **το αρνάκι** *to arnakee*

lamp **η λάμπα** *ee lamba*

to land *(plane)* **προσγειώνω** *prosyeeono*

landslide **η καθίζηση** *ee katheezeesee*

language **η γλώσσα** *ee ghlosa*

laptop **το λάπτοπ** *to laptop*

large **μεγάλος** *meghalos*

last **τελευταίος** *telefteos*

late (in the day) **αργά** argha
I am late (for an appointment) **έχω αργήσει** ekho aryeesee
later αργότερα arghotera
laundrette το πλυντήριο to pleendeereeo
laundry service η υπηρεσία πλυντηρίου ee eepeereseea pleendeereeoo
lavatory η τουαλέτα ee tooaleta
lawyer ο / η δικηγόρος o / ee dheekeeghoros
laxative το καθαρτικό to katharteeko
lay-by η βοηθητική λωρίδα ee voeetheeteekee loreedha
lazy τεμπέλης tembelees
lead (electric) **το καλώδιο** to kalodheeo
leader (guide) **ο / η ξεναγός** o / ee ksenaghos
leadfree αμόλυβδος amoleevdhos
leaf το φύλλο to feelo
leak η διαρροή ee dheearoee
to learn μαθαίνω matheno
least: *at least* **τουλάχιστο** toolakheesto
leather το δέρμα to dherma
leather goods τα δερμάτινα είδη ta dhermateena eedhee
to leave (go away) **φεύγω** fevgho
leek το πράσσο to praso
left: *(on/to the) left* **αριστερά** areestera
left-luggage (office) **η φύλαξη αποσκευών** ee feelaksee aposkevon
leg το πόδι to podhee
leggings οι περισκελίδες ee pereeskeleedhes
lemon το λεμόνι to lemonee
lemonade η λεμονάδα ee lemonadha
lemon tea το τσάι με λεμόνι to tsaee me lemonee
to lend δανείζω dhaneezo
length το μήκος to meekos
lens ο φακός o fakos
lentils οι φακές ee fakes
less: *less milk* **λιγότερο γάλα** leeghotero ghala
lesson το μάθημα to matheema
to let (allow) **επιτρέπω** epeetrepo (hire out) **νοικιάζω** neekyazo
letter το γράμμα to ghrama
letterbox το γραμματοκιβώτιο to ghramatokeevotyo
lettuce το μαρούλι to maroolee
level crossing η σιδηροδρομική διασταύρωση ee seedheerodhromeekee dheeastavrosee
library η βιβλιοθήκη ee veevleeotheekee
licence η άδεια ee adheea
to lie down ξαπλώνω ksaplono
lifeboat η ναυαγοσωστική λέμβος ee navaghososteekee lemvos
lifeguard ο ναυαγοσώστης o navaghosostees
life insurance η ασφάλεια ζωής ee asfaleea zoees
life jacket το σωσίβιο to soseeveeo
lift το ασανσέρ to asanser
lift pass (skiing) **το εισιτήριο** to eeseeteereeo
light το φως to fos
light bulb ο γλόμπος o ghlobos

lighter *(to light a cigarette)* **ο αναπτήρας** *o anapteeras*

lightning ο κεραυνός *o keravnos*

to like : ***I like* μου αρέσει** *moo aresee*

lilo το φουσκωτό στρώμα *to fooskoto stroma*

lime *(fruit)* **το γλυκολέμονο** *to ghleekolemono*

line η γραμμή *ee ghramee*

lip reading η χειλοανάγνωση *ee kheeloanaghnosee*

lip salve το προστατευτικό στικ *to prostatefteeko stick*

lipstick το κραγιόν *to krayon*

liqueur το λικέρ *to leeker*

to listen ακούω *akoo-o*

litre το λίτρο *to leetro*

litter τα σκουπίδια *ta skoopeedhya*

little μικρός *meekros*
***a little* λίγο** *leegho*

to live μένω *meno*
***he lives in London* μένει στο Λονδίνο** *menee sto londheeno*

liver το συκώτι *to seekotee*

living room το καθιστικό *to katheesteeko*

lizard η σαύρα *ee savra*

lobster ο αστακός *o astakos*

local τοπικός *topeekos*

lock η κλειδαριά *ee kleedharya*

to lock κλειδώνω *kleedhono*
***I'm locked out* κλειδώθηκα έξω** *kleedhotheeka ekso*

locker *(luggage)* **η θήκη** *ee theekee*

log book η άδεια κυκλοφορίας *ee adheea keekloforeeas*

lollipop το γλειφιτζούρι *to ghleefeedzooree*

London το Λονδίνο *to londheeno*

long μακρύς *makrees*

to look at κοιτάζω *keetazo*

to look after φροντίζω *frondeezo*

to look for ψάχνω *psakhno*

lorry το φορτηγό *to forteegho*

to lose χάνω *khano*

lost χαμένος *khamenos*
***I've lost my wallet* έχασα το πορτοφόλι μου** *ekhasa to portofolee moo*
***I am lost* χάθηκα** *khatheeka*

lost-property office το γραφείο απωλεσθέντων αντικειμένων *to ghrafeeo apolesthendon andeekeemenon*

lot : ***a lot (of)*** **πολύς** *polees*

lotion η λοσιόν *ee losyon*

loud δυνατός *dheenatos*

lounge *(at airport)* **η αίθουσα** *ee ethoosa*
(in hotel, house) **το σαλόνι** *to salonee*

to love αγαπώ *aghapo*

low χαμηλός *khameelos*

low-alcohol beer η μπίρα χαμηλή σε αλκοόλ *ee beera khameelee se alko-ol*

low-fat λαϊτ *laeet*

luggage οι αποσκευές *ee aposkeves*

luggage allowance το επιτρεπόμενο βάρος αποσκευών *to epeetrepomeno varos aposkevon*

luggage rack ο χώρος αποσκευών *o khoros aposkevon*

luggage tag η ετικέτα *ee eteeketa*

luggage trolley το καροτσάκι αποσκευών *to karotsakee aposkevon*

lump **η εξόγκωση** *ee eksogosee*

lunch **το μεσημεριανό** *to meseemereeano*

lung **ο πνεύμονας** *o pnevmonas*

luxury **η πολυτέλεια** *ee poleeteleea*

M

machine **η μηχανή** *ee meekhanee*

mad **τρελός** *trelos*

magazine **το περιοδικό** *to pereeodheeko*

magnifying glass **ο μεγενθυτικός φακός** *o meyentheeteekos fakos*

maiden name **το πατρώνυμο** *to patroneemo*

main course *(of meal)* **το κύριο πιάτο** *to keereeo pyato*

mains *(electric)* **ο κεντρικός αγωγός** *o kendreekos aghoghos*

to make **κάνω** *kano*

make-up **το μακιγιάζ** *to makeeyaz*

male **αρσενικός** *arseneekos*

man *(mankind)* **ο άνθρωπος** *o anthropos*
(as opposed to woman) **ο άντρας** *o andras*

manager **ο διαχειριστής** *o dheeakheereestees*

many **πολλοί** *polee*
many people **πολλοί άνθρωποι** *polee anthropee*

map **ο χάρτης** *o khartees*

marble **το μάρμαρο** *to marmaro*

margarine **η μαργαρίνη** *ee marghareenee*

marina **η μαρίνα** *ee mareena*

market **η αγορά** *ee aghora*

market day **η μέρα της αγοράς** *ee mera tees aghoras*

marmalade **η μαρμελάδα πορτοκαλιού** *ee marmeladha portokalyoo*

marriage certificate **το πιστοποιητικό γάμου** *to peestopyeeteeko ghamoo*

married **παντρεμένος** *pandremenos*

mass *(in church)* **η Θεία Λειτουργία** *ee theea leetooryeea*

match *(game)* **ο αγώνας** *o aghonas*

matches **τα σπίρτα** *ta speerta*

material **το υλικό** *to eeleeko*

matter : ***it doesn't matter*** **δεν πειράζει** *dhen peerazee*
what's the matter with you? **τι έχεις;** *tee ekhees*

mayonnaise **η μαγιονέζα** *ee mayoneza*

meal **το γεύμα** *to yevma*

to mean **εννοώ** *eno-o*

measles **η ιλαρά** *ee eelara*

meat **το κρέας** *to kreas*

mechanic **ο μηχανικός** *o meekhaneekos*

medicine *(drug)* **το φάρμακο** *to farmako*

Mediterranean **η Μεσόγειος** *ee mesoyeeos*

medium sweet *(wine)* **μέτριο γλυκύ** *metreeo ghleekee*
(steak, size) **μέτριο** *metreeo*

to meet **συναντώ** *seenando*

meeting **η συνάντηση** *ee seenandeesee*

melon **το πεπόνι** *to peponee*
(watermelon) **το καρπούζι** *to karpoozee*

member *(of club)* **το μέλος** *to melos*

men **οι άντρες** *ee andres*

menu ο κατάλογος *o kataloghos* // το μενού *to menoo*

message το μήνυμα *to meeneema*

metal το μέταλο *to metalo*

meter ο μετρητής *o metreetees*

metre το μέτρο *to metro*

microwave *(oven)* ο φούρνος μικροκυμάτων *o foornos meekrokeematon*

midday το μεσημέρι *to meseemeree*

midnight τα μεσάνυχτα *ta mesaneekhta*

migraine η ημικρανία *ee eemeekraneea*

mile το μίλι *to meelee*

milk το γάλα *to ghala*

milkshake το μιλκσέικ *to meelkseyk*

millimetre το χιλιοστόμετρο *to kheelyostometro*

million το εκατομμύριο *to ekatomeereeo*

mince ο κιμάς *o keemas*

to mind : *do you mind if...?* σας ενοχλεί αν...; *sas enokhlee an...*

mineral water το επιτραπέζιο νερό *to epeetrapezeeo nero (sparkling)* το αεριούχο μεταλλικό νερό *to aeryookho metaleeko nero*

minimum ελάχιστος *elakheestos*

minor road ο δευτερεύων δρόμος *o dhefterevon dhromos*

mint *(herb)* ο δυόσμος *o dheeosmos*

minute το λεπτό *to lepto*

mirror ο καθρέφτης *o kathreftees*

to miss *(train, etc.)* χάνω *khano*

Miss η Δεσποινίς *ee dhespeenees*

missing χαμένος *khamenos*
he's missing λείπει *leepee*

mistake το λάθος *to lathos*

misunderstanding η παρεξήγηση *ee parekseeyeesee*

mobile phone το κινητό (τηλέφωνο) *to keeneeto (teelefono)*

moisturizer η υδατική κρέμα *ee eedhateekee krema*

monastery το μοναστήρι *to monasteeree*

money τα χρήματα *ta khreemata* // τα λεφτά *ta lefta*

money order η ταχυδρομική επιταγή *ee takheedhromeekee epeetayee*

month ο μήνας *o meenas*

monument το μνημείο *to mneemeeo*

moon το φεγγάρι *to fengaree*

more περισσότερο *pereesotero*
more bread κι άλλο ψωμί *kee alo psomee*

morning το πρωί *to proee*

mosaic το μωσαϊκό *to mosaeeko*

mosque το τζαμί *to dzamee*

mosquito το κουνούπι *to koonoopee*

most το περισσότερο *to pereesotero*

moth η πεταλουδίτσα *ee petaloodheetsa*

mother η μητέρα *ee meetera*

mother-in-law η πεθερά *ee pethera*

motor η μηχανή *ee meekhanee*

motorbike η μοτοσικλέτα *ee motoseekleta*

motorboat το ταχύπλοο *to takheeplo-o*

motorway ο αυτοκινητόδρομος *o aftokeeneetodhromos*

mountain το βουνό *to voono*

mouse το ποντίκι *to pondeekee*

mousse το μους *to moos*

moustache το μουστάκι *to moostakee*

mouth το στόμα *to stoma*

to move κινούμαι *keenoome*

Mr Κύριος *keereeos*

Mrs Κυρία *keereea*

much πολύς *polees*
too much πάρα πολύ *para polee*
very much πάρα πολύ *para polee*

mumps οι μαγουλάδες *ee maghooladhes*

muscle ο μυς *o mees*

museum το μουσείο *to mooseeo*

mushroom το μανιτάρι *to maneetaree*

music η μουσική *ee mooseekee*

mussel το μύδι *to meedhee*

must : ***I must go*** πρέπει να πάω *prepee na pao*
you must go πρέπει να πας *prepee na pas*
he / she must go πρέπει να πάει *prepee na paee*
we must go πρέπει να πάμε *prepee na pame*

mustard η μουστάρδα *ee moostardha*

N

nail *(metal)* το καρφί *to karfee*
(on finger, toe) το νύχι *to neekhee*

nail polish το βερνίκι νυχιών *to verneekee neekhyon*

nail polish remover το ασετόν *to aseton*

nailbrush η βούρτσα των νυχιών *ee voortsa ton neekhyon*

naked γυμνός *yeemnos*

name το όνομα *to onoma*

napkin η πετσέτα *ee petseta*

nappy η πάνα *ee pana*

narrow στενός *stenos*

nationality η υπηκοότητα *ee eepeeko-oteeta*

navy blue μπλε μαρέν *ble maren*

near κοντά *konda*

necessary απαραίτητος *apareteetos*

neck ο λαιμός *o lemos*

necklace το κολιέ *to kolye*

to need : ***I need...*** χρειάζομαι... *khreeazome...*

needle η βελόνα *ee velona*
a needle and thread βελόνα και κλωστή *velona ke klostee*

negative *(photography)* το αρνητικό *to arneeteeko*

neighbour ο γείτονας / η γειτόνισσα *o yeetonas / ee yeetoneesa*

nephew ο ανιψιός *o aneepsyos*

never ποτέ *pote*
I never go there δεν πηγαίνω ποτέ εκεί *dhen peeyeno pote ekee*

new καινούριος *kenooryos*

news *(TV, radio)* οι ειδήσεις *ee eedheesees*

newspaper η εφημερίδα *ee efeemereedha*

New Year : ***happy New Year!*** καλή χρονιά! *kalee khronya*

New Zealand η Νέα Ζηλανδία *ee nea zeelandheea*

next επόμενος *epomenos*

nice *(thing)* ωραίος *oreos*
(person) καλός *kalos*

niece η ανιψιά *ee aneepsya*

night **η νύχτα** *ee neekhta*

nightclub **το νυχτερινό κέντρο** *to neekhtereeno kendro*

nightdress **το νυχτικό** *to neekhteeko*

no **όχι** *okhee*

nobody **κανένας** *kanenas*

noise **ο θόρυβος** *o thoreevos*

non-alcoholic **μη οινοπνευματώδης** *mee eenopnevmatodhees*

none **κανένα** *kanena*

non-smoking **μη καπνίζοντες** *mee kapneezondes*

north **ο βορράς** *o voras*

Nothern Ireland **η Βόρεια Ιρλανδία** *ee voreea eerlandheea*

nose **η μύτη** *ee meetee*

not **μη** *mee* // **δεν** *dhen*
I am not **δεν είμαι** *dhen eeme*
don't stop **μη σταματάς** *mee stamatas*

note (banknote) **το χαρτονόμισμα** *to khartonomeesma*
(letter) **το σημείωμα** *to seemeeoma*

note pad **το σημειωματάριο** *to seemeeomatareeo*

nothing **τίποτα** *teepota*

now **τώρα** *tora*

nudist beach **η παραλία γυμνιστών** *ee paraleea yeemneeston*

number **ο αριθμός** *o areethmos*

number plate **η πινακίδα κυκλοφορίας** *ee peenakeedha keekloforeeas*

nurse **η νοσοκόμα** *ee nosokoma*

nut (peanut) **το φιστίκι** *to feesteekee*
(walnut) **το καρύδι** *to kareedhee*
(hazelnut) **το φουντούκι** *to foondookee*
(for bolt) **το παξιμάδι** *to pakseemadhee*

O

oar **το κουπί** *to koopee*

occasionally **κάπου-κάπου** *kapoo-kapoo*

octopus **το χταπόδι** *to khtapodhee*

odd number **ο μονός αριθμός** *o monos areethmos*

of : ***of course*** **βέβαια** *vevea*

off (light, machine, etc) **σβυστός** *sveestos*
it's off (rotten) **είναι χαλασμένο** *eene khalasmeno*

to offer **προσφέρω** *prosfero*

office **το γραφείο** *to ghrafeeo*

often **συχνά** *seekhna*

oil **το λάδι** *to ladhee*

oil filter **το φίλτρο του λαδιού** *to feeltro too ladhyoo*

ointment **η αλοιφή** *ee aleefee*

OK **εντάξει** *endaksee*

old (person) **ηλικιωμένος** *eeleekyomenos*
(thing) **παλιός** *palyos*
how old are you? **πόσων χρονών είστε;** *poson khronon eeste*

olive oil **το ελαιόλαδο** *to eleoladho*

olives **οι ελιές** *ee elyes*

omelette **η ομελέτα** *ee omeleta*

on **πάνω** *pano*
(light, TV) **ανοιχτός** *aneekhtos*
on the table **(πάνω) στο τραπέζι** *(pano) sto trapezee*

once **μία φορά** *meea fora*

one **ένας / μία / ένα** *enas (masculine) / meea (feminine) / ena (neuter)*

one-way *(street)* **ο μονόδρομος** *o monodhromos* *(ticket)* **το απλό εισιτήριο** *to aplo eeseeteereeo*

onion **το κρεμμύδι** *to kremeedhee*

only **μόνο** *mono*

to open **ανοίγω** *aneegho*

open *adj* **ανοικτός** *aneektos*

operator *(telephone)* **η τηλεφωνήτρια** *ee teelefoneetreea*

opposite **απέναντι** *apenandee*

or **ή** *ee*

orange *(fruit)* **το πορτοκάλι** *to portokalee* *(colour)* **πορτοκαλί** *portokalee*

orange juice **ο χυμός πορτοκαλιού** *o kheemos portokalyoo*

orchard **το περιβόλι** *to pereevolee*

to order **παραγγέλλω** *parangelo*

organize **οργανώνω** *orghanono*

original **αρχικός** *arkheekos*

Orthodox *(religion)* **ορθόδοξος** *orthodhoksos*

other **άλλος** *alos*

out *(light, etc.)* **σβησμένος** *sveesmenos* ***he's out*** **λείπει** *leepee*

outdoors **στην ύπαιθρο** *steen eepethro*

outside **έξω** *ekso*

outskirts **τα περίχωρα** *ta pereekhora*

oven **ο φούρνος** *o foornos*

over **πάνω από** *pano apo* ***over there*** **εκεί πέρα** *ekee pera*

to owe : ***you owe me*** **μου χρωστάς** *moo khrostas*

owner **ο ιδιοκτήτης** *o eedheeokteetees*

oxygen **το οξυγόνο** *to okseeghono*

oyster **το στρείδι** *to streedhee*

P

to pack **πακετάρω** *paketaro*

package **το δέμα** *to dhema*

package tour **η οργανωμένη εκδρομή** *ee orghanomenee ekdhromee*

packet **το πακέτο** *to paketo*

paddling pool **η λιμνούλα για παιδιά** *ee leemnoola ya pedhya*

padlock **το λουκέτο** *to looketo*

paid **πληρωμένος** *pleeromenos*

pain **ο πόνος** *o ponos*

painful **οδυνηρός** *odheeneeros* ***it's painful*** **πονάει** *ponaee*

painkiller **το παυσίπονο** *to pafseepono*

painting **ο πίνακας** *o peenakas*

pair **το ζευγάρι** *to zevgharee*

palace **το παλάτι** *to palatee*

pale **χλομός** *khlomos*

pan **η κατσαρόλα** *ee katsarola*

pancake **η κρέπα** *ee krepa*

panties **η κυλότα** *ee keelota*

pants *(men's underpants)* **το σλιπ** *to sleep*

panties *(women's)* **η κυλότα** *ee keelota*

paper **το χαρτί** *to khartee*

parcel **το δέμα** *to dhema*

pardon **παρακαλώ** *parakalo* ***I beg your pardon*** **με συγχωρείτε** *me seenkhoreete*

parents **οι γονείς** *o ghonees*

park *n* **το πάρκο** *to parko*

to park *(in car)* **παρκάρω** *parkaro*

parsley **ο μαϊντανός** *o ma-eendanos*

part **το μέρος** *to meros*

party *(group)* **η ομάδα** *ee omadha* *(celebration)* **το πάρτυ** *to party*

passenger **ο επιβάτης** *o epeevatees*

passport **το διαβατήριο** *to dheeavateereeo*

passport control **ο έλεγχος διαβατηρίων** *o elengkhos dheeavateereeon*

pasta **τα ζυμαρικά** *ta zeemareeka*

pastry **η ζύμη** *ee zeemee* *(cake)* **το γλύκισμα** *to ghleekeesma*

path **το μονοπάτι** *to monopatee*

pavement **το πεζοδρόμιο** *to pezodhromeeo*

to pay **πληρώνω** *pleerono*

payment **η πληρωμή** *ee pleeromee*

peach **το ροδάκινο** *to rodhakeeno*

peak hour **η ώρα αιχμής** *ee ora ekhmees*

peanut **το φιστίκι** *to feesteekee*

pear **το αχλάδι** *to akhladhee*

peas **ο αρακάς** *o arakas*

pebble **το πετραδάκι** *to petradhakee*

pedestrian *(person)* **ο πεζός** *o pezos*

pedestrian crossing **η διασταύρωση πεζών** *ee dheeastavrosee pezon*

to peel **ξεφλουδίζω** *ksefloodheezo*

peg *(for tent)* **ο πάσσαλος** *o pasalos* *(for clothes)* **το μανταλάκι** *to mandalakee*

pen **το στύλο** *to steelo*

pencil **το μολύβι** *to moleevee*

penicillin **η πενικιλλίνη** *ee peneekeeleenee*

penknife **ο σουγιάς** *o sooyas*

pensioner **ο / η συνταξιούχος** *o / ee seendaksyookhos*

pepper *(spice)* **το πιπέρι** *to peeperee* *(vegetable)* **η πιπεριά** *ee peeperya*

per : ***per hour*** **την ώρα** *teen ora*

perfect **τέλειος** *teleeos*

performance **η παράσταση** *ee parastasee*

perfume **το άρωμα** *to aroma*

perhaps **ίσως** *eesos*

period *(menstruation)* **η περίοδος** *ee pereeodhos*

perm **η περμανάντ** *ee permanand*

permit **άδεια** *adheea*

person **το πρόσωπο** *to prosopo*

personal stereo **το προσωπικό στερεοφωνικό** *to prosopeeko stereofoneeko*

pet **το κατικοίδιο ζώο** *to kateekeedhyo zo-o*

petrol **η βενζίνη** *ee venzeenee*

petrol station **το βενζινάδικο** *to venzeenadheeko* // **το πρατήριο βενζίνης** *to prateereeo venzeenees*

phone *see* **telephone**

phonecard **η τηλεκάρτα** *ee teelekarta*

photocopy **η φωτοτυπία** *ee fototeepeea*

photograph **η φωτογραφία** *ee fotoghrafeea*

phrase book **το βιβλιαράκι φράσεων** *to veevleearakee fraseon*

picture η εικόνα *ee eekona*

pie η πίτα *ee peeta*

piece το κομμάτι *to komatee*

pier η αποβάθρα *ee apovathra*

pill το χάπι *to khapee*

pillow το μαξιλάρι *to makseelaree*

pillowcase η μαξιλαροθήκη *ee makseelarotheekee*

pin η καρφίτσα *ee karfeetsa*

pine το πεύκο *to pefko*

pineapple ο ανανάς *o ananas*

pink ροζ *roz*

pipe η πίπα *ee peepa*

pistachio nut το φυστίκι Αιγίνης *to feesteekee eyeenees*

plaster (for broken limb) ο γύψος *o yeepsos*

plastic πλαστικός *plasteekos*

plate το πιάτο *to pyato*

platform η αποβάθρα *ee apovathra*

to play παίζω *pezo*

playroom το δωμάτιο των παιδιών *to dhomateeo ton pedhyon*

please παρακαλώ *parakalo*

pleased ευχαριστημένος *efkhareesteemenos*

pliers η πένσα *ee pensa*

plug (electric) η πρίζα *ee preeza*

plum το δαμάσκηνο *to damaskeeno*

plumber ο υδραυλικός *o eedhravleekos*

poisonous δηλητηριώδης *dheeleeteereeodhees*

police η αστυνομία *ee asteenomeea*

policeman ο αστυνόμος *o asteenomos*

police station το αστυνομικό τμήμα *to asteenomeeko tmeema*

polish (for shoes) το βερνίκι *to verneekee*

polluted μολυσμένος *moleesmenos*

pollution η ρύπανση *ee reepansee*

pony trekking η ιππασία *ee eepaseea*

pool (for swimming) η πισίνα *ee peeseena*

popular δημοφιλής *dheemofeelees*
(fashionable) κοσμικός *kosmeekos*

pork το χοιρινό *to kheereeno*

port (harbour) το λιμάνι *to leemanee*

porter ο αχθοφόρος *o akhthoforos*

possible δυνατός *dheenatos*

to post (letter) ταχυδρομώ *takheedhromo*

postbox το ταχυδρομικό κουτί *to takheedhromeeko kootee*

postcard η καρτποστάλ *ee kartpostal*

postcode ο κωδικός *o kodheekos*

post office το ταχυδρομείο *to takheedhromeeo*

pot η κατσαρόλα *ee katsarola*

potato η πατάτα *ee patata*

pottery τα κεραμικά *to kerameeka*

pound (money) η λίρα *ee leera*

powdered milk το γάλα σε σκόνη *to ghala se skonee*

pram το καροτσάκι *to karotsakee*

prawn η γαρίδα *ee ghareedha*

to prefer προτιμώ *proteemo*

pregnant έγγυος *engeeos*

to prepare ετοιμάζω *eteemazo*

prescription **η συνταγή** *ee seendayee*

present *(gift)* **το δώρο** *to dhoro*

pretty **ωραίος** *oreos*

price **η τιμή** *ee teemee*

price list **ο τιμοκατάλογος** *o teemokataloghos*

priest **ο παπάς** *o papas*

private **ιδιωτικός** *eedheeoteekos*

prize **το βραβείο** *to vraveeo*

probably **πιθανώς** *peethanos*

problem **το πρόβλημα** *to provleema*

programme **το πρόγραμμα** *to proghrama*

prohibited **απαγορευμένος** *apaghorevmenos*

to pronounce **προφέρω** *profero*
how do you pronounce this? **πώς το προφέρετε;** *pos to proferete*

Protestant **διαμαρτυρόμενος** *dheeamarteeromenos*

prune **το δαμάσκηνο ξερό** *to dhamaskeeno ksero*

public **δημόσιος** *dheemoseeos*

public holiday **η γιορτή** *ee yortee*

to pull **τραβώ** *travo*

pullover **το πουλόβερ** *to poolover*

puncture **το τρύπημα** *to treepeema*

purple **πορφυρός** *porfeeros*

purse **το πορτοφόλι** *to portofolee*

to push **σπρώχνω** *sprokhno*

push chair **το καροτσάκι (μωρού)** *to karotsakee (moroo)*

to put **βάζω** *vazo*
to put down **βάζω κάτω** *vazo kato*

pyjamas **οι πιζάμες** *ee peezames*

Q

quality **η ποιότητα** *ee peeoteeta*

quay **η προκυμαία** *ee prokeemea*

queen **η βασίλισσα** *ee vaseeleesa*

question **η ερώτηση** *ee eroteesee*

queue **η ουρά** *ee oora*

quick **γρήγορος** *ghreeghoros*

quickly **γρήγορα** *ghreeghora*

quiet **ήσυχος** *eeseekhos*

quilt *(duvet)* **το πάπλωμα** *to paploma*

R

rabbit **το κουνέλι** *to koonelee*

rabies **η λύσσα** *ee leesa*

racket **η ρακέτα** *ee raketa*

radiator *(car)* **το ψυγείο** *to pseeyeeo*

radio **το ραδιόφωνο** *to radheeofono*

radish **το ραπανάκι** *to rapanakee*

railway station **ο σιδηροδρομικός σταθμός** *o seedheerodhromeekos stathmos*

rain **η βροχή** *ee vrokhee*

raincoat **το αδιάβροχο** *to adheeavrokho*

raining : *it's raining* **βρέχει** *vrekhee*

raisin **η σταφίδα** *ee stafeedha*

rare **σπάνιος** *spanyos*
(steak) **μισοψημένος** *meesopseemenos*

rash *(skin)* **το εξάνθημα** *to eksantheema*

raspberries **τα βατόμουρα** *ta vatomoora*

rat **ο αρουραίος** *o arooreos*

rate **ο ρυθμός** *o reethmos*
rate of exchange **η ισοτιμία** *ee eesoteemeea*

raw **ωμός** *omos*

razor **το ξυράφι** *to kseerafee*

razor blade **το ξυραφάκι** *to kseerafakee*

to read **διαβάζω** *dheeavazo*

ready **έτοιμος** *eteemos*

real **πραγματικός** *praghmateekos*

reason **ο λόγος** *o loghos*

receipt **η απόδειξη** *ee apodheeksee*

recently **τελευταία** *teleftea*

reception *(desk)* **η ρεσεψιόν** *ee resepsyon*

recipe **η συνταγή** *ee seendayee*

to recommend **συνιστώ** *seeneesto*

record *(music, etc.)* **ο δίσκος** *o dheeskos*

red **κόκκινος** *kokeenos*

reduction **η έκπτωση** *ee ekptosee*

refill **το ανταλλακτικό** *to andalakteeko*

refund **η επιστροφή χρημάτων** *e epeestrofee khreematon*

registered *(letter)* **συστημένο** *seesteemeno*

regulations **οι κανονισμοί** *ee kanoneesmee*

to reimburse **αποζημιώνω** *apozeemeeono*

relations *(family)* **οι συγγενείς** *ee seengenees*

to relax **ξεκουράζομαι** *ksekoorazome*

reliable *(person)* **αξιόπιστος** *akseeopeestos*
(car, method) **δοκιμασμένος** *dhokeemasmenos*

to remain **απομένω** *apomeno*

to remember **θυμάμαι** *theemame*

to rent **νοικιάζω** *neekyazo*

rental **το νοίκι** *to neekee*

to repair **επιδιορθώνω** *epeedheeorthono*

to repeat **επαναλαμβάνω** *epanalamvano*

reservation **η κράτηση** *ee krateesee*

to reserve **κρατώ** *krato*

reserved **κρατημένος** *krateemenos*

rest **ξεκούραση** *ksekoorasee*
the rest **οι υπόλοιποι** *ee eepoleepee*

to rest **ξεκουράζομαι** *ksekoorazome*

restaurant **το εστιατόριο** *to esteeatoreeo*

restaurant car **το βαγόνι ρεστωράν** *to vaghonee restoran*

to retire **βγαίνω στη σύνταξη** *vyeno stee seendaksee*

retired **συνταξιούχος** *seendaksyookhos*

to return *(go back, give back)* **επιστρέφω** *epeestrefo*

return ticket **το εισιτήριο με επιστροφή** *to eeseeteereeo me epeestrofee*

reverse-charge call **κλήση πληρωτέα από τον παραλήπτη** *kleesee pleerotea apo ton paraleeptee*

rheumatism **οι ρευματισμοί** *ee revmateesmee*

rice **το ρύζι** *to reezee*

rich *(person, food)* **πλούσιος** *plooseeos*

riding *(equestrian)* **η ιππασία** *ee eepaseea*

right *(correct, accurate)* **σωστός** *sostos*
(on/to the) right δεξιά *dheksya*

ring **το δαχτυλίδι** *to dhakhteeleedhee*

ripe **ώριμος** *oreemos*

river **το ποτάμι** *to potamee*

road **ο δρόμος** *o dhromos*

road map **ο οδικός χάρτης** *o odheekos khartees*

roast **το ψητό** *to pseeto*

to rob **ληστεύω** *leestevo*

roll *(of bread)* **το ψωμάκι** *to psomakee*

roof **η στέγη** *ee steyee*

roof rack **η σχάρα** *ee skhara*

room *(in house, etc.)* **το δωμάτιο** *o dhomateeo*
(space) **ο χώρος** *o khoros*

room service **η υπηρεσία δωματίου** *ee eepeereseea dhomateeoo*

rope **το σχοινί** *to skheenee*

rosé **ροζέ** *roze*

rotten *(fruit)* **χαλασμένος** *khalasmenos*

rough *(sea)* **τρικυμισμένη** *treekeemeesmenee*

round *(shape)* **στρογγυλός** *strongeelos*
round Greece **γύρω στην Ελλάδα** *yeero steen eladha*

route **ο δρόμος** *o dhromos*

to row *(boat)* **κάνω κουπί** *kano koopee*

rowing boat **η βάρκα με κουπιά** *ee varka me koopya*

royal **βασιλικός** *vaseeleekos*

rubber *(substance)* **το καουτσούκ** *to ka-ootsook*
(eraser) **η γόμα** *ee goma*

rubber band **το λαστιχάκι** *to lasteekhakee*

rubbish **τα σκουπίδια** *ta skoopeedhya*

rucksack **ο σάκκος** *o sakos*

ruins **τα ερείπια** *ta ereepya*

rum **το ρούμι** *to roomee*

to run **τρέχω** *trekho*

rush hour **η ώρα αιχμής** *ee ora ekhmees*

rusty **σκουριασμένος** *skooryasmenos*

S

sad **λυπημένος** *leepeemenos*

safe *adj (harmless)* **αβλαβής** *avlavees*
(not dangerous) **ακίνδυνος** *akeendheenos*
(secure, sure) **ασφαλής** *asfalees*

safe *n* **το χρηματοκιβώτιο** *to khreematokeevotyo*

safety pin **η παραμάνα** *ee paramana*

sailing **η ιστιοπλοΐα** *ee eesteeoploeea*

salad **η σαλάτα** *ee salata*

salad dressing **το λαδολέμονο** *to ladholemono*

sale *(in shop)* **το ξεπούλημα** *to ksepooleema*

salmon **ο σολομός** *o solomos*

salt **το αλάτι** *to alatee*

same **ίδιος** *eedheeos*

sand **η άμμος** *ee amos*

sandals **τα πέδιλα** *ta pedheela*

sandwich **το σάντουϊτς** *to sandwich*

sanitary towel **η σερβιέτα** *ee servyeta*

sardine **η σαρδέλα** *ee sardhela*

sauce **η σάλτσα** *ee saltsa*

saucepan **η κατσαρόλα** *ee katsarola*

saucer **το πιατάκι** *to pyatakee*

sausage **το λουκάνικο** *to lookaneeko*

savoury **πικάντικος** *peekandeekos*

to say **λέω** *leo*

scarf *(long)* **το κασκόλ** *to kaskol* *(square)* **το μαντήλι** *to mandeelee*

school **το σχολείο** *to skholeeo* *(for 12- to 15-year-olds)* **το γυμνάσιο** *to yeemnaseeo* *(for 15- to 18-year-olds)* **το λύκειο** *to leekeeo*

scissors **το ψαλίδι** *to psaleedhee*

Scotland **η Σκωτία** *ee skoteea*

Scottish *(person)* **ο Σκωτσέζος / η Σκωτσέζα** *o skotsezos / ee skotseza*

screw **η βίδα** *ee veedha*

screwdriver **το κατσαβίδι** *to katsaveedhee*

sculpture **το γλυπτό** *to ghleepto*

sea **η θάλασσα** *ee thalasa*

seafood **τα θαλασσινά** *ta thalaseena*

seasickness **η ναυτία** *ee nafteea*

seaside *(beach, seafront)* **η παραλία** *ee paraleea*

seat *(in theatre)* **η θέση** *ee thesee* *(in car, etc.)* **το κάθισμα** *to katheesma*

second **δεύτερος** *dhefteros*

second class *(ticket, etc.)* **δεύτερη θέση** *dhefteree thesee*

second-hand **μεταχειρισμένος** *metakheereesmenos*

to see **βλέπω** *vlepo*

self-service **το σελφ σέρβις** *to self service*

to sell **πουλώ** *poolo*

Sellotape® **το σελοτέιπ** *to seloteyp*

send **στέλνω** *stelno*

separate **χωριστός** *khoreestos*

serious **σοβαρός** *sovaros*

to serve **σερβίρω** *serveero*

service *(in restaurant, etc.)* **η εξυπηρέτηση** *ee ekseepeereteesee*

service charge **το ποσοστό υπηρεσίας** *to pososto eepeereseeas*

set menu **το καθορισμένο μενού** *to kathoreesmeno menoo*

several **διάφοροι** *dheeaforee*

to sew **ράβω** *ravo*

shade **η σκιά** *ee skeea*

shallow **ρηχός** *reekhos*

shampoo **το σαμπουάν** *to sambooan*

shampoo and set **λούσιμο και στέγνωμα** *looseemo ke steghnoma*

to share **μοιράζω** *meerazo*

to shave **ξυρίζομαι** *kseereezome*

shaving cream **η κρέμα ξυρίσματος** *ee krema kseereesmatos*

she **αυτή** *aftee*

sheep **το πρόβατο** *to provato*

sheet **το σεντόνι** *to sendonee*

shellfish **τα όστρακα** *ta ostraka*

ship **το πλοίο** *to pleeo*

shirt **το πουκάμισο** *to pookameeso*

shock absorber **το αμορτισέρ** *to amorteeser*

shoe **το παπούτσι** *to papootsee*

to shop ψωνίζω *psoneezo*

shop το μαγαζί *to maghazee*

shop assistant *(woman)* η πωλήτρια *ee poleetreea* *(man)* ο πωλητής *o poleetees*

short κοντός *kondos*

short cut ο συντομότερος δρόμος *o seendomoteros dhromos*

shorts το σορτς *to shorts*

show *n (in theatre, etc.)* η παράσταση *ee parastasee*

to show δείχνω *dheekhno*

shower *(in bath)* το ντους *to doos* *(rain)* η μπόρα *ee bora*

shrimp η γαρίδα *ee ghareedha*

shut *(closed)* κλειστός *kleestos*

to shut κλείνω *kleeno*

shutters τα παντζούρια *ta pantzooreea*

sick *(ill)* άρρωστος *arostos*
to be sick *(vomit)* κάνω εμετό *kano emeto*

sightseeing : ***to go sightseeing*** επισκέπτομαι τα αξιοθέατα *epeeskeptome ta akseeotheata*

sign *(roadsign, notice, etc.)* η πινακίδα *ee peenakeedha*

signature η υπογραφή *ee eepoghrafee*

silk το μετάξι *to metaksee*

silver ασημένιος *aseemeneeos*

similar παρόμοιος *paromeeos*

simple απλός *aplos*

to sing τραγουδώ *traghoodho*

single *(not married)* ελεύθερος *eleftheros*
(not double) μονός *monos*

single bed το μονό κρεββάτι *to mono krevatee*

single room το μονόκλινο δωμάτιο *to monokleeno dhomateeo*

sink ο νεροχύτης *o nerokheetees*

sister η αδελφή *ee adhelfee*

to sit *(down)* κάθομαι *kathome*

size *(of clothes, shoes)* το νούμερο *to noomero*

ski το σκι *to skee*

to ski κάνω σκι *kano skee*

ski jacket το μπουφάν του σκι *to boofan too skee*

ski pants το παντελόνι του σκι *to pandelonee too skee*

ski pole το ραβδί του σκι *to ravdhee too skee*

ski run η διαδρομή του σκι *ee dheeadhromee too skee*

ski suit τα ρούχα του σκι *ta rookha too skee*

skimmed milk το αποβουτυρωμένο γάλα *to apovooteeromeno ghala*

skin το δέρμα *to dherma*

skin diving το υποβρύχιο κολύμπι *to eepovreekheeo koleembee*

skirt η φούστα *ee foosta*

sky ο ουρανός *o ooranos*

to sleep κοιμούμαι *keemoome*

sleeper το βαγκόν-λι *to vagon-lee*

sleeping bag το υπνόσακος *o eepnosakos*

sleeping pill το υπνωτικό χάπι *to eepnoteeko khapee*

slice η φέτα *ee feta*

slide *(photography)* το σλάιντ *to slide*

slippery γλιστερός *ghleesteros*

slow σιγά *seegha*

small μικρός *meekros*

smaller (than) **μικρότερος (από)** *meekroteros (apo)*

smell **η μυρωδιά** *ee meerodhya*

smile **το χαμόγελο** *to khamoyelo*

to smile **χαμογελώ** *khamoyelo*

smoke **ο καπνός** *o kapnos*

to smoke **καπνίζω** *kapneezo*

smoked **καπνιστός** *kapneestos*

snack bar **το σνακ μπαρ** *to snack bar*

snake **το φίδι** *to feedhee*

snorkel **ο αναπνευστήρας** *o anapnevsteeras*

snow **το χιόνι** *to khyonee*

snowed up **αποκλεισμένος από το χιόνι** *apokleesmenos apo to khyonee*

snowing : ***it's snowing*** **χιονίζει** *khyoneezee*

so *(that's why)* **γι'αυτό** *yee afto*
so much **τόσο πολύ** *toso polee*
so pretty **τόσο ωραίος** *toso oreos*
so that *(in order to)* **για να** *ya na*

soap **το σαπούνι** *to sapoonee*

soap powder **το απορρυπαντικό** *to aporeepandeeko*

sober **ξεμέθυστος** *ksemetheestos*

sock **η κάλτσα** *ee kaltsa*

socket *(electrical)* **η πρίζα** *ee preeza*

soda *(water)* **η σόδα** *ee sodha*

soft **μαλακός** *malakos*

soft drink **το αναψυκτικό** *to anapseekteeko*

some **μερικοί** *mereekee*

someone **κάποιος** *kapyos*

something **κάτι** *katee*

sometimes **κάποτε** *kapote*

son **ο γιος** *o yos*

song **το τραγούδι** *to traghoodhee*

soon **σύντομα** *seendoma*
as soon as possible **το συντομότερο** *to seendomotero*
sooner **νωρίτερα** *noreetera*

sore : ***it's sore*** **πονάει** *ponaee*

sorry : ***I'm sorry*** *(apology)* **συγγνώμη** *seeghnomee*
(regret) **λυπούμαι** *leepoome*

sort **το είδος** *to eedhos*

soup **η σούπα** *ee soopa*

south **ο νότος** *o notos*

souvenir **το σουβενίρ** *to sooveneer*

space *(room)* **ο χώρος** *o khoros*

spanner **το κλειδί** *to kleedhee*

spare wheel **η ρεζέρβα** *ee rezerva*

spark plug **το μπουζί** *to boozee*

sparkling *(wine)* **αφρώδης** *afrodhees*

to speak **μιλώ** *meelo*

special **ειδικός** *eedheekos*

speciality *(in restaurant)* **η σπεσιαλιτέ** *ee spesyaleete*

speed **η ταχύτητα** *ee takheeteeta*

speed limit **το όριο ταχύτητας** *to oreeo takheeteetas*

spell *(to write)* **γράφω** *ghrafo*
how do you spell it? **πώς γράφεται;** *pos ghrafete*

spicy **πικάντικος** *peekandeekos*

spinach **το σπανάκι** *to spanakee*

spirits **τα οινοπνευματώδη ποτά** *ta eenopnevmatodhee pota*

sponge **το σφουγγάρι** *to sfoongaree*

spoon **το κουτάλι** *to kootalee*

sport **το σπορ** *to spor*

spring *(season)* **η άνοιξη** *ee aneeksee*

square (in town) **η πλατεία** ee plateea

squash (sport) **το σκουός** to skoo-os
orange squash **η πορτοκαλάδα** ee portokaladha
lemon squash **η λεμονάδα** ee lemonadha

squid **το καλαμάρι** to kalamaree

stadium **το στάδιο** to stadheeo

stairs **η σκάλα** ee skala

stalls (in theatre) **η πλατεία** ee plateea

stamp **το γραμματόσημο** to ghramatoseemo

star (in sky) **το άστρο** to astro

to start **αρχίζω** arkheezo

starter (in meal) **το ορεκτικό** to orekteeko

station **ο σταθμός** o stathmos

stationer's **το χαρτοπωλείο** to khartopoleeo

to stay **μένω** meno

steak **η μπριζόλα** ee breezola

steep **ανηφορικός** aneeforeekos

sterling **η αγγλική λίρα** ee angleekee leera

steward (on a ship) **ο καμαρότος** o kamarotos
(on plane) **ο αεροσυνοδός** o aeroseenodhos

stewardess (on plane) **η αεροσυνοδός** ee aeroseenodhos

sticking plaster **ο λευκοπλάστης** o lefkoplastees

still (yet) **ακόμα** akoma
(immobile) **ακίνητος** akeeneetos
(water) **μη αεριούχο** mee aeryookho

sting **το τσίμπημα** to tseembeema

stomach **το στομάχι** to stomakhee

stomach upset **η στομαχική διαταραχή** ee stomakheekee dheeatarakhee

to stop **σταματώ** stamato

storm (thunder) **η καταιγίδα** ee kateyeedha

straight : *straight on* **ευθεία** eftheea

straw (for drinking) **το καλαμάκι** to kalamakee

strawberry **η φράουλα** ee fraoola

street **ο δρόμος** o dhromos

street plan **ο οδικός χάρτης** o odheekos khartees

string **ο σπάγγος** o spangos

striped **ριγωτός** reeghotos

strong **δυνατός** dheenatos

stuck (jammed) **κολλημένος** koleemenos

student **ο φοιτητής / η φοιτήτρια** o feeteetees / ee feeteetreea

stung : *I've been stung by something* **κάτι με τσίμπησε** katee me tseembeese

stupid **ανόητος** anoeetos

suddenly **ξαφνικά** ksafneeka

suede **το καστόρι** to kastoree

sugar **η ζάχαρη** ee zakharee

suit (man's) **το κοστούμι** to kostoomee
(woman's) **το ταγιέρ** to ta-yer

suitcase **η βαλίτσα** ee valeetsa

summer **το καλοκαίρι** to kalokeree

sun **ο ήλιος** o eeleeos

to sunbathe **κάνω ηλιοθεραπεία** kano eeleeotherapeea

sun block **το αντιηλιακό** to andee-eelyako

sunburn (painful) **το κάψιμο από τον ήλιο** to kapseemo apo ton eeleeo

sunglasses τα γυαλιά του ήλιου *ta yalya too eeleeoo*

sunny *(weather)* **ηλιόλουστος** *eelyoloostos*

sunrise η ανατολή *ee anatolee*

sunset το ηλιοβασίλεμα *to eeleeovaseelema*

sunshade η ομπρέλα *ee ombrela*

sunstroke η ηλίαση *ee eeleeasee*

suntan lotion το λάδι για τον ήλιο *to ladhee ya ton eeleeo*

supermarket το σούπερμάρκετ *to supermarket*

supper το δείπνο *to dheepno*

supplement το συμπλήρωμα *to seembleeroma*

surcharge η επιβάρυνση *ee epeevareensee*

surfboard η σανίδα σέρφινγκ *ee saneedha surfing*

surfing το σέρφινγκ *to surfing*

surname το επώνυμο *to eponeemo*

surrounded by τριγυρισμένος από *treeyeereesmenos apo*

suspension η ανάρτηση *ee anarteesee*

to sweat ιδρώνω *eedhrono*

sweater το πουλόβερ *to poolover*

sweet *adj (taste)* **γλυκός** *ghleekos*

sweet *n* **το γλυκό** *to ghleeko*

sweets οι καραμέλες *ee karameles*

sweetener η ζαχαρίνη *ee zakhareenee*

to swim κολυμπώ *koleembo*

swimming pool η πισίνα *ee peeseena*

swimsuit το μαγιό *to ma-yo*

swing *(for children)* **η κούνια** *ee koonya*

switch ο διακόπτης *o dheeakoptees*

to switch on ανάβω *anavo*

to switch off σβήνω *sveeno*

swollen *(ankle, etc.)* **πρησμένος** *preesmenos*

synagogue η συναγωγή *ee seenayoyee*

T

table το τραπέζι *to trapezee*

tablecloth το τραπεζομάντηλο *to trapezomandeelo*

tablespoon το κουτάλι *to kootalee*

tablet το χάπι *to khapee*

table tennis το πινγκ πονγκ *to ping pong*

to take παίρνω *perno*

to take out βγάζω *vghazo* *(from bank account)* **αποσύρω** *aposeero*

to talk μιλώ *meelo*

tall ψηλός *pseelos*

tame *(animal)* **ήμερος** *eemeros*

tampons τα ταμπόν *ta tambon*

tap η βρύση *ee vreesee*

tape recorder το μαγνητόφωνο *to maghneetofono* *(cassette player)* **το κασετόφωνο** *to kasetofono*

to taste δοκιμάζω *dhokeemazo*

taste *n* **η γεύση** *ee yefsee*

tax ο φόρος *o foros*

taxi το ταξί *to taksee*

taxi rank η πιάτσα για ταξί *ee pyatsa ya taksee*

tea το τσάι *to tsaee*

tea bag το φακελλάκι τσαγιού *to fakelakee tsa-yoo*

to teach διδάσκω *dheedhasko*

teacher **ο δάσκαλος / η δασκάλα** *o dhaskalos / ee dhaskala*

teapot **η τσαγιέρα** *ee tsa-yera*

tear *(in eye)* **το δάκρυ** *to dhakree* *(in material)* **το σχίσιμο** *to skheeseemo*

teaspoon **το κουταλάκι** *to kootalakee*

teat **η ρώγα** *ee rogha*

teeth **τα δόντια** *ta dhondeea*

telegram **το τηλεγράφημα** *to teeleghrafeema*

telephone **το τηλέφωνο** *to teelefono*

telephone box **ο τηλεφωνικός θάλαμος** *o teelefoneekos thalamos*

telephone call **το τηλεφώνημα** *to teelefoneema*

telephone directory **ο τηλεφωνικός κατάλογος** *o teelefoneekos kataloghos*

television **η τηλεόραση** *ee teeleorasee*

telex **το τέλεξ** *to telex*

to tell **λέγω** *legho* *(story)* **διηγούμαι** *dhee-eeghoome*

temperature **η θερμοκρασία** *ee thermokraseea*
to have a temperature **έχω πυρετό** *ekho peereto*

temple **ο ναός** *o naos*

temporary **προσωρινός** *prosoreenos*

tennis **το τένις** *to tenees*

tennis ball **η μπάλα του τένις** *ee bala too tennis*

tennis court **το γήπεδο του τένις** *to yeepedho too tenees*

tennis racket **η ρακέτα του τένις** *ee raketa too tenees*

tent **η σκηνή** *ee skeenee*

tent peg **ο πάσσαλος της σκηνής** *o pasalos tees skeenees*

terminus **το τέρμα** *to terma*

terrace **η ταράτσα** *ee taratsa*

thank you **ευχαριστώ** *efkhareesto*

that **εκείνος** *ekeenos*
that book **εκείνο το βιβλίο** *ekeeno to veevleeo*
that one **εκείνο** *ekeeno*

theatre **το θέατρο** *to theatro*

then **τότε** *tote*

there **εκεί** *ekee*
there is **υπάρχει** *eeparkhee*
there are **υπάρχουν** *eeparkhoon*

thermometer **το θερμόμετρο** *to thermometro*

these **αυτοί / αυτές / αυτά** *aftee (masculine) / aftes (feminine) / afta (neuter)*
these books **αυτά τα βιβλία** *afta ta veevleea*

they **αυτοί** *aftee* see GRAMMAR

thick **χοντρός** *khontros*

thief **ο κλέφτης** *o kleftees*

thin **λεπτός** *leptos*

thing **το πράγμα** *to praghma*

third **τρίτος** *treetos*

thirsty : ***I'm thirsty*** **διψάω** *dheepsao*

this **αυτός / αυτή / αυτό** *aftos (masculine) / aftee (feminine) / afto (neuter)*
this book **αυτό το βιβλίο** *afto to veevleeo*
this one **αυτό** *afto*

those **εκείνοι** *ekeenee*
those books **εκείνα τα βιβλία** *ekeena ta veevleea*

thread **η κλωστή** *ee klostee*

throat **ο λαιμός** *o lemos*

throat lozenges **οι παστίλιες για το λαιμό** *ee pasteelyes ya to lemo*

through διαμέσου *dheeamesoo*

thunder ο κεραυνός *o keravnos*

thunderstorm η θύελλα *ee theeela*

ticket το εισιτήριο *to eeseeteereeo*

ticket collector ο ελεγκτής *o elengtees*

ticket office η θυρίδα *ee theereedha*

tie η γραβάτα *ee ghravata*

tight σφιχτός *sfeekhtos*

tights το καλσόν *to kalson*

till *(cash)* **το ταμείο** *to tameeo*

till *(until)* **μέχρι** *mekhree*

time *(by the clock)* **η ώρα** *ee ora*
what time is it? **τι ώρα είναι;** *tee ora eene*

timetable *(buses, trains, etc)* **το δρομολόγιο** *to dromoloyeeo* *(school, shop opening hours etc)* **το ωράριο** *to orareeo*

tin η κονσέρβα *ee konserva*

tinfoil το αλουμινόχαρτο *to aloomeenokharto*

tin-opener το ανοιχτήρι για κονσέρβες *to aneekhteeree ya konserves*

tip *(to waiter, etc.)* **το πουρμπουάρ** *to poorbooar*

tipped *(cigarettes)* **με φίλτρο** *me feeltro*

tired κουρασμένος *koorasmenos*

tissue το χαρτομάντηλο *to khartomandeelo*

to σε *se*
to the **στο / στη / στο** *sto (masculine) stee (feminine) sto (neuter)*
to Greece **στην Ελλάδα** *steen eladha*

toast η φρυγανιά *ee freeghanya*

tobacco ο καπνός *o kapnos*

tobacconists το καπνοπωλείο *to kapnopoleeo*

today σήμερα *seemera*

together μαζί *mazee*

toilet η τουαλέτα *ee tooaleta*

toilet paper το χαρτί υγείας *to khartee eeyeeas*

toll τα διόδια *ta dheeodheea*

tomato η ντομάτα *ee domata*

tomato juice ο χυμός ντομάτας *o kheemos domatas*

tomorrow αύριο *avreeo*

tongue η γλώσσα *ee ghlosa*

tonic water το τόνικ *to toneek*

tonight απόψε *apopse*

too *(also)* **επίσης** *epeesees*
(too much) **πάρα πολύ** *para polee*

tooth το δόντι *to dhondee*

toothache ο πονόδοντος *o ponodhondos*

toothbrush η οδοντόβουρτσα *ee odhontovoortsa*

toothpaste η οδοντόκρεμα *ee odhondokrema*

top το πάνω μέρος *to pano meros*
(of mountain) **η κορυφή** *ee koreefee*

torch ο φακός *o fakos*

torn σχισμένος *skheesmenos*

total το σύνολο *to seenolo*

tough *(of meat)* **σκληρός** *skleeros*

tour η εκδρομή *ee ekdhromee*

tourist ο τουρίστας / η τουρίστρια *o tooreestas / ee tooreestreea*

tourist office το τουριστικό γραφείο *to tooreesteeko ghrafeeo*

tourist ticket **το τουριστικό εισιτήριο** *to tooreesteeko eeseeteereeo*

to tow **ρυμουλκώ** *reemoolko*

towel **η πετσέτα** *ee petseta*

tower **ο πύργος** *o peerghos*

town **η πόλη** *ee polee*

town centre **το κέντρο της πόλης** *to kendro tees polees*

town hall **το δημαρχείο** *to dheemarkheeo*

town plan **ο χάρτης της πόλης** *o khartees tees polees*

towrope **το σχοινί ρυμούλκησης** *to skheenee reemoolkeesees*

toy **το παιχνίδι** *to pekhneedhee*

traditional **παραδοσιακός** *paradhosyakos*

traffic **η κυκλοφορία** *ee keekloforeea*

traffic lights **τα φανάρια (της τροχαίας)** *ta fanareea (tees trokheas)*

trailer **το τρέιλερ** *to trailer*

train **το τρένο** *to treno*

training shoes **τα αθλητικά παπούτσια** *ta athleeteeka papootsya*

tram **το τραμ** *to tram*

to translate **μεταφράζω** *metafrazo*

translation **η μετάφραση** *ee metafrasee*

to travel **ταξιδεύω** *takseedhevo*

travel agent **ο ταξιδιωτικός πράκτορας** *o takseedhyoteekos praktoras*

travellers' cheques **τα ταξιδιωτικά τσεκ** *ta takseedhyoteeka tsek*

tray **ο δίσκος** *o dheeskos*

tree **το δέντρο** *to dhendro*

trim *n (hair)* **το κόψιμο** *to kopseemo*

trip **η εκδρομή** *ee ekdhromee*

trolley bus **το τρόλεϊ** *to troley*

trouble **ο μπελάς** *o belas*

trousers **το παντελόνι** *to pandelonee*

trout **η πέστροφα** *ee pestrofa*

true **αληθινός** *aleetheenos*

trunk **το μπαούλο** *to baoolo*

trunks **το μαγιό** *to ma-yo*

to try **προσπαθώ** *prospatho*

to try on **δοκιμάζω** *dhokeemazo*

T-shirt **το μπλουζάκι** *to bloozakee*

tuna **ο τόνος** *o tonos*

tunnel **η σήραγγα** *ee seeranga*

turkey **η γαλοπούλα** *ee ghalopoola*

to turn **στρίβω** *streevo*

turnip **η ρέβα** *ee reva*

to turn off *(on a journey)* **στρίβω** *streevo*
(radio, etc.) **κλείνω** *kleeno*
(engine, light) **σβήνω** *sveeno*

to turn on *(radio, TV)* **ανοίγω** *aneegho*
(engine, light) **ανάβω** *anavo*

TV **η τηλεόραση** *ee teeleorasee*

tweezers **το τσιμπίδι** *to tseembeedhee*

twice **δύο φορές** *dheeo fores*

twin **ο δίδυμος** *o dheedheemos*

twin-bedded **το δίκλινο δωμάτιο** *to dheekleeno dhomateeo*

to type **δακτυλογραφώ** *dhakteeloghrafo*

typical **τυπικός** *teepeekos*

tyre **το λάστιχο** *to lasteekho*

tyre pressure **η πίεση στα λάστιχα** *ee peeyesee sta lasteekha*

U

ugly **άσχημος** *askheemos*

umbrella **η ομπρέλα** *ee ombrela*

uncle **ο θείος** *o theeos*

uncomfortable **άβολος** *avolos*

unconscious **αναίσθητος** *anestheetos*

under **κάτω από** *kato apo*

underground *(railway)* **το μετρό** *to metro*

underpants see **pants**

underpass **η υπόγεια διάβαση** *ee eepoyeea dheeavasee*

to understand **καταλαβαίνω** *katalaveno*

underwear **τα εσώρουχα** *ta esorookha*

unemployed **άνεργος** *anerghos*

unfasten **λύνω** *leeno*

United States **οι Ηνωμένες Πολιτείες** *ee eenomenes poleeteeyes*

university **το πανεπιστήμιο** *to panepeesteemeeo*

unleaded petrol **η αμόλυβδη βενζίνη** *ee amoleevdhee venzeenee*

to unpack *(case)* **αδειάζω** *adheeazo*

up *(out of bed)* **ξύπνιος** *kseepneeos*
to go up **ανεβαίνω** *aneveno*

upstairs **πάνω** *pano*

urgently **επειγόντως** *epeeghondos*

urine **τα ούρα** *ta oora*

urn **ο αμφορέας** *o amforeas*

to use **χρησιμοποιώ** *khreeseemopyo*

useful **χρήσιμος** *khreeseemos*

usual **συνηθισμένος** *seeneetheesmenos*

usually **συνήθως** *seeneethos*

V

vacancy *(room)* **το διαθέσιμο δωμάτιο** *to dheeatheseemo dhomateeo*

vacuum cleaner **η ηλεκτρική σκούπα** *ee eelektreekee skoopa*

valid **έγκυρος** *engkeeros*

valley **η κοιλάδα** *ee keeladha*

valuable **πολύτιμος** *poleeteemos*

valuables **τα πολύτιμα αντικείμενα** *ta poleeteema andeekeemena*

value **η αξία** *ee akseea*

van **το φορτηγάκι** *to forteeghakee*

vase **το βάζο** *to vazo*

VAT **ο ΦΠΑ** *o fee pee a*

veal **το μοσχάρι** *to moskharee*

vegetables **τα λαχανικά** *ta lakhaneeka*

vegetarian **ο χορτοφάγος** *o khortofaghos*

vein **η φλέβα** *ee fleva*

velvet **το βελούδο** *to veloodho*

ventilator **ο εξαεριστήρας** *o eksaereesteeras*

very **πολύ** *polee*

vest **η φανέλα** *ee fanela*

via **μέσω** *meso*

video **το βίντεο** *to veedeo*

video camera **η βιντεοκάμερα** *ee veedeokamera*

video recorder **το βίντεο** *to veedeeo*

view **η θέα** *ee thea*

villa **η βίλλα** *ee veela*

village **το χωριό** *to khoryo*

vine leaves **τα κληματόφυλλα** *ta kleematofeela*

vinegar **το ξύδι** *to kseedhee*

visa **η βίζα** *ee veesa*

to visit **επισκέπτομαι** *epeeskeptome*

visit **επίσκεψη** *ee epeeskepsee*

vitamin **η βιταμίνη** *ee veetameenee*

vodka **η βότκα** *ee votka*

voice **η φωνή** *ee fonee*

volleyball **το βόλεϊ** *to volay*

voltage **η τάση** *ee tasee*

W

wage **ο μισθός** *o meesthos*

waist **η μέση** *ee mesee*

to wait for **περιμένω** *pereemeno*

waiter **το γκαρσόνι** *to garsonee*

waiting room **η αίθουσα αναμονής** *ee ethoosa anamonees*

waitress **η σερβιτόρα** *ee serveetora*

Wales **η Ουαλία** *ee ooaleea*

walk **ο περίπατος** *o pereepatos*

to walk **περπατώ** *perpato*

walking stick **το μπαστούνι** *to bastoonee*

wall **ο τοίχος** *o teekhos*

wallet **το πορτοφόλι** *to portofolee*

walnut **το καρύδι** *to kareedhee*

to want **θέλω** *thelo*

war **ο πόλεμος** *o polemos*

wardrobe **η γκαρνταρόμπα** *ee gardaroba*

warm **ζεστός** *zestos*

warning triangle **το τρίγωνο αυτοκινήτου** *to treeghono aftokeeneetoo*

to wash *(clothes)* **πλένω** *pleno*
(oneself) **πλένομαι** *plenome*

washbasin **ο νιπτήρας** *o neepteeras*

washing machine **το πλυντήριο** *to pleendeereeo*

washing powder **το απορρυπαντικό** *to aporeepandeeko*

washing-up liquid **το υγρό για τα πιάτα** *to eeghro ya ta pyata*

wasp **η σφήκα** *ee sfeeka*

waste bin **το καλάθι των αχρήστων** *to kalathee ton akhreeston*

watch *n* **το ρολόι** *to roloee*

to watch *(TV)* **βλέπω** *vlepo*
(someone's luggage) **προσέχω** *prosekho*

watchstrap **το λουρί του ρολογιού** *to looree too roloyoo*

water **το νερό** *to nero*
fresh water **το γλυκό νερό** *to ghleeko nero*
salt water **το αλμυρό νερό** *to almeero nero*

waterfall **ο καταρράκτης** *o kataraktees*

water heater **ο θερμοσίφωνας** *o thermoseefonas*

water-skiing **το θαλάσσιο σκι** *to thalaseeo skee*

watermelon **το καρπούζι** *to karpoozee*

waterproof **αδιάβροχος** *adheeavrokhos*

wave *(on sea)* **το κύμα** *to keema*

wax **το κερί** *to keree*

way *(method)* **ο τρόπος** *o tropos*
this way **από 'δω** *apodho*
that way **από 'κει** *apokee*

we **εμείς** *emees*

weak **αδύνατος** *adheenatos*

to wear **φορώ** *foro*

weather **ο καιρός** *o keros*

wedding **ο γάμος** *o ghamos*

week **η εβδομάδα** *ee evdhomadha*

weekday **η καθημερινή** *ee katheemereenee*

weekend **το σαββατοκύριακο** *to savatokeereeako*

weekly *(rate, etc.)* **εβδομαδιαίος** *evdhomadhyeos*

weight **το βάρος** *to varos*

welcome **καλώς ήλθατε** *kalos eelthate*

well *(healthy)* **υγιής** *eeyee-ees*

well done *(steak)* **καλοψημένος** *kalopseemenos*

Welsh *(person)* **ο Ουαλός / η Ουαλή** *o ooalos / ee ooalee*

west **η δύση** *ee dheesee*

wet *(damp)* **βρεγμένος** *vreghmenos* *(weather)* **βροχερός** *vrokheros*

wetsuit **η στολή για υποβρύχιο ψάρεμα** *ee stolee ya eepovreekheeo psarema*

what? **τι;** *tee*
what is it? **τι είναι;** *tee eene*

wheel **ο τροχός** *o trokhos*

wheelchair **η αναπηρική καρέκλα** *ee anapeereekee karekla*

when? **πότε;** *pote*

where? **πού;** *poo*

which? **ποιος;** *pyos (masculine)*
ποια; *pya (feminine)*
ποιο; *pyo (neuter)*
which is it? **ποιο είναι;** *pyo eene*

while **ενώ** *eno*

whipped cream **η σαντιγύ** *ee sandeeyee*

whisky **το ουίσκυ** *to whisky*

white **άσπρος** *aspros*

who? **ποιος;** *pyos*

whole **όλος** *olos*

wholemeal bread **ψωμί ολικής αλέσεως** *psomee oleekees aleseos*

whose : *whose is it?* **ποιου είναι;** *pyoo eene*

why? **γιατί;** *yatee*

wide **πλατύς** *platees*

wife **η σύζυγος** *ee seezeeghos*

wind **ο αέρας** *o aeras*

window **το παράθυρο** *to paratheero*

windmill **ο ανεμόμυλος** *o anemomeelos*

windscreen **το παρμπρίζ** *to parbreez*

windsurfing **το γουιντσέρφινγκ** *to windsurfing*

wine **το κρασί** *to krasee*

wine list **ο κατάλογος των κρασιών** *o kataloghos ton krasyon*

wine shop **η κάβα** *ee kava*

winter **ο χειμώνας** *o kheemonas*

with **με** *me*

without **χωρίς** *khorees*

woman **η γυναίκα** *ee yeeneka*

wood **το ξύλο** *to kseelo*

wool **το μαλλί** *to malee*

word **η λέξη** *ee leksee*

work **η δουλειά** *ee dhoolya*

to work *(person)* **δουλεύω** *dhoolevo*
(machine) **λειτουργεί** *leetooryee*

worried **ανήσυχος** *aneeseekhos*

worse **χειρότερος** *kheeroteros*

worth : *20 euros worth of unleaded petrol* **Είκοσι ευρώ αμόλυβδη βενζίνη** *eekosee evro amoleevdhee venzeenee*

to wrap (up) **τυλίγω** *teeleegho*

wrapping paper **το χαρτί περιτυλίγματος** *to khartee pereeteeleeghmatos*

to write **γράφω** *ghrafo*

writing paper **το χαρτί αλληλογραφίας** *to khartee aleeloghrafeeas*

wrong **λάθος** *lathos*
you're wrong **κάνετε λάθος** *kanete lathos*

Y

yacht **το γιοτ** *to yacht*

year **ο χρόνος** *o khronos*

yellow **κίτρινος** *keetreenos*

yes **ναι** *ne*

yesterday **χτες** *khtes*

yet **ακόμα** *akoma*
not yet **όχι ακόμα** *okhee akoma*

yoghurt **το γιαούρτι** *to yaoortee*

you *(singular/plural)* **εσύ / εσείς** *esee / esees*

young **νέος** *neos*

youth hostel **ο ξενώνας νεότητος** *o ksenonas neoteetos*

Z

zero **το μηδέν** *to meedhen*

zip **το φερμουάρ** *to fermooar*

zone **η ζώνη** *ee zonee*

zoo **ο ζωολογικός κήπος** *o zo-oloyeekos keepos*

DICTIONARY

greek-english

α Α

αβγό (το) egg
αβγά ημέρας newly-laid eggs

άγαλμα (το) statue

αγάπη (η) love

αγαπώ to love

αγγελία (η) announcement

άγγελος (ο) angel

Αγγλία (η) England

αγγλικός/ή/ό English *(thing)*

Άγγλος/Αγγλίδα (ο/η) Englishman/Englishwoman

αγγούρι (το) cucumber

άγιος/α/ο holy ; saint
Άγιον Όρος (το) Mount Athos

αγκινάρα (η) artichoke

άγκυρα (η) anchor

αγορά (η) agora ; market

αγοράζω to buy

αγοραστής (ο) buyer

αγόρι (το) young boy

άδεια (η) permit ; licence
άδεια οδήγησης driving licence

άδειος/α/ο empty

αδελφή (η) sister

αδελφός (ο) brother

αδιάβροχο (το) raincoat

αδιέξοδο (το) cul-de-sac ; no through road

αδίκημα (το) offence

αέρας (ο) wind

αερογραμμές (οι) airways
Βρετανικές Αερογραμμές British Airways
Κυπριακές Αερογραμμές Cyprus Airways

αεροδρόμιο (το) airport

αεροπλάνο (το) aeroplane

αεροπορία (η) air force
Ολυμπιακή Αεροπορία Olympic Airways

αεροπορικό εισιτήριο (το) air ticket

αεροπορικώς by air

αζήτητος/η/ο unclaimed

Αθήνα (η) Athens

αθλητικό κέντρο (το) sports centre

αθλητισμός (ο) sports

Αιγαίο (το) the Aegean Sea

αίθουσα (η) room
αίθουσα αναμονής waiting room
αίθουσα αναχωρήσεων departure lounge

αιμορραγώ to bleed

αίμα (το) blood

αίτημα (το) demand

αίτηση (η) application

ακάθαρτος/η/ο dirty

ακουστικά (τα) earphones
ακουστικά βαρυκοΐας hearing aids

ακουστικό (το) receiver *(telephone)*

ακούω to hear

άκρη (η) edge

Ακρόπολη (η) the Acropolis

ακτή (η) beach ; shore

ακτινογραφία (η) X-ray

ακυρώνω to cancel

αλάτι (το) salt

αλεύρι (το) flour

αλλαγή (η) change

αλλάζω to change
δεν αλλάζονται goods will not be exchanged

αλληλογραφία (η) correspondence

αλληλογραφώ to correspond

αλλοδαπός/ή foreign national
αστυνομία αλλοδαπών immigration police

αλμυρός/ή/ό salty

αλυσίδα (η) chain

αμάξι (το) car ; vehicle

αμάξωμα (το) body *(of car)*

αμερικάνικος/η/ο American *(thing)*

Αμερικανός/Αμερικανίδα American *(man/woman)*

Αμερική (η) America

αμέσως at once ; immediately

αμήν amen

άμμος (η) sand

αμμουδιά (η) sandy beach

αμοιβή (η) reward ; fare ; salary ; payment

αμπέλι (το) vine

αμύγδαλο (το) almond

αμφιθέατρο (το) amphitheatre

αμφορέας (ο) jar ; amphora

αν if

αναβολή (η) delay

ανάβω to switch on

αναγγελία (η) announcement

αναζήτηση (η) search

ανάκριση (η) interrogation

ανάκτορα (τα) palace

αναμονή (η) waiting
αίθουσα αναμονής waiting room

ανανάς (ο) pineapple

ανανεώνω to renew

ανάπηρος/η/ο handicapped ; disabled

αναπληρώνω to replace

αναπτήρας (ο) cigarette lighter

ανασκαφή (η) excavation

ανατολή (η) east ; sunrise

ανατολικός/ή/ό eastern

ΑΝΑΧΩΡΗΣΕΙΣ
DEPARTURES

αναψυκτήριο (το) refreshment room

αναψυκτικό (το) soft drink

αναψυχή (η) recreation ; pleasure

άνδρας (ο) man

ΑΝΔΡΕΣ GENTS

ανδρική μόδα (η) men's fashions

ανεμιστήρας (ο) fan

άνθη (τα) flowers *(only on signs)*

ανθοπωλείο (το) florist's

άνθρωπος (ο) man

ανοίγω to open

ΑΝΟΙΚΤΟ OPEN

άνοιξη (η) spring *(season)*

ανταλλαγή (η) exchange

ανταλλακτικά (τα) spare parts

αντιβιοτικά (τα) antibiotics

αντίγραφο (το) copy ; reproduction

αντίκες (οι) antiques

αντικλεπτικά (τα) anti-theft devices

αντίο goodbye

αντιπηκτικό (το) antifreeze

αντιπρόσωπος (ο) representative

αντλία (η) pump
αντλία βενζίνης petrol pump

αντρόγυνο (το) couple

ανώμαλος/η/ο uneven ; rough

αξεσουάρ (τα) accessories
αξεσουάρ αυτοκινήτου car accessories

αξία (η) value

αξία διαδρομής fare

αξιοθέατα (τα) the sights

απαγορεύω to forbid ; no...
απαγορεύεται η αναμονή no waiting
απαγορεύεται η διάβαση keep off
απαγορεύεται η είσοδος no entry
απαγορεύεται το κάπνισμα no smoking
απαγορεύεται η στάθμευση no parking

απαγορεύονται τα σκυλιά no dogs
απαγορεύεται η φωτογράφηση no photography
απαγορεύεται το κολύμπι no swimming
απαγορεύεται η κατασκήνωση no camping

απαίτηση (η) claim

απεργία (η) strike

απογείωση (η) takeoff

απόγευμα (το) afternoon

απόδειξη (η) receipt

αποθήκη (η) warehouse ; store-room

αποκλειστικός/ή/ό exclusive

απόκριες (οι) carnival

αποσκευές (οι) luggage
αναζήτηση αποσκευών left-luggage *(office)*

απόχη (η) fishing/butterfly net

απόψε tonight

ΑΠΡΙΛΙΟΣ APRIL

αργότερα later

αρέσω to please
μου αρέσει I like
δεν μου αρέσει I don't like
σου αρέσει you like
δεν σου αρέσει you don't like

αριθμός (ο) number
αριθμός διαβατηρίου passport number
αριθμός πτήσεως flight number
αριθμός τηλεφώνου telephone number

αριστερά left *(opposite of right)*

αρνί (το) lamb

αρρώστια (η) illness

άρρωστος/η/ο ill

αρτοποιείο (η) bakery

αρχαιολογικός χώρος (ο) archaeological site

αρχαίος/α/ο ancient

αρχή (η) start

αρχίζω to begin ; to start

άρωμα (το) perfume

ασανσέρ (το) lift ; elevator

ασθενής (ο/η) patient

άσθμα (το) asthma

άσκοπος/η/ο improper
άσκοπη χρήση improper use

ασπιρίνη (η) aspirin

άσπρος/η/ο white

αστακός (ο) lobster

αστικός νομισματοδέκτης (ο) coin-operated phone for local calls

αστυνομία (η) police
αστυνομία αλλοδαπών immigration police
Ελληνική αστυνομία Greek police

αστυνομική διάταξη (η) police notice

αστυνομικό τμήμα (το) police station

αστυνομικός σταθμός (ο) police station

αστυνόμος (ο) policeman

αστυφύλακας (ο) town policeman

ασφάλεια (η) insurance ; fuse

ασφάλεια έναντι κλοπής theft insurance
ασφάλεια έναντι τρίτων third-party insurance
ασφάλεια ζωής life insurance

ασφάλιση (η) insurance
πλήρης ασφάλιση comprehensive insurance
ιατρική ασφάλιση medical insurance

ατμοπλοϊκό εισιτήριο (το) boat ticket

ατομικός/ή/ό personal

άτομο (το) person
άτομο τρίτης ηλικίας pensioner

ατύχημα (το) accident

αυγή (η) dawn

αυγό (το) egg

ΑΥΓΟΥΣΤΟΣ AUGUST

αυτοκίνητο (το) car
ενοικιάσεις αυτοκινήτων car hire
συνεργείο αυτοκινήτων car repairs

αυτοκινητόδρομος (ο) motorway

αυτόματος/η/ο automatic

άφιξη (η) arrival

ΑΦΙΞΕΙΣ ARRIVALS

αφορολόγητα (τα) duty-free goods

Αφροδίτη Aphrodite ; Venus

αχλάδι (το) pear

άχρηστα (τα) waste

αψίδα (η) arch

β Β

βαγόνι (το) carriage *(train)*

βάζω to put

βαλβίδα (η) valve

βαλίτσα (η) suitcase

βαμβακερός/ή/ό *(made of)* cotton

βαρέλι (το) barrel
μπίρα από βαρέλι draught beer

βαρελίσιο κρασί (το) house wine

βάρκα (η) boat

βάρος (το) weight

βαφή (η) paint ; dye ; painting ; dyeing

βάφω to paint

βγάζω to take off

βγαίνω to go out

βελόνα (η) needle

βενζίνη (η) petrol ; gasoline

βήχας (ο) cough

βιβλίο (το) book

βιβλιοθήκη (η) bookcase ; library
Δημοτική Βιβλιοθήκη Public Library
Κεντρική Βιβλιοθήκη Central Library

βιβλιοπωλείο (το) bookshop

Βίβλος (η) the Bible

βιταμίνη (η) vitamin

βιτρίνα (η) shop window

βλέπω to see

βοδινό κρέας beef

βοήθεια (η) help
οδική βοήθεια breakdown service
πρώτες βοήθειες casualty *(hospital)*

βόμβα (η) bomb

βόρειος/α/ο northern

βορράς (ο) north

βουλή (η) parliament

βουνό (το) mountain

βούρτσα (η) brush

βούτυρο (το) butter

βράδυ (το) evening

βραδινό (το) evening meal

βράζω to boil

βραστός/ή/ό boiled

Βρετανία (η) Britain

βρετανικός/ή/ό British *(thing)*

Βρετανός/Βρετανίδα (ο/η) British *(man/woman)*

βρέχει it is raining

βροχή (η) rain

γ Γ

γάιδαρος (ο) donkey

γάλα (το) milk

γαλάζιος/α/ο blue ; light blue

γαλακτοπωλείο (το) dairy shop

Γαλλία (η) France

γαλλικός/ή/ό French *(thing)*

Γάλλος/Γαλλίδα (ο/η) French *(man/woman)*

γαλοπούλα (η) turkey

γάμος (ο) wedding ; marriage

γαμήλια δεξίωση wedding reception

γαρίδα (η) shrimp ; prawn

γειά σας hello ; goodbye *(formal)*

γειά σου hello ; goodbye *(informal)*

γεμάτος/η/ο full

γενέθλια (τα) birthday

γενικός/ή/ό general
Γενικό Νοσοκομείο General Hospital

γέννηση (η) birth

Γερμανία (η) Germany

γερμανικός/ή/ό German *(thing)*

Γερμανός/Γερμανίδα (ο/η) German *(man/woman)*

γεμιστός/ή/ό stuffed

γεύμα (το) meal

γέφυρα (η) bridge

για for

γιαγιά (η) grandmother

γιαούρτι (το) yoghurt

γιασεμί (το) jasmine

γιατί; why?

γιατρός (ο/η) doctor

γίνομαι to become
γίνονται δεκτές πιστωτικές κάρτες we accept credit cards

γιορτή (η) festival ; celebration ; name day

γιος (ο) son

γιοτ (το) yacht

γκάζι (το) accelerator *(car)* ; gas

γκαλερί art gallery ; art sales

γκαράζ (το) garage

γκαρσόν (το)/γκαρσόνι (το) waiter

γλυκός/ιά/ό sweet
γλυκό (το)/γλυκά (τα) cakes and pastries ; desserts
γλυκό ταψιού traditional pastries with syrup

γλύπτης/γλύπτρια (ο/η) sculptor

γλυπτική (η) sculpture

γλώσσα (η) tongue ; language ; sole *(fish)*

γονείς (οι) parents

γουιντσέρφινγκ (το) windsurfing

γράμμα (το) letter
γράμμα κατεπείγον express letter
γράμμα συστημένο recorded delivery

γραμμάριο (το) gram

γραμματοκιβώτιο (το) letter box

γραμματόσημο (το) stamp

γραφείο (το) office ; desk
Γραφείο Τουρισμού Tourist Office

γρήγορα quickly

γρίπη (η) influenza

γυαλί (το) glass
γυαλιά (τα) glasses
γυαλιά ηλίου sunglasses

γυαλικός/ή/ό made of glass

γυναίκα (η) woman

ΓΥΝΑΙΚΩΝ LADIES

γύρω round ; about

γωνία (η) corner

δ Δ

δακτυλίδι (το) ring *(for finger)*

δαμάσκηνο (το) plum

δαντέλα (η) lace

δασκάλα (η) teacher *(female)*

δάσκαλος (ο) teacher *(male)*

δάσος (το) forest

δείπνο (το) dinner

δέκα ten

ΔΕΚΕΜΒΡΙΟΣ
DECEMBER

δελτίο (το) card ; coupon
δελτίο αφίξεως arrival card

δελφίνι (το) dolphin
ιπτάμενο δελφίνι hydrofoil

Δελφοί (οι) Delphi

Δεμέστιχα dry wine *(white or red)*

δεν not
δεν δίνεται ρέστα no change given

ΔΕΝ ΛΕΙΤΟΥΡΓΕΙ
OUT OF ORDER

δεξιά right *(opposite of left)*

δέρμα (το) skin ; leather

δεσποινίς/δεσποινίδα (η) Miss

ΔΕΥΤΕΡΑ MONDAY

δεύτερος/η/ο second

δηλητήριο poison

δήλωση (η) announcement
δήλωση συναλλάγματος currency declaration
είδη προς δήλωση goods to declare
ουδέν προς δήλωση nothing to declare

δημαρχείο (το) town hall

δημόσιος/α/ο public
δημόσια έργα road works
δημόσιος κήπος public gardens

δημοτικός/ή/ό public
Δημοτική Αγορά public market
Δημοτική Βιβλιοθήκη Public Library

διάβαση (η) crossing
διάβαση πεζών pedestrian crossing
υπόγεια διάβαση πεζών pedestrian subway

διαβατήριο (το) passport
αριθμός διαβατηρίου passport number
έλεγχος διαβατηρίων passport control

διαβήτης (ο) diabetes

διαδρομή (η) route

δίαιτα (η) diet

διακεκριμένος/η/ο distinguished
διακεκριμένη θέση business class

διακοπές (οι) holidays

διάλειμμα (το) interval ; break

διαμέρισμα (το) flat ; apartment

διανυχτερεύει open all night

διάρκεια (η) duration
κατά τη διάρκεια της ημέρας during the day

διασκέδαση (η) entertainment

κέντρο διασκεδάσεως nightclub

διασταύρωση (η) crossroads ; junction

διατηρώ to keep ; to preserve
διατηρείτε την πόλη καθαρή keep the town clean

διεθνής/ής/ές international

διερμηνέας (ο/η) interpreter

διεύθυνση (η) address

διευθυντής (ο) manager

δικαστήριο (το) court

δικηγόρος (ο/η) lawyer

δίνω to give

διπλός/ή/ό double
διπλό δωμάτιο double room
διπλό κρεββάτι double bed

δισκοθήκη (η) disco *(Cyprus)* ; music collection

δίσκος (ο) record

δίχτυ (το) net

διψώ to be thirsty

δολάριο (το) dollar

δόντι (το) tooth

δράμα (το) drama ; play

δραχμή (η) drachma

δρομολόγιο (το) timetable ; route
δρομολόγια εξωτερικού international routes
δρομολόγια εσωτερικού domestic routes

δρόμος (ο) street ; way

δύση (η) west ; sunset

δυσκοιλιότητα (η) constipation

δυστύχημα (το) accident ; mishap

δυτικός/ή/ό western

Δωδεκάνησα (τα) the Dodecanese

δωμάτιο (το) room

δωρεάν free of charge

δώρο (το) present ; gift

ε Ε

εβδομάδα (η) week

εγγραφή (η) registration

εγγύηση (η) guarantee

έγχρωμος/η/ο coloured
έγχρωμες φωτογραφίες colour photographs

εδώ here

ΕΕ EU

εθνικός/ή/ό national
Εθνικό Θέατρο National Theatre
εθνική οδός motorway
Εθνικός Κήπος National Garden *(in Athens)*
εθνικός ύμνος national anthem

έθνος (το) nation

εθνικότητα nationality

ειδικός/ή/ό special ; specialist

είδος (το) kind ; sort
είδη goods
είδη προς δήλωση goods to declare
είδη εξοχής camping equipment
είδη καπνιστού tobacconist
είδη κήπου garden centre

εισιτήριο (το) ticket
απλό εισιτήριο single ticket
εισιτήριο με επιστροφή return ticket
ατμοπλοϊκό εισιτήριο boat ticket
σιδηροδρομικό εισιτήριο rail ticket
φοιτητικό εισιτήριο student ticket

ΕΙΣΟΔΟΣ ENTRANCE

εισπράκτορας (ο) conductor *(on bus)*
χωρίς εισπράκτορα pay as you enter ; prepaid

εκδόσεις εισιτηρίων ticket office

εκδοτήρια (τα) ticket machines

εκεί there

έκθεση (η) exhibition

εκθεσιακό κέντρο exhibition centre

εκκλησία (η) church ; chapel

έκπτωση (η) discount

ΕΚΠΤΩΣΕΙΣ SALE

εκτελούνται έργα road works

εκτός except ; unless
εκτός λειτουργίας out of order

έλα! come on! *(singular)*

έλάτε! come on! *(plural)*

ελαιόλαδο (το) olive oil

ελαστικό (το) tyre
σέρβις ελαστικών tyre service

ελαττώνω to reduce ; to decrease
ελαττώσατε ταχύτητα reduce speed

έλεγχος (ο) control
έλεγχος διαβατηρίων passport control
έλεγχος εισιτηρίων check-in
έλεγχος ελαστικών tyre check
αγορανομικός έλεγχος approved prices

ΕΛΕΥΘΕΡΟ FREE

ελιά (η) olive ; olive tree

έλκος (το) ulcer

Ελλάδα (η) Greece

Έλληνας/Ελληνίδα (ο/η) Greek *(man/woman)*

ελληνικά (τα) Greek *(language)*

ελληνικός/ή/ό Greek *(thing)*
Ελληνικά Ταχυδρομεία Greek Post Office (ELTA)
Ελληνική Δημοκρατία Republic of Greece
Ελληνικής κατασκευής Made in Greece
Ελληνικός Οργανισμός Τουρισμού Greek Tourist Organisation (EOT)
Ελληνικό προϊόν product of Greece

ΕΛΞΑΤΕ PULL

εμπρός forward ; in front

εμφανίζω to develop *(film)*

εμφάνιση (η) film development

εναντίον against

έναρξη (η) opening ; beginning

ένας/μία/ένα one

ένδυμα (το) article of clothing
έτοιμα ενδύματα ready-to-wear clothing

ένεση (η) injection

ενήλικος (ο) adult

εννέα/εννιά nine

ενοικιάζω to rent ; to hire
ενοικιάζεται to let

ενοικιάσεις for hire

ενοίκιο (το) rent

ενορία (η) parish

εντάξει all right ; OK

εντομοκτόνο (το) insecticide

έντυπο (το) form *(to fill in)*

έξι six

ΕΞΟΔΟΣ EXIT

εξοχή (η) countryside

εξυπηρέτηση (η) service

εξυπηρετώ to serve

έξω out ; outside

εξωλέμβιες (οι) outboard motorboats

εξώστης (ο) circle ; balcony *(theatre)*

εξωτερικός/ή/ό external
το εξωτερικό abroad

εξωτερικού letters abroad *(on postbox)*
πτήσεις εξωτερικού international flights

ΕΟΚ EEC (EC)

ΕΟΤ Greek/Hellenic Tourist Organization

επάγγελμα (το) occupation ; profession

επείγον/επείγουσα urgent ; express
επείγοντα περιστατικά casualty department

επιβάτης/τρια (ο/η) passenger
διερχόμενοι επιβάτες passengers in transit

επιβεβαιώνω to confirm

επιβίβαση (η) boarding
κάρτα επιβιβάσεως boarding card

επιδόρπιο (το) dessert

επικίνδυνος/η/ο dangerous

επίσης also ; the same to you

επισκεπτήριο (το) visiting hours

επισκέπτης (ο) visitor

επισκευή (η) repair
επισκευές repairs

επίσκεψη (η) visit
ώρες επισκέψεων visiting hours

επιστολή (η) letter
επιστολή επείγουσα urgent or express letter
επιστολή συστημένη registered letter

επιστροφή (η) return ; return ticket
επιστροφή νομισμάτων returned coins
επιστροφές returned goods ; refunds

επιταγή (η) cheque ; invoice
ταχυδρομική επιταγή postal order

επόμενος/η/ο next

εποχή (η) season

επτά/εφτά seven

Επτάνησα (τα) Ionian Islands

επώνυμο (το) surname ; last name

έργα (τα) works

έργα χειρός (τα) handcrafts

εργαλείο (το) tool

έργο (κινηματογραφικό) film

εργοστάσιο (το) factory

έργο τέχνης (το) artwork

έρχομαι to come

ερώτηση (η) question

εστιατόριο (το) restaurant

εσώρουχα (τα) underwear ; lingerie

εσωτερικός/ή/ό internal
εσωτερικού inland *(on post boxes)* ; domestic
πτήσεις εσωτερικού domestic flights

εταιρ(ε)ία (η) company ; firm

έτος (το) year

έτσι so ; like this

ευθεία (η) straight line
κατ΄ ευθείαν straight on

εύθυνη (η) responsibility

ευκαιρία (η) opportunity ; bargain

ευκολία (η) ease ; convenience
ευκολίες πληρωμής credit terms

ευρωπαϊκός/ή/ό European

Ευρώπη (η) Europe

ευχαριστώ thank you

εφημερίδα (η) newspaper

ζ Ζ

ζάλη (η) dizziness

ζαμπόν (το) ham

ζάχαρη (η) sugar

ζαχαροπλαστείο (το) patisserie

ζέστη (η) heat
κάνει ζέστη it's hot

ζευγάρι (το) couple

ζημιά (η) damage
πάσα ζημιά τιμωρείται anyone causing damage will be prosecuted

ζητώ to ask ; to seek

ζυγαριά (η) scales *(for weighing)*

ζυμαρικά (τα) pasta products

ζωγραφική (η) painting *(art)*

ζώνη (η) belt
ζώνη ασφαλείας safety belt ; seat belt

ζώο (το) animal

ζωολογικός κήπος (ο) zoo

η Η

η the *(with feminine nouns)*

ή or

ηλεκτρικός/ή/ό electrical

ηλεκτρισμός (ο) electricity

ηλεκτρονικός/ή/ό electronic

ηλιακός/ή/ό solar

ηλίαση (η) sunstroke

ηλικία (η) age

ηλιοβασίλεμα (το) sunset

ηλιοθεραπεία (η) sunbathing

ήλιος (ο) sun

Ήλιος a dry white wine from Rhodes

ημέρα (η) day

ημερήσιος/α/ο daily

ΗΜΕΡΟΜΗΝΙΑ DATE

ημερομηνία αναχωρήσεως date of departure
ημερομηνία αφίξεως date of arrival
ημερομηνία γεννήσεως date of birth
ημερομηνία λήξης expiry date

ημιδιατροφή (η) half board

Ηνωμένο Βασίλειο (το) United Kingdom (UK)

ΗΠΑ USA

Ηνωμένες Πολιτείες της Αμερικής United States of America

ησυχία (η) calmness ; quiet

ήσυχος/η/ο calm ; quiet

θ Θ

θάλασσα (η) sea

θαλάσσιος/α/ο of the sea
θαλάσσιο αλεξίπτωτο paragliding
θαλάσσιο σκι water-skiing

θέατρο (το) theatre

θέλω to want ; to need

Θεός (ο) God

θεός/θεά (ο/η) god ; goddess

Θεοτόκος (η) Virgin Mary

θεραπεία (η) treatment

θερινός/ή/ό summer
θερινές διακοπές summer holidays
θερινό θέρετρο summer resort

θέρμανση (η) heating

θερμίδα (η) calorie

θερμοστάτης (ο) thermostat

θέση (η) place ; seat
διακεκριμένη θέση business class
κράτηση θέσης seat reservation
οικονομική θέση economy class
πρώτη θέση first class

Θεσσαλονίκη (η) Salonica/Thessaloniki

θύελλα (η) storm

θύρα (η) gate *(airport)*

θυρίδα (η) ticket window

θυρωρείο (το) porter's lodge

ι Ι

ΙΑΝΟΥΑΡΙΟΣ JANUARY

ιατρική περίθαλψη (η) medical treatment

ιατρός (ο/η) doctor

ιδιοκτήτης/τρια (ο/η) owner

ΙΔΙΩΤΙΚΟΣ ΧΩΡΟΣ PRIVATE

Ιόνιο Πέλαγος (το) Ionian sea

Ιόνιοι Νήσοι (οι) Ionian Islands

ΙΟΥΛΙΟΣ JULY

ΙΟΥΝΙΟΣ JUNE

ιππασία (η) horse riding

ιπποδρομίες (οι) horse racing

ιππόδρομος (ο) racetrack

ιππόκαμπος (ο) sea-horse

ιπτάμενο δελφίνι hydrofoil (flying dolphin)

Ισθμός της Κορίνθου Corinth canal

ΙΣΟΓΕΙΟ GROUND FLOOR

ισοτιμία (η) exchange rate

Ισπανία (η) Spain

ισπανικός/ή/ό Spanish *(thing)*

Ισπανός/ίδα (ο/η) Spaniard *(man/woman)*

ιστιοπλοΐα (η) sailing

Ιταλία (η) Italy

ιταλικός/ή/ό Italian *(thing)*

Ιταλός/ίδα (ο/η) Italian *(man/woman)*

ιχθυοπωλείο (το) fishmonger's

κ Κ

κάβα (η) wine merchant; off-licence

κάβουρας (ο) crab

καζίνο (το) casino

καθαριστήριο (το) dry-cleaner's

καθαρίστρια (η) cleaner

καθαρός/ή/ό clean

κάθε every ; each

καθεδρικός ναός (ο) cathedral

καθημερινός/ή/ό daily
καθημερινά δρομολόγια daily departures

κάθισμα (το) seat

καθολικός/ή/ό Catholic ; total

καθυστέρηση (η) delay

και and

καιρός (ο) weather ; time

κακάο (το) cocoa ; chocolate flavour

κακοκαιρία (η) bad weather

καλά well ; all right

καλάθι (το) basket

καλαμαράκια (τα) small squid *(dish)*

καλαμάρι (το) squid ; calamari

καλημέρα good morning

καληνύχτα good night

καλησπέρα good evening

καλοκαίρι (το) summer

καλοριφέρ (το) central heating ; radiator

καλοψημένο well done *(meat)*

καλσόν (το) tights

κάλτσα (η) sock ; stocking

καμαριέρα (η) chambermaid

κάμερα (η) camcorder

καμπίνα (η) cabin

κανάλι (το) canal ; channel *(TV)*

κανέλα (η) cinnamon

κανένας no-one

κάνω to do

καπέλο (το) hat

καπετάνιος (ο) captain *(of ship)*

καπνίζω to smoke
μην καπνίζετε no smoking

καπνιστός/ή/ό smoked
καπνιστός σολομός smoked salmon
καπνιστό χοιρινό smoked ham
καπνιστό ψάρι smoked fish
καπνιστό τυρί smoked cheese

κάπνισμα (το) smoking
απαγορεύεται το κάπνισμα no smoking

καπνιστής (ο) smoker
είδη καπνιστού tobacconist's

καπνοπωλείο (το) tobacconist

καπνός (ο) smoke

κάποτε sometimes ; one time

καράβι (το) boat ; ship

καραμέλα (η) sweet

κάρβουνο (το) coal
στα κάρβουνα charcoal-grilled

καρδιά (η) heart

καρναβάλι (το) carnival

καροτσάκι (το) pushchair

καρπούζι (το) watermelon

κάρτα (η) card ; postcard
κάρτα απεριόριστων διαδρομών rail card for unlimited monthly travel
κάρτα επιβιβάσεως boarding card
επαγγελματική κάρτα business card
μόνο με κάρτα cardholders only
πιστωτική κάρτα credit card
κάρτα αναλήψεως ATM card ; cash card

καρτοτηλέφωνο (το) card phone

καρτποστάλ (το) postcard

καρύδα (η) coconut

καρύδι (το) walnut

καρχαρίας (ο) shark

κασέτα (η) tape *(for recording)*

κασετόφωνο (το) tape recorder

κάστανο (το) chestnut

κάστρο (το) castle ; fortress

κατάθεση (η) deposit ; statement to police

καταιγίδα (η) storm

καταλαβαίνω to understand
καταλαβαίνεις; do you understand? *(familiar form)*
καταλαβαίνετε; do you understand? *(polite form)*

κατάλογος (ο) list ; menu ; directory
τηλεφωνικός κατάλογος telephone directory

καταπραϋντικό (το) tranquillizer

κατασκήνωση (η) camping

κατάσταση (η) condition ; situation

κατάστημα (το) shop

κατάστρωμα (το) deck

κατεπείγον/ κατεπείγουσα urgent ; express

κατεψυγμένος/η/ο frozen

κατηγορία (η) class *(of hotel)*

κατσαρόλα (η) saucepan ; pot

κατσίκα (η) goat

κατσικάκι (το) kid *(young goat)*

κάτω under ; lower; down

καύσιμα (τα) fuel

καφέ brown

καφενείο (το) coffee house

καφές (ο) coffee *(usually Greek)*
καφές βαρύς γλυκός very sweet strong coffee
καφές γλυκός sweet coffee
καφές μέτριος medium sweet coffee
καφές σκέτος strong black coffee
καφές στιγμιαίος instant coffee *(Nescafé)*
καφές φραπέ iced coffee *(Nescafé)*

καφετερία (η) cafeteria

καφετιέρα (η) coffee maker

κέικ (το) cake

κεντρικός/ή/ό central

ΚΕΝΤΡΟ CENTRE

κέντρο (το) centre
κέντρο αλλοδαπών immigration office
κέντρο διασκεδάσεως nightclub
κέντρο εκδόσεως ticket office
κέντρο υγείας health centre
αθλητικό κέντρο sports centre
τηλεφωνικό κέντρο telephone exchange

κεράσι (το) cherry

Κέρκυρα (η) Corfu

κέρμα (το) coin

κερνώ to buy a drink

κεφάλι (το) head

κεφτέδες (οι) meatballs

κήπος (ο) garden
δημόσιος κήπος public garden
ζωολογικός κήπος zoo

κιβώτιο (το) large box
κιβώτιο ταχυτήτων gearbox

κιλό (το) kilo

κίνδυνος (ο) danger
κίνδυνος θανάτου extreme danger

κινηματογράφος (ο) cinema

κινητό (το) mobile phone

κινητήρας (ο) engine

κίτρινος/η/ο yellow

κλαμπ (το) club

κλειδί (το) key ; spanner

κλείνω to close

ΚΛΕΙΣΤΟ CLOSED

κλέφτης (ο) thief

κλέφτικο (το) lamb dish

κλήση (η) summons

κλήση τροχαίας (η) traffic ticket

κλίμα (το) climate

κλινική (η) clinic ; hospital ; ward

κοιμάμαι to sleep

κοινωνικός/ή/ό social
κοινωνικές ασφαλίσεις national insurance

κόκκινος/η/ο red

κολοκυθάκι (το) courgette

κολοκύθι (το) marrow

κόλπος (ο) gulf ; vagina

κολύμπι (το) swimming

κολυμπώ to swim

κολώνα (η) pillar ; column

κομμωτήριο (το) hairdresser's

κομμωτής/μώτρια (ο/η) hairstylist

κομπόστα (η) stewed fruit ; compote

κομωδία (η) comedy

κονιάκ (το) cognac ; brandy

κονσέρβα (η) tinned food

κονσέρτο (το) concert

κοντά near

κόρη (η) daughter

κορίτσι (το) young girl

κόρνα (η) horn *(in car)*

κόσμημα (το) jewellery

κοσμηματαπωλείο (το) jewellery shop

κοστούμι (το) man's suit

κότα (η) hen

κοτολέτα (η) chop

κοτόπουλο (το) chicken

κουβέρτα (η) blanket

κουζίνα (η) kitchen ; cuisine
ελληνική κουζίνα Greek cuisine

κουμπί (το) button

κουνέλι (το) rabbit

κουνούπι (το) mosquito

κουνουπίδι (το) cauliflower

κουπί (το) oar

κουρείο (το) barber's shop

κουταλάκι (το) teaspoon

κουτάλι (το) tablespoon

κουτί (το) box

κραγιόν (το) lipstick

κρασί (το) wine
κρασί γλυκό sweet wine
κρασί ξηρό dry wine
κρασί κόκκινο red wine
κρασί λευκό white wine
κρασί ροζέ rosé wine

κρατήσεις (οι) bookings ; reservations
κρατήσεις ξενοδοχείων hotel bookings

κράτηση (η) reservation
κράτηση θέσης seat reservation

κρέας (το) meat
κρέας αρνίσιο lamb
κρέας βοδινό beef
κρέας μοσχαρίσιο beef
κρέας χοιρινό pork

κρεββάτι (το) bed

κρεββατοκάμαρα (η) bedroom

κρέμα (η) cream

κρεμμύδι (το) onion

κρεοπωλείο (το) butcher's shop

Κρήτη (η) Crete

κρουαζιέρα (η) cruise

κρύος/α/ο cold

κτηνιατρείο (το) veterinary surgery

κυβέρνηση (η) government

κυβερνήτης (ο) captain *(of aircraft)*

Κυκλάδες (οι) Cyclades *(islands)*

κύκλος (ο) circle

κυκλοφορία (η) traffic ; circulation

κυλικείο (το) canteen ; cafeteria

Κύπρος (η) Cyprus

Κύπριος/Κυπρία (ο/η) from Cyprus ; Cypriot *(man/woman)*

κυρία (η) Mrs ; lady

ΚΥΡΙΑΚΗ SUNDAY

κύριος (ο) Mr ; gentleman

κωδικός (ο) code
ταχυδρομικός κωδικός postcode
τηλεφωνικός κωδικός dialling code ; area code

λ Λ

λάδι (το) oil
λάδι ελιάς olive oil

λαϊκός/ή/ό popular ; folk
λαϊκή αγορά market
λαϊκή μουσική popular music
λαϊκή τέχνη folk art

λάστιχο (το) tyre ; rubber ; elastic

λαχανικά (τα) vegetables

λαχείο (το) lottery ticket

λεμονάδα (η) lemon squash ; lemonade

λεμόνι (το) lemon
χυμός λεμονιού lemon juice

λεξικό (το) dictionary

λεπτό (το) minute

λεπτός/ή/ό thin ; slim

λευκός/ή/ό white

λεφτά (τα) money

λεωφορείο (το) bus

λεωφόρος (η) avenue

λήξη (η) expiry

λιανικός/ή/ό retail
λιανική πώληση retail sale

λίγος/η/ο a few ; a little
λίγο ψημένο rare *(meat)*

λικέρ (το) liqueur

λιμάνι (το) port ; harbour

Λιμενικό Σώμα (το) coastguard

λίμνη (η) lake

λίρα (η) pound

λίτρο (το) litre

λογαριασμός (ο) bill

λουκάνικο (το) sausage

λουκανόπιτα (η) sausage pie

λουκούμι (το) Turkish delight

λουλούδι (το) flower

λύσσα (η) rabies

μ Μ

μαγαζί (το) shop

μαγειρεύω to cook

μαγιό (το) swimsuit

μαϊντανός (ο) parsley

ΜΑΙΟΣ MAY

μακαρόνια (τα) macaroni ; spaghetti dishes

μάλιστα yes ; of course

μαλλί (το) wool

μαλλιά (τα) hair

μάλλινος/η/ο woollen

μαμά (η) mum

μανιτάρια (τα) mushrooms

μανταρίνι (το) mandarin orange ; tangerine

μαντήλι (το) handkerchief

μαξιλάρι (το) pillow ; cushion

μαργαρίνη (η) margarine

μαργαριτάρι (το) pearl

μάρμαρο (το) marble

μαρμάρινος/η/ο made of marble

μαρμελάδα (η) jam

μαρούλι (το) lettuce

ΜΑΡΤΙΟΣ MARCH

μαύρος/η/ο black

μαχαίρι (το) knife

μαχαιροπήρουνα (τα) cutlery

με with

μεγάλος/η/ο large ; big

μέγαρο (το) hall ; palace ; block of apartments
μέγαρο μουσικής concert hall
μέγαρο αστυνομίας police headquarters

μέγεθος (το) size

μεζεδάκια (τα) selection of appetizers and salads served as a starter *(like tapas)*

μέλι (το) honey

μελιτζάνα (η) aubergine ; eggplant

μέλος (το) member

μενού (το) menu

μέρα (η) day

μερίδα (η) portion

μέσα in ; inside

μεσάνυχτα (τα) midnight

μεσημέρι (το) midday

μεσημεριανό (το) midday meal

Μεσόγειος (η) Mediterranean Sea

μέσω via

μετά after

μετάξι (το) silk

μεταξύ between ; among
εν τω μεταξύ meanwhile

μεταφράζω to translate

μεταχειρισμένος/η/ο used ; second-hand

μετεωρολογικό δελτίο (το) weather forecast

μετρητά (τα) cash

μετρό (το) underground *(railway)*

μη... do not...
μη καπνίζετε no smoking
μην κόπτετε άνθη do not pick flowers
μην πατάτε το πράσινο keep off the grass
μη ρίπτετε σκουπίδια no dumping *(rubbish)*
μη σταθμεύετε no parking

μηδέν zero

μήλο (το) apple

μηλόπιτα (η) apple pie

μήνας (ο) month
μήνας του μέλιτος honeymoon

μητέρα (η) mother

μηχανή (η) machine ; engine

μηχανικός (ο) mechanic ; engineer

μία a(n) ; one *(with feminine nouns)*

μικρός/ή/ό small

μιλάω/μιλω to speak

μόδα (η) fashion

μολύβι (το) pencil

μόλυνση (η) infection ; pollution

μοναστήρι (το) monastery

μονόδρομος (ο) one-way street

μονοπάτι (το) path

μόνος/η/ο alone ; only
μόνο είσοδος/έξοδος entrance/exit only

μονός/ή/ό single ; alone

μοσχάρι (το) calf ; beef

μοτοσυκλέτα (η) motorcycle

ΜΟΥΣΕΙΟ MUSEUM

Αρχαιολογικό Μουσείο Archaeological Museum
Μουσείο Λαϊκής Τέχνης Folk Museum

μουσική (η) music

μουστάρδα (η) mustard

μπακάλης (ο) grocer

μπαμπάς (ο) dad

μπανάνα (η) banana

μπάνιο (το) bathroom ; bath

μπαρμπούνι (το) red mullet

μπαταρία (η) battery

μπέικον (το) bacon

μπιζέλια (τα) peas

μπίρα (η) beer

μπισκότο (το) biscuit

μπλε blue

μπλούζα (η) blouse

μπογιά (η) paint

μπουζούκι (το) bouzouki

μπουκάλι (το) bottle
μεγάλο μπουκάλι large bottle
μικρό μπουκάλι half-bottle

μπουρνούζι (το) bathrobe

μπριζόλα (η) chop ; steak

μπύρα (η) beer

Μυκήναι Mycenae

Μυκηναϊκός πολιτισμός (ο) Mycenean civilization

μύτη (η) nose

μωρό (το) baby
 για **μωρά** for babies

μωσαϊκό (το) mosaic

ν Ν

ναι yes

ναός (ο) temple ; church
 καθεδρικός ναός cathedral

ναύλο (το) boat fare

νάιλον (το) nylon

ναυλωμένος/η/ο chartered
 ναυλωμένη πτήση charter flight

ναυτία (η) travel sickness

ναυτικός όμιλος (ο) sailing club

νεκρός/ή/ό dead

νεκροταφείο (το) cemetery

νεοελληνικά (τα) Modern Greek

νερό (το) water
 επιτραπέζιο νερό still mineral water
 μεταλλικό νερό mineral water
 πόσιμο νερό drinking water

νεφρός (ο) kidney

νηπιαγωγείο (το) nursery school

νησί (το) island

νησίδα (η) traffic island

νίκη (η) victory

ΝΟΕΜΒΡΙΟΣ
NOVEMBER

νοίκι (το) rent

νομίζω to think

νόμισμα (το) coin ; currency
 επιστροφή νομισμάτων returned coins

νομισματοδέχτης (ο) coin-operated phone

νοσοκομείο (το) hospital

νοσοκόμος/α (ο/η) nurse

νότιος/α/ο southern

νότος (ο) south

νούμερο (το) number

ντομάτα (η) tomato

ντουζίνα (η) dozen

ντους (το) shower *(in bath)*

νυκτερινός/ή/ό all-night *(chemists, etc)*

νύχτα (η) night

ξ Ξ

ξεκουράζω to have a rest ; to relax

ξεναγός (ο/η) guide

ξενοδοχείο (το) hotel
 κρατήσεις ξενοδοχείων hotel reservations

ξένος/η/ο strange ; foreign
 ξένος/η (ο/η) foreigner ; visitor

ξενώνας (ο) guesthouse

ξέρω to know

ξεχνώ to forget

ξηρός/ή/ό dry
 ξηροί καρποί dried fruit and nuts

ξιφίας (ο) swordfish

ξύδι (το) vinegar

ξύλο (το) wood

ξυριστική μηχανή (η) safety razor

ο Ο

οδηγία (η) instruction
 οδηγίες χρήσεως instructions for use

οδηγός (ο) driver ; guidebook

οδηγώ to drive

οδική βοήθεια (η) breakdown service

οδοντιατρείο (το) dental surgery

οδοντίατρος (ο/η) dentist

οδοντόβουρτσα (η) toothbrush

οδοντόκρεμα (η) toothpaste

οδοντοστοιχία (η) denture(s)

οδός (η) road ; street

οικογένεια (η) family

οικονομική θέση (η) economy class

οινομαγειρείον (το) licensed restaurant with traditional cuisine

οινοπνευματώδη ποτά (τα) spirits

οκτώ/οχτώ eight

ΟΚΤΩΒΡΙΟΣ OCTOBER

ολισθηρόν οδόστρωμα (το) slippery road surface

όλος/η/ο all of

Ολυμπία (η) Olympia

ολυμπιακός/ή/ό Olympic
Ολυμπιακή Αεροπορία Olympic Airways
Ολυμπιακό Στάδιο Olympic stadium
Ολυμπιακοί Αγώνες Olympic games

Όλυμπος (ο) Mount Olympus

ομελέτα (η) omelette

όμιλος (ο) club
ναυτικός όμιλος sailing club

ομπρέλα (η) umbrella

όνομα (το) name

ονοματεπώνυμο (το) full name

όπερα (η) opera

οπτικός (ο) optician

οργανισμός (ο) organization
Οργανισμός Σιδηροδρόμων Ελλάδος (ΟΣΕ) Greek Railways

οργανωμένος/η/ο organized
οργανωμένα ταξίδια organized tours

ορειβασία (η) mountaineering

ορεκτικό (το) starter ; appetizer

όρεξη (η) appetite
καλή όρεξη enjoy your meal!

ορθόδοξος/η/ο orthodox

όρος (ο) condition
όροι ενοικιάσεως conditions of hire

όροφος (ο) floor ; storey

ΟΣΕ Greek Railways

ΟΤΕ Greek Telecom

ούζο (το) ouzo

ουρά (η) tail ; queue

όχι no

π Π

παγάκι (το) ice cube

παϊδάκι (το) lamb chop

πάγος (ο) ice

παίρνω to take

παγωμένος/η/ο frozen

παγωτό (το) ice cream

παιδικός/ή/ό for children
παιδικά children's wear
παιδικός σταθμός crèche

πακέτο (το) parcel ; packet

παλτό (το) coat

πάνα (η) nappy

Παναγία (η) the Virgin Mary

πανεπιστήμιο (το) university

πανσιόν (η) guesthouse

πάντα/πάντοτε always

παντελόνι (το) trousers

παντοπωλείο (το) grocer's

πάνω up

παπάς (ο) priest

πάπλωμα (το) duvet

παππούς (ο) grandfather

παπούτσι (το) shoe

παραγγελία (η) order

παραγγέλνω to order

παραγωγή (η) production
Ελληνικής παραγωγής produce of Greece

παράθυρο (το) window

παρακαλώ please

παρακαμπτήριος (ο) by-pass

παραλία (η) seashore ; beach

παράξενος/η/ο strange

ΠΑΡΑΣΚΕΥΗ FRIDAY

παράσταση (η) performance

παρέα (η) company ; group

Παρθενώνας (ο) the Parthenon

πάρκο (το) park

παρμπρίζ (το) windscreen

πάστα (η) pastry ; cake

παστέλι (το) honey and sesame seed bar

Πάσχα (το) Easter

πατάτα (η) potato
πατάτες πουρέ creamed/mashed potatoes
πατάτες τηγανητές chips
πατάτες φούρνου roast potatoes

πατέρας (ο) father

παυσίπονο (το) painkiller

πάω to go

πεζοδρόμιο (το) pavement

ΠΕΖΟΔΡΟΜΟΣ
PEDESTRIAN AREA

πεζός (ο) pedestrian

Πειραιάς (ο) Piraeus

πελάτης/τίσσα (ο/η) customer

Πελοπόννησος (η) Peloponnese

ΠΕΜΠΤΗ THURSDAY

πένα (η) pen ; penny

πεπόνι (το) melon

περιοδικό (το) magazine

περιοχή (η) area

περίπατος (ο) walk

περίπτερο (το) kiosk

περιστέρι (το) pigeon ; dove

πέτρα (η) stone

πετρέλαιο (το) diesel fuel

πετρινός/ή/ό made of stone

πετσέτα (η) towel

πεύκο (το) pine tree

πηγαίνω to go

πιάτο (το) plate ; dish

ΠΙΕΣΑΤΕ PUSH

πίεση (η) pressure
πίεση αίματος blood pressure

πιλότος (ο) pilot

πινακίδα (η) sign ; number plate
πινακίδα κυκλοφορίας number plate

πινακοθήκη (η) art gallery ; collection of paintings

πίπα (η) pipe

πιπέρι (το) pepper
πιπεριές γεμιστές stuffed peppers

πισίνα (η) swimming pool

πιστοποιητικό (το) certificate

πιστωτική κάρτα (η) credit card

πίσω behind ; back

πίτα (η) pie

πιζάμα (η) pyjamas

πίτσα (η) pizza

πιτσαρία (η) pizzeria

πλαζ (η) beach

πλάι next to

πλατεία (η) square

πλατίνες (οι) points *(in car)*

πλεκτά (τα) knitwear

ΠΛΗΡΟΦΟΡΙΕΣ
INFORMATION

πληροφορίες δρομολογίων travel information

πλήρωμα (το) crew
τα μέλη του πληρώματος crew members

πληρωμή (η) payment
ευκολίες πληρωμής credit facilities
προς πληρωμή insert money

πληρώνω to pay

πλοίο (το) ship

πλυντήριο (το) washing machine
πλυντήριο αυτοκινήτων car wash
πλυντήριο πιάτων dish washer

ποδηλάτης (ο) cyclist

ποδήλατο (το) bicycle
ποδήλατο της θάλασσας pedalo

πόδι (το) foot ; leg

ποδόσφαιρο (το) football

ποιος/ποια/ποιο who ; which

ποιότητα (η) quality

πόλη (η) town ; city

πολίτης (ο) citizen

πολιτική (η) politics

πολυκατάστημα (το) department store

πολυκατοικία (η) block of flats

πολύς/πολλή/πολύ much ; many

πονόδοντος (ο) toothache

πονοκέφαλος (ο) headache

πονόλαιμος (ο) sore throat

πόνος (ο) pain

πόρτα (η) door

πορτοκαλάδα (η) orange squash

πορτοκάλι (το) orange
χυμός πορτοκαλιού orange juice

πορτοφόλι (το) wallet

πόσα; how many?

πόσο; how much?
πόσο κάνει; how much is it?
πόσο κοστίζει; how much does it cost?

ποσοστό (το) rate ; percentage
ποσοστό υπηρεσίας service charge
συμπεριλαμβανομένου ποσοστού υπηρεσίας service included

ποσότητα (η) quantity

ποτάμι (το) river

πότε; when?

ποτέ never

ποτήρι (το) glass *(for drinking)*

ποτό (το) drink

πού; where?

πουκάμισο (το) shirt

πούλμαν (το) coach

πουλώ to sell

πουρμπουάρ (το) tip *(to waiter, etc)*

πούρο (το) cigar

πράκτορας (ο) agent

πρακτορείο (το) agency

πράσινος/η/ο green

πρατήριο (το) specialist shop
πρατήριο βενζίνης petrol station
πρατήριο άρτου baker's

πρεσβεία (η) embassy

πρίζα (η) socket

πριν before

πρόγραμμα (το) programme

πρόεδρος (ο) president
προεδρικό μέγαρο presidential palace

προειδοποίηση (η) warning

προϊόν (το) product
Ελληνικό προϊόν product of Greece

προκαταβολή (η) deposit

προκρατήσεις (οι) advance bookings

προορισμός (ο) destination

προπληρώνω to pay in advance

Προ-πο (το) Greek football pools

προσγείωση (η) landing

προσδεθείτε fasten safety belts

πρόσκληση (η) invitation

προσοχή (η) attention

προτεστάντης (ο) protestant

πρόστιμο (το) fine

πρόχειρος/η/ο handy ; impromptu ; rough
πρόχειρο φαγητό snack

πρωί (το) morning

πρωινός/ή/ό morning

πρωινό (το) breakfast

πρωτεύουσα (η) capital city

πρωτομαγιά (η) May Day

πρώτος/η/ο first
πρώτες βοήθειες first aid
πρώτη θέση first class

πρωτοχρονιά (η) New Years Day

πτήση (η) flight
πτήσεις εξωτερικού international flights
πτήσεις εσωτερικού domestic flights
αριθμός πτήσης flight number
ναυλωμένη πτήση charter flight
τακτικές πτήσεις scheduled flights

πυροσβεστήρας (ο) fire extinguisher

πυροσβέστης (ο) fireman

πυροσβεστική (η) fire brigade
πυροσβεστική υπηρεσία fire service
πυροσβεστικός σταθμός fire station

πώληση (η) sale
λιανική πώληση retail sale
χονδρική πώληση wholesale

πωλητής/ήτρια(ο/η) sales assistant

ΠΩΛΕΙΤΑΙ FOR SALE

πώς; how?

ρ Ρ

ρεζέρβα (η) spare wheel

ρεσεψιόν (η) reception *(desk)*

ρέστα (τα) change *(money)*

ρετσίνα (η) retsina

ρεύμα (το) current ; electricity

ρόδα (η) wheel

ροδάκινο (το) peach

ρόδι (το) pomegranate

Ρόδος (η) Rhodes (island)

ρολόι (το) watch ; clock

ρούμι (το) rum

ρύζι (το) rice

ρυμουλκώ to tow

σ ς Σ

ΣΑΒΒΑΤΟ SATURDAY

Σαββατοκύριακο (το) weekend

σακάκι (το) jacket *(menswear)*

σαλάμι (το) salami

σαλάτα (η) salad

σαλιγκάρι (το) snail

σάλτσα (η) sauce

σαμπάνια (η) champagne

σαμπουάν (το) shampoo

σάντουιτς (το) sandwich

σαπούνι (το) soap

σβήνω to extinguish
σβήσατε τα τσιγάρα σας extinguish cigarettes

ΣΕΠΤΕΜΒΡΙΟΣ
SEPTEMBER

σέρβις (το) service

σεφ (ο) chef

σήμα (το) sign ; signal
σήμα κατατεθέν trademark
σήμα κινδύνου emergency signal

σήμερα today

σιγά slowly

σιδηρόδρομος (ο) railway
σιδηροδρομικός σταθμός railway station
σιδηροδρομικώς by rail

σκάλα (η) ladder ; staircase

σκαλί (το) step

σκέτος/η/ο plain
καφές σκέτος black coffee

σκηνή (η) tent ; stage

σκι (το) ski
θαλάσσιο σκι water-skiing

σκοινί (το) rope

σκορδαλιά (η) garlic and potato mash

σκόρδο (ο) garlic

σκουπίδια (τα) rubbish ; refuse

σκυλί (το) dog

Σκωτία (η) Scotland

σκωτσέζικος/η/ο (η) Scottish *(thing)*

Σκωτσέζος/Σκωτσέζα (ο/η) Scotsman/Scotswoman

σόδα (η) soda

σοκολάτα (η) chocolate

σολομός (ο) salmon

σόμπα (η) stove ; heater

σούβλα (η) skewer

σουβλάκι (το) meat cooked on skewer

σούπα (η) soup

σοφέρ(ο) chauffeur

σπανάκι (το) spinach

σπανακόπιτα (η) spinach pie

σπαράγγι (το) asparagus

σπεσιαλιτέ της κουζίνας todays special dish

σπίρτο (το) match

σπίτι (το) house ; home

σπιτικός/ή/ο homemade

σπορ (τα) sports

Σποράδες (οι) the Sporades

στάδιο (το) stadium ; stage

σταθμεύω to park
ανώτατος χρόνος σταθμεύσεως maximum parking time
απαγορεύεται η στάθμευση no parking
μη σταθμεύετε no parking
χώρος σταθμεύσεως parking area

σταθμός (ο) station
πυροσβεστικός σταθμός fire station
σιδηροδρομικός σταθμός railway station
σταθμός υπεραστικών λεωφορείων bus station *(intercity)*

σταμάτα! stop!

στάση (η) stop
στάση εργασίας strike
στάσις ΗΛΠΑΠ trolley bus stop
στάση λεωφορείου bus stop

σταυροδρόμι (το) crossroads

σταφίδα (η) raisin

σταφύλι (το) grape

στεγνοκαθαριστήριο (το) dry-cleaner's

στιγμή (η) moment

στοά (η) arcade

στροφή (η) turn ; bend

στρώμα (το) mattress

στυλό (η) pen

συγγνώμη sorry ; excuse me

συγχαρητήρια congratulations

συγχωρώ:με συγχωρείτε excuse me

σύζυγος (ο/η) husband/wife

σύκο (το) fig

συκώτι (το) liver

συλλυπητήρια (τα) condolences

συμπεριλαμβάνω to include

συμπλέκτης (ο) clutch *(of car)*

συμπληρώνω to fill in

σύμπτωμα (το) symptom

συμφωνία (η) agreement

συμφωνώ to agree

συνάλλαγμα (το) foreign exchange
 δήλωση συναλλάγματος currency declaration
 η τιμή του συναλλάγματος exchange rate

συνάντηση (η) meeting

συναντώ to meet

συναυλία (η) concert

συνεργείο (το) workshop ; garage for car repairs
 συνεργείο αυτοκινήτων car repairs

σύνθεση (η) ingredients ; flower arrangement

σύνολο (το) total

σύνορα (τα) border ; frontier

συνταγή (η) prescription ; recipe

ΣΥΡΑΤΕ PULL

σύστημα κλιματισμού (το) air conditioning

συστημένη επιστολή (η) recorded delivery

συχνά often

σφράγισμα (το) filling *(in tooth)*

σχηματίζω to form
 σχηματίστε τον αριθμό dial the number

σχολείο (το) school

σχολή (η) school
 σχολή οδηγών driving school
 σχολή σκι ski school

σώζω to save ; to rescue

σώμα (το) body

σωσίβιο (το) life jacket

τ Τ

ταβέρνα (η) tavern with traditional food and wine

ταινία (η) film ; strip ; tape

ΤΑΜΕΙΟ CASH DESK

ταμίας (ο/η) cashier

ταμιευτήριο (το) savings bank

ταξί (το) taxi
 αγοραίο ταξί minicab *(no meter)*
 γραφείο ταξί taxi office
 ραδιό ταξί radio taxi

ταξίδι (το) journey ; tour
 καλό ταξίδι have a good trip
 ταξιδιωτικό γραφείο travel agent
 οργανωμένα ταξίδια organized tours

ταξιθέτης/τρια (ο/η) theatre attendant

ταραμοσαλάτα (η) taramosalata

ταυτότητα (η) identity ; identity card

ταχεία (η) express train

ταχυδρομείο (το) post office
Ελληνικά Ταχυδρομεία (ΕΛΤΑ) Greek Post Office

ταχυδρομικά (τέλη) postage
ταχυδρομικές επιταγές postal orders
ταχυδρομικός κώδικας postcode
ταχυδρομικώς by post

ταχύμετρο (το) speedometer

ταχύτητα/ταχύτης (η) speed
κιβώτιο ταχύτητων gearbox

τελευταίος/α/ο last

τέλος (το) end ; tax ; duty
ταχυδρομικά τέλη postage
οδικά τέλη road tax
τέλος πάντων well ; anyway *(to start sentence)*

τελωνείο (το) customs

τένις (το) tennis

τέντα (η) awning

τέρμα (το) terminus ; end of route

ΤΕΤΑΡΤΗ WEDNESDAY

τέχνη (η) art
λαϊκή τέχνη folk art

τζαμί (το) mosque

τζάμι (το) glass *(of window)*

τζατζίκι (το) tsatsiki *(yoghurt, cucumber and garlic)*

τηγανίτα (η) pancake

τηλεκάρτα (η) phonecard

τηλεόραση (η) television

τηλεπικοινωνίες (οι) telecommunications

τηλεφώνημα (το) telephone call

ΤΗΛΕΦΩΝΟ
TELEPHONE

τηλεφωνικός θάλαμος phone box
τηλεφωνικός κατάλογος telephone directory
τηλεφωνικός κωδικός dialling code ; area code

τι; what?
τι είναι; what is it?

τιμή (η) price ; honour
τιμή εισιτηρίου price of ticket ; fare

τιμοκατάλογος (ο) price list

τιμολόγιο (το) invoice

τιμόνι (το) steering wheel

τιμωρώ to punish

τίποτα nothing
έχετε τίποτα να δηλώσετε have you anything to declare

τμήμα (το) department ; police station

το it ; the *(with neuter nouns)*

τοιχοκόλληση (η) bill posting

τόκος (ο) interest *(bank)*

τόνος (ο) ton ; tuna fish

τοστ (το) toasted sandwich

ΤΟΥΑΛΕΤΕΣ TOILETS

τουρισμός (ο) tourism

τουρίστας/στρια (ο/η) tourist

τουριστικός/ή/ό tourist
τουριστικά είδη souvenirs
τουριστική αστυνομία Tourist Police

Τουρκία (η) Turkey

τραγούδι (το) song

τραγωδία (η) tragedy

τράπεζα (η) bank

τραπεζαρία (η) dining room

τραπέζι (το) table

τρένο (το) train

ΤΡΙΤΗ TUESDAY

τρόλεϊ (το) trolley bus

τροφή (η) food

τροχαία (η) traffic police

τροχός (ο) wheel

τροχόσπιτο (το) caravan ; mobile home

τρώγω/τρώω to eat

τσάι (το) tea

τσάντα (η) bag

τσάρτερ (το) charter flight

τσιγάρο (το) cigarette

τυρί (το) cheese

τυρόπιτα (η) cheese pie

τυφλός/ή/ό blind

υ Υ

υγεία (η) health
στην υγειά σας your health ; cheers

υγειονομικός έλεγχος (ο) health inspection

Ύδρα (η) Hydra (island)

Υμηττός (ο) Mount Hymettos

υπεραγορά (η) supermarket

υπεραστικό λεωφορείο (το) long-distance coach

υπερωκεάνιο (το) liner

υπηρεσία (η) service
ποσοστό υπηρεσίας service charge

υπηρέτης (ο) servant

υπηρέτρια (η) maid

υπόγειος/α/ο underground
υπόγεια διάβαση πεζών pedestrian subway
υπόγειος σιδηρόδρομος underground *(railway)*

υπολογιστής (ο) computer

υπουργείο (το) ministry

υψηλός/ή/ό high
υψηλή τάση high voltage

ύφασμα (το) fabric ; cloth
υφάσματα textiles
υφάσματα επιπλώσεων upholstery fabrics

ύψος (το) height
ύψος περιορισμένο height limit

φ Φ

φαγητό (το) food ; meal

φαΐ (το) food

φακός (ο) lens ; torch
φακοί επαφής contact lenses

φακές (οι) lentils

φανάρι (το) traffic light ; lantern

φαξ (το) fax

φαρμακείο (το) chemist's

φαρμάκι (το) poison

φάρμακο (το) medicine

φάρος (ο) lighthouse

φασολάκι (το) green bean

φασόλι (το) haricot bean

φάω to eat

ΦΕΒΡΟΥΑΡΙΟΣ
FEBRUARY

φεριμπότ (το) ferry boat

φέτα (η) feta cheese ; slice

φιλενάδα (η) girlfriend

φιλέτο (το) fillet of meat

φιλμ (το) film
εμφανίσεις φιλμ film developing

φίλος/η (ο/η) friend

φίλτρο (το) filter
φίλτρο αέρος air filter
φίλτρο λαδιού oil filter
καφές φίλτρου filter coffee

φις (το) plug *(electric)*

φλας (το) flash *(camera)* ; indicators *(on car)*

φοιτητής/φοιτήτρια (ο/η) student

φοιτητικό εισιτήριο (το) student fare

φόρεμα (το) dress

φορολογημένα είδη duty-paid goods

φόρος (ο) tax
  συμπεριλαμβανομένων φόρων including taxes

φουντούκι (το) hazelnut

φούρνος (ο) oven ; bakery

φουσκωτά σκάφη (τα) inflatable boats

ΦΠΑ (ο) VAT

φράουλα (η) strawberry

φρένο (το) brake *(in car)*

φρέσκος/ια/ο fresh

φρούτο (το) fruit

φρουτοσαλάτα (η) fruit salad

φύλακας (ο) guard

φύλαξη αποσκευών (η) left-luggage office

φυστίκι (το) peanut
  φυστίκια Αιγίνης pistachio nuts

φυτό (το) plant

φως (το) light

φωτιά (η) fire

φωτογραφία (η) photograph
  έγχρωμες φωτογραφίες colour photographs

φωτογραφίζω to take photographs
  μη φωτογραφίζετε no photographs

φωτογραφική μηχανή (η) camera

φωτοτυπία (η) photocopy

χ Χ

χαίρετε hello *(polite)*

χάπι (το) pill

χάρτης (ο) map
  οδικός χάρτης road map

χαρτί (το) paper
  χαρτί κουζίνας kitchen paper

χαρτικά (τα) stationery

χαρτονόμισμα (το) banknote

χαρτοπωλείο (το) stationer's shop

χασάπικο (το) butcher's shop

χειροποίητος/η/ο handmade

χειρούργος (ο) surgeon

χειρόφρενο (το) handbrake

χέρι (το) hand

χιλιόμετρο (το) kilometre

χιόνι (το) snow

χοιρινό (το) pork

χορός (ο) dance

χορτοφάγος (ο/η) vegetarian

χορωδία (η) choir

χουρμάς (ο) date *(fruit)*

χρειάζομαι to need

χρήματα (τα) money

χρηματοκιβώτιο (το) safe *(for valuables)*

χρήση (η) use
  οδηγίες χρήσεως instructions for use

χρήσιμος/η/ο useful

χρησιμοποιώ to use

χριστιανός/ή Christian

Χριστούγεννα (τα) Christmas
  Καλά Χριστούγεννα Merry Christmas

χρόνος (ο) time ; year

χρυσαφικά (τα) jewellery

χρυσός/ή/ό *(made of)* gold
  Χρυσός Οδηγός Yellow Pages

χρώμα (το) colour ; paint

χταπόδι (το) octopus

χτένα (η) comb

χτες yesterday

χυμός (ο) juice
χυμός λεμονιού lemon juice
χυμός πορτοκαλιού orange juice

χώρα (η) country

χωράφια (τα) fields

χωριάτικο ψωμί (το) bread *(round, flat loaf)*

χωριό (το) village

χωρίς without
χωρίς εισπράκτορα exact fare ; prepaid ticket

χώρος (ο) area ; site
αρχαιολογικός χώρος archaeological site
ιδιωτικός χώρος private land
χώρος σταθμεύσεως parking area

ψ Ψ

ψάρεμα (το) fishing

ψαρεύω to fish

ψάρι (το) fish

ψαρόβαρκα (η) fishing boat

ψαροταβέρνα (η) fish tavern

ψημένος/η/ο cooked ; roasted ; grilled

ψητός/ή/ό roast ; grilled

ψυγείο (το) fridge

ψύχω to cool

ψωμάς (ο) baker

ψωμί (το) bread

ω Ω

ΩΘΗΣΑΤΕ PUSH

ωτοστόπ (το) hitchhiking

ώρα (η) time ; hour
ώρες επισκέψεως visiting hours
ώρες λειτουργίας opening hours
ώρες συναλλαγής banking hours
της ώρας freshly cooked *(food)*

ωραίος/α/ο beautiful

ωράριο (το) timetable

ως as

ωστόσο however

HOW GREEK WORKS

The following basic rules of Greek grammar will help you make full use of the information in this book.

Greek grammar is rather complicated by the fact that pronouns, nouns and adjectives change their ending according to their function in the sentence, according to whether they are singular or plural, or whether they are masculine, feminine or neuter (rather like German). We give a basic outline of the grammar, but for a more full explanation you should consult a Greek grammar book.

GREEK ALPHABET

Greek is spelt exactly as it sounds. The only difficulty may occur with letters which have the same sound, e.g. **υ**, **η**, **ι**, **ει** and **οι** are all pronounced '*ee*'.

The names of the 24 letters of the Greek alphabet are given below:

			SOUND
α, Α	**άλφα**	***a**lfa*	*a*
β, Β	**βήτα**	*v**ee**ta*	*v*
γ, Γ	**γάμα**	*gh**a**ma*	*gh*
δ, Δ	**δέλτα**	*dh**e**lta*	*dh*
ε, Ε	**έψιλον**	***e**pseelon*	*e*
ζ, Ζ	**ζήτα**	***zee**ta*	*z*
η, Η	**ήτα**	***ee**ta*	*ee*
θ, Θ	**θήτα**	*th**ee**ta*	*th*
ι, Ι	**γιώτα**	*y**o**ta*	*ee*
κ, Κ	**κάπα**	*k**a**pa*	*k*
λ, Λ	**λάμδα**	*l**a**mdha*	*l*
μ, Μ	**μι**	*mee*	*m*
ν, Ν	**νι**	*nee*	*n*
ξ, Ξ	**ξι**	*ksee*	*ks*
ο, Ο	**όμικρον**	***o**meekron*	*o*
π, Π	**πι**	*pee*	*p*
ρ, Ρ	**ρο**	*ro*	*r*
σ, ς, Σ	**σίγμα**	*s**ee**ghma*	*s*
τ, Τ	**ταυ**	*taf*	*t*
υ, Υ	**ύψιλον**	***ee**pseelon*	*ee*
φ, Φ	**φι**	*fee*	*f*
χ, Χ	**χι**	*khee*	*kh*
ψ, Ψ	**ψι**	*psee*	*ps*
ω, Ω	**ωμέγα**	*om**e**gha*	*o*

NOUNS

*A **noun** is a word such as **car**, **horse** or **Mary** which is used to refer to a person or thing.*

Greek nouns can be *masculine, feminine* or *neuter* and the words for **the** and **a** (the articles) change according to the gender of the noun.

ο *(o)*	= **the** with *masculine* nouns
η *(ee)*	= **the** with *feminine* nouns
το *(to)*	= **the** with *neuter* nouns
ένας *(**e**nas)*	= **a** with *masculine* nouns
μία *(**mee**a)*	= **a** with *feminine* nouns
ένα *(**e**na)*	= **a** with *neuter* nouns

The article is the most reliable indication of the gender of a noun, i.e. whether it is *masculine, feminine* or *neuter*.

In the dictionary sections you will come across examples like this: **ο / η γιατρός** *(yatr**o**s)* **doctor**. This means that the same ending is used for men as well as women doctors i.e. **ο γιατρός** is a male doctor, **η γιατρός** is a female doctor.

You will also encounter entries like **ο Άγγλος / η Αγγλίδα** indicating that an **Englishman** is referred to as **ο Άγγλος** *(**a**nglos)* while an **Englishwoman** is **η Αγγλίδα** *(angl**ee**dha)*.

Masculine endings of nouns

The most common endings of *masculine* nouns are **-ος** *(os)*, **-ας** *(as)*, **-ης** *(ees)*, e.g.

ο καιρός *(ker**o**s)*	**the weather**
ο πατέρας *(pat**e**ras)*	**the father**
ο κυβερνήτης *(keevern**ee**tees)*	**the captain** *(of aeroplane)*

Feminine endings of nouns

The most common endings of *feminine* nouns are **-α** (a), **-η** *(ee)*, e.g.

η μητέρα *(meet**e**ra)*	**the mother**
η Κρήτη *(kr**ee**tee)*	**Crete**

Neuter endings of nouns

The most common *neuter* endings are: **-ο** (o), **-ι** (ee), e.g.

το κτίριο *(kt**ee**reeo)*	**the building**
το πορτοκάλι *(portok**a**lee)*	**the orange** *(fruit)*

PLURALS

The article **the** changes in the plural. For *masculine* (**ο**) and *feminine* (**η**) nouns it becomes **οι** *(ee)*. For *neuter* nouns (**το**) it becomes **τα** *(ta)*.

Nouns have different endings in the plural. *Masculine* nouns change from **-ος** to **-οι** and from **-ας** and **-ης** to **-ες**. *Feminine* nouns change from **-α** and **-η** to **-ες**. *Neuter* nouns have an **-α** ending in the plural.

Examples:

masculine	**ο βράχος** *(o vr**a**khos)*	**the rock**
	οι βράχοι *(ee vr**a**khee)*	**the rocks**
	ο άντρας *(o **a**ndhras)*	**the man**
	οι άντρες *(ee **a**ndhres)*	**the men**
feminine	**η κυρία** *(ee keer**ee**a)*	**the lady**
	οι κυρίες *(ee keer**ee**-es)*	**the ladies**
	η αδελφή *(ee adhelf**ee**)*	**the sister**
	οι αδελφές *(ee adelf**es**)*	**the sisters**
neuter	**το κτίριο** *(to kt**ee**reeo)*	**the building**
	τα κτίρια *(ta kt**ee**reea)*	**the buildings**
	το κλειδί *(to kleedh**ee**)*	**the key**
	τα κλειδιά *(ta kleedhee**a**)*	**the keys**

ADJECTIVES

*An **adjective** is a word such as **small**, **pretty** or **practical** that describes a person or thing, or gives extra information about them.*

Adjective endings must agree with the gender and number of the noun they describe, e.g.

ο καλός πατέρας *(kal**o**s pat**e**ras)*	**the good father**
η καλή κυρία *(kal**ee** keer**ee**a)*	**the good lady**
οι καλοί πατέρες *(kal**ee** pat**e**res)*	**the good fathers**
οι καλές κυρίες *(kal**e**s keer**ee**es)*	**the good ladies**

You will see that in the Greek-English dictionary section of this book, all adjectives are given with their endings clearly marked e.g.

κρύος/α/ο *(kr**ee**-os/a/o)*	**cold**

The most common adjectival endings are **-ος** *(os)* for *masculine*, **-η** *(ee)* for *feminine* and **-ο** *(o)* for *neuter*.

In Greek, adjectives can come before or after the noun they describe.

POSSESSIVE ADJECTIVES

In Greek the possessive adjective: my, your, his, etc. follow the noun. And they don't change even if the noun is *masculine*, *feminine*, *singular* or *plural*. The article will still go in front of the noun.

my	**μου**	*moo*
your	**σου**	*soo*
his	**του**	*too*
her	**της**	*tees*
its	**του/της**	*too/tees*
our	**μας**	*mas*
your *(plural)*	**σας**	*sas**
their	**τους**	*toos*

**This is also the polite form*

my key	**το κλειδί μου**	*to kleedh**ee** moo*
your room	**το δωμάτιό σας**	*to dhom**a**tee**o** sas*

VERBS

*A **verb** is a word such as **sing**, **walk** or **cry** which is used with a subject to say what someone or something does or what happens to them. **Regular verbs** follow the same pattern or endings. **Irregular verbs** do not follow a regular pattern so you need to learn their different endings.*

The most essential verbs in Greek are the verbs **είμαι I am** and **έχω I have**. Unlike verbs in English, Greek verbs have a different ending for each person and number.

to be

είμαι	**I am**	***ee**me*
είσαι	**you are**	***ee**se*
είναι	**he/she/it is**	***ee**ne*
είμαστε	**we are**	***ee**maste*
είστε	**you are**	***ee**ste**
είναι	**they are**	***ee**ne*

* *This form is also used when addressing people we do not know very well; it is generally referred to as the polite plural (like the French 'vous').*

NOTE: While in English it is necessary to use the personal pronoun i.e. **we**, **you** etc, in order to distinguish between **we are**, **you are** etc, in Greek this function is carried out by the different endings of the verb itself. This way in Greek, **we are** and **they are** can be simply **είμαστε** *(**ee**maste)*, **είναι** *(**ee**ne)*.

to have

έχω	**I have**	*e*kho
έχεις	**you have**	*e*khees
έχει	**he/she/it has**	*e*khee
έχουμε	**we have**	*e*khoome
έχετε	**you have**	*e*khete
έχουν	**they have**	*e*khoon

NOTE: As above, **I have** can be expressed in Greek with simply the verb **έχω**; each ending is particular to a specific person.

Verbs in Greek in the active voice, end in **-ω** *(o)* or **-ώ** *(**o**)*. This is the ending with which they generally appear in dictionaries. Please note that in everyday speech a more usual ending for **-ώ** *(**o**)* is **-άω** *(**a**o)*. If a verb does not have an active voice form, in a dictionary it will appear with the ending **-μαι** *(-me)*, e.g. **λυπάμαι** *(leep**a**me)* **to be sad** or **sorry**, **θυμάμαι** *(theem**a**me)* **to remember**.

The verb **αγαπώ** *aghap**o*** **to love** has typical endings for verbs ending in **-ώ** *(-**o**)* while those ending in **-ω** *(-o)* follow the pattern of **έχω** *(**e**kho)* above.

αγαπώ/άω *(aghap**o**/**a**o)*	**I love**
αγαπάς *(aghap**a**s)*	**you love**
αγαπά *(aghap**a**)*	**he/she/it loves**
αγαπούμε *(aghap**oo**me)*	**we love**
αγαπάτε *(aghap**a**te)*	**you love**
αγαπούν *(aghap**oo**n)*	**they love**

In Greek, there are two ways of addressing people, depending on their age, social or professional position, and how formal or informal the relationship is between two people. e.g. an older person will probably speak to a much younger one using the singular (informal way) but the younger person will use the plural (formal) unless well acquainted. Similarly two friends will speak to each other using the informal singular:

Τι κάνεις; *(tee k**a**nees)*	**How are you?**
Καλά, εσύ; *(kal**a** es**ee**)*	**Fine, and you?**

While two acquaintances will address each other in a more formal way using the second person plural, like this:

Τι κάνετε; *(tee k**a**nete)*	**How are you?**
Καλά, εσείς; *(kal**a** es**ee**s)*	**Fine, and you?**

PERSONAL PRONOUNS

*A **pronoun** is a word that you use to refer to someone or something when you do not need to use a noun, often because the person or thing has been mentioned earlier. Examples are **it**, **she**, **something** and **him**.*

There are times when the pronoun needs to be used, for example, in conjunction with the verb in order to establish the sex of the person involved, i.e. **he** or **she**, or indeed **it**.

εγώ	**I**	*egh**o***
εσύ	**you**	*es**ee***
αυτός	**he**	*aft**o**s*
αυτή	**she**	*aft**ee***
αυτό	**it**	*aft**o***
εμείς	**we**	*em**ee**s*
εσείς	**you**	*es**ee**s*
αυτοί	**they** *(masc.)*	*aft**ee***
αυτές	**they** *(fem.)*	*aft**e**s*
αυτά	**they** *(neut.)*	*aft**a***

Thus: **αυτός έχει** *(aft**o**s **e**khee)* **he has**

αυτή έχει *(aft**ee** **e**khee)* **she has**

NEGATIVE

To make a sentence negative, you put **δεν** (*dhen*) immediately before the verb, e.g.

δεν ξέρω *dhen ks**e**ro* **I don't know**

δεν έχω... *dhen **e**kho* **I have no...**

FUTURE

The future tense is made by adding **θα** *tha* immediately before the verb, e.g.

θα πάω *tha pao* **I shall go**

θα δεν πάω *tha dhen pao* **I shall not go**